Cognitive Explorations of Translation

Continuum Studies in Translation
Series Editor: Jeremy Munday, Centre for Translation Studies, University of Leeds

Published in association with the International Association for Translation and Intercultural Studies (IATIS), Continuum Studies in Translation aims to present a series of books focused around central issues in translation and interpreting. Using case studies drawn from a wide range of different countries and languages, each book presents a comprehensive examination of current areas of research within translation studies written by academics at the forefront of the field. The thought-provoking books in this series are aimed at advanced students and researchers of translation studies.

Translation as Intervention
Edited by Jeremy Munday

Translator and Interpreter Training: Issues, Methods and Debates
Edited by John Kearns

Translation: Theory and Practice in Dialogue
Edited by Rebecca Hyde Parker, Karla L. Guadarrama García and Antoinette Fawcett

Translation Studies in Africa: Central Issues in Interpreting and Literary and Media Translation
Edited by Judith Inggs and Libby Meintjes

Cognitive Explorations of Translation

Edited by
Sharon O'Brien

Continuum Studies in Translation

continuum

Continuum International Publishing Group

The Tower Building	80 Maiden Lane
11 York Road	Suite 704
London	New York
SE1 7NX	NY 10038

www.continuumbooks.com

British Library Cataloguing-in-Publication Data
A catalogue record for this book is available from the British Library.

ISBN: 978-1-4411-8949-3 (hardcover)
ISBN: 978-1-4411-7268-6 (paperback)

Library of Congress Cataloging-in-Publication Data
Cognitive explorations of translation / edited by Sharon O'Brien.
    p. cm. -- (Continuum studies in translation)
    Includes index.
    ISBN 978-1-4411-8949-3 (hardcover) – ISBN 978-1-4411-7268-6 (pbk.) 1. Translating and interpreting–Psychological aspects. 2. Cognitive psychology. I. O'Brien, Sharon, 1969- II. Title. III. Series.

    P306.2.C555 2010
    418'.02019–dc22

2010012773

Typeset by Fakenham Photosetting Ltd, Fakenham, Norfolk
Printed and bound in India by Replika Press Pvt Ltd

Table of Contents

Series Editor's Preface

The International Association for Translation and Intercultural Studies (IATIS) provides a global forum for scholars and researchers concerned with translation and other forms of intercultural communication.

The Association facilitates the exchange of knowledge and resources among scholars in different parts of the world, stimulates interaction between researchers from diverse traditions, and encourages scholars across the globe to explore issues of mutual concern and intellectual interest.

Among the Association's activities are the organization of conferences and workshops, the creation of web-based resources and the publication of newsletters and scholarly books and journals.

The Translation Series published by Continuum in conjunction with IATIS is a key publication for the Association. It addresses the scholarly community at large, as well as the Association's members. Each volume presents a thematically coherent collection of essays, under the co-ordination of a prominent guest editor. The series thus seeks to be a prime instrument for the promotion and dissemination of innovative research, sound scholarship and critical thought in all areas that fall within the Association's purview.

Jeremy Munday
University of Leeds, UK

Introduction

Sharon O'Brien

Dublin City University, Ireland

This volume arose out of the special panel on Cognitive Explorations of Translation which was part of the 3rd conference of the International Association for Translation and Interpreting Studies (IATIS), held at Monash University, Melbourne, Australia from 8–10 July 2009.

In 2000, Riitta Jääskeläinen commented that the discipline of translation studies has traditionally focused on texts, languages and cultures and has not been much interested in how the human mind works. The unfortunate consequence of this lack of interest, again according to Jääskeläinen (ibid: 72), was that 'process-oriented research efforts may lack the explanatory power required to draw reliable generalizations which are necessary for building viable theories and creating testable hypotheses'. It is now ten years on from those comments, and I wonder how much progress has been made? Although cognition-oriented research in translation is not new, there is certainly evidence of an increasing interest in how the translator's mind works; this evidence can be seen, for example, in recent volumes of the Copenhagen Studies in Language Series (Göpferich et al. 2008, Göpferich et al. 2009, Mees et al. 2009); the edited volume by Shreve and Angelone (2010) and now in this volume. However, the primary focus in translation studies is still text, language and culture, and *how* translation happens is still a somewhat peripheral question. Progress has been made, as can be seen from the research published here and in the aforementioned volumes, but we are still grappling with questions of methodology and searching for synergies between translation and interpreting research[1], as well as with sister disciplines such as linguistics, psycholinguistics and cognitive science, to mention a few.

Investigating the brain and how it functions is not a simple task and this may explain why progress is slow. Some may question the importance of this sub-domain of research in translation studies, but any research that helps understand the complex task that is translation or, indeed, the functioning of the human brain is, I would argue, valuable and should stand firm alongside other 'ways of seeing'.

Cognitive-oriented research is perhaps also impeded by the fact that those who situate themselves in 'Translation Studies' are not, on the whole, cognitive scientists, biologists, or psychologists. But some remain undeterred by the challenges and forge ahead, little by little, with their investigations of translation processes. In this regard we are engaging in 'disciplinary nomadism', as Cronin puts it (2003: 112). The research methods are becoming more varied and adventurous, as will be seen in the contributions published here.

The theoretical and methodological framework for cognitive explorations of translation come primarily from cognitive psychology and Ericsson and Simon's framework (1984/1993), which is based on the view of human cognition as information processing and on the assumption that we are able to report accurately on what is being processed in our working memory at any point in time. If reporting occurs simultaneously with a task, it is called a 'concurrent verbalization', but if the reporting occurs once a task has been completed, it is termed a 'retrospective verbalization'. The term used for what is happening during verbalization is 'thinking aloud' and the product of thinking aloud (i.e. the verbalization and its transcription) is a 'think-aloud protocol' (TAP for short). Göpferich et al. (this volume) argue for the use of a more specialized term 'Translation Process Protocol' (or TPP) to designate a TAP that includes not only what was said during translation but also actions that occur during the process, such as consulting a dictionary.

Thinking aloud gives insight into the cognitive processes for *consciously* processed information but not for automated cognitive processes, which do not enter short-term memory (STM), and as a consequence we are not conscious of them. This is just one of the weaknesses of the thinking-aloud method. There are many other proposed weaknesses. For example, it has been shown to slow down the primary task (Krings 2001); if the task is very demanding (e.g. during simultaneous interpreting), all available cognitive processes might be used up, leaving no 'room' for verbalization; if retrospective verbalization is employed, memory failure can affect data quality and reliability; some research participants are more suited to verbalization than others and, arguably, training is required before engaging participants in thinking aloud, etc. On the topic of retrospective verbalization, Muñoz Martín (2010) casts doubt on whether translators can tap the same mental processes that occurred during translation, and he suggests that it is more plausible to assume that during retrospection translators are in fact constructing knowledge of what they *think* happened during the translation process. For additional issues regarding TAP as a research method, see Jääskeläinen (this volume).

Despite its weaknesses, thinking aloud has and is still being fruitfully employed to gain a better understanding of translation processes. However, new methods have emerged or, to be more precise, have been borrowed from other disciplines, which support and sometimes replace TAP as a research method. These include keyboard logging, screen recording, eye tracking and physiological measures, all of which are represented in the IATIS 2010 Yearbook contributions.

Keyboard logging involves the use of computer software to log every key pressed on the keyboard, including deletions, scrolling up and down, cutting and pasting actions, switches between mouse and keyboard, and even 'inactivity', recorded as pauses. Keyboard logging is a technique used in Human-Computer Interaction research (Lazar et al. 2010) and in writing process research (Van Waes and Leijten 2006). A keyboard-logging tool called Translog has been designed specifically for translation process research (Jakobsen and Schou 1999) and its use is in evidence in several contributions here. Translog records the keys pressed during the production of a translation and produces a log file which can then be analysed in a systematic way.

Keyboard logging has been used to investigate a variety of questions around translation processes. For example, what can revisions of text tell us about the linearity (or non-linearity) and phases of the translation process? What evidence is there for the existence of specific 'units of translation', punctuated by pauses? What can we deduce about cognitive effort by investigating the number and duration of pauses and their locations in the text? What differences are there between expert and novice translators? From a human-computer interaction perspective, do expert translators make more efficient use of the keyboard than novices? What effect does time pressure have on the revision process. And so on ...

Translog also produces a screen recording so the researcher can play back, at varying speeds, what actually happened on the translator's monitor during the translation process. This is known as 'screen recording' and can be used to supplement the keyboard-logging data as well as data derived from thinking aloud, and other methods such as questionnaires or surveys. The screen recording and keyboard data provide evidence of what the translator actually did during the translation process as opposed to what they *think* they did (the latter data being provided via verbalizations). Screen recordings can be used to aid retrospective verbalizations ('cued retrospective protocols'); in this scenario the translator watches the screen recording and uses it as an aid to construct a representation of what s/he was thinking or doing during the translation process. Other, non-translation specific, computer programs exist for recording screen activity. Camtasia Studio and Proxy Pro are two that are commonly used in translation process research.

Eye-tracking systems use cameras to track the position of a user's (in our context: translator's) eyes on a user interface. Infrared light is reflected off parts of the eye and specialized software, running in the background during a recording session, records the eye movement data.

While we are processing information, our eyes engage in either rapid movements, known as 'saccades' or in longer, sweeping movements, with the latter providing evidence of attention shifts. Forward and backward saccades are normal in reading processes and provide information, about for example the readability or comprehensibility of a text (cf. Rayner 1998), the reader type (Hyönä and Nurminen 2006), or indeed about the expertise of the reader (Moravcsik and Kintsch 1995, Kaakinen et al. 2003). Longer sweeps of the eye, on the other hand, can provide evidence of attention shifts between source and target text (Jensen, this volume). This type of data could be used to investigate the parts of a text that are difficult to comprehend, or to compare monolingual reading processes with 'reading for translation' (see for example Jakobsen and Jensen 2008). Alternatively, if one is interested in the interaction between translators and technology, eye tracking can be used to measure the usability of translation tools. The eye-tracking software also transforms the raw eye movement data into graphic representations such as gaze plots (which give a static view of the scan path of the user) or heatmaps (which show where the majority of gazes were for a group of participants in a task), giving an interesting perspective on translators' focus of attention during the translation process and what features in tools are most or least used.

In addition to providing interesting data on eye movements, eye-tracking equipment also records measures which have been shown to be indicative of cognitive effort (Rayner 1998, Radach et al. 2004). These measures include fixations (duration and number) and pupil dilation. Fixations are defined as 'eye movements which stabilize the retina over a stationary object of interest' (Duchowski 2003: 43). Fixations are measured in milliseconds. It has been found that the average fixation during monolingual reading is between 200 and 250 milliseconds, with 175 milliseconds being used as the minimal threshold. It is generally accepted that fixation duration and number are reliable indicators of cognitive load (Rayner 1998). Using these measures, we can, for example, learn about the cognitive effort involved in translating a particular text for a specific translator or groups of translators, we can investigate differences in expertise by comparing experts with novice translators, we can investigate how difficult it is to edit a 95 per cent fuzzy match proposal from a translation memory (TM) versus a 75 per cent match, or we can compare the editing of a TM match with editing raw Machine Translation output (cf. O'Brien 2006, 2008). These are just some examples of how eye tracking has been used in the past few years in translation process research, yet we have not yet posed all the questions we might possibly investigate using eye-tracking systems. The complexity of implementing eye-tracking systems in a research study should not be underestimated (O'Brien 2009); it has been described as a 'high-cost, high-reward endeavour' (Lazar et al. 2010: 349). When paired with other methods such as TAP or keyboard logging, there is no question as to the richness of the data that are produced.

Can translation be stressful, frustrating? What degree of cognitive effort is involved in editing partial matches (of varying quality) from a translation memory system? Does time pressure add to the stress level? Do inadequate subtitles frustrate viewers? All these questions can be researched using questionnaires, for example, or interviews. However, such techniques rely on the perception, opinions and recall of the research participant. Physiological measures represent an alternative or complementary way of directly recording the stress, frustration or other range of emotions that might be experienced during the translation process. These measures are based on the fact that the human body is essentially an electrical system and that the flow of electricity changes, depending on the level of stress, arousal or frustration we are experiencing (Lazar et al. ibid: 350). Galvanic skin response, blood-volume pressure and electroencephalography (EEG) are typical physiological measures used in research on cognition. The skin response test measures the flow of electricity through the skin which increases when we sweat more in response to specific emotions. Blood-volume pressure can be used as an indicator of anxiety (ibid: 353). And electroencephalography (EEG) uses electrodes to measure activity in the brain, in a millisecond timeframe, in response to different stimuli or emotions. Functional Magnetic Resonance Imaging (fMRI), on the other hand, measures blood flow and oxygenation in the brain and works in timeframes of seconds, rather than milliseconds.

Physiological measures are relatively new to translation process research, but have been used to some extent in interpreting research (e.g. Fabbro et al. 1990; Kurz 1994; Rinne et al. 2000). However, Moser-Mercer (2000: 86) points out that results from interpreting studies employing physiogical techniques should be 'viewed with caution' as articulatory artifacts can be produced, and Shlesinger (2000) also highlights automatization as a problem here, which leads to a difficulty in separating out the cognitive components of the process that one might wish to study.

The implementation of physiological measures is not straightforward nor without drawbacks, as we have noted. It may require expertise in, for example, galvanic skin tests, as well as access to the necessary equipment. The interpretation of data produced in these tests is also not without challenges. However, as a means of directly recording the translator's (or interpreter's) physiological responses to the emotions experienced during translation (or interpretation), they open up intriguing possibilities, and potentially overcome some of the shortcomings of the thinking aloud technique, as well as those of questionnaires and interviews.

Earlier we mentioned the significance of Ericsson and Simon's *Protocol Analysis: Verbal Reports as Data* (1984/1993) for translation process research. In her article in this volume, Riitta Jääskeläinen brings us 'back to basics': she questions the validity of the decision to found translation process research on Ericsson and Simon's framework and wonders whether it is wise to continue to do so without testing the framework's applicability to the study of cognitive processes in translation. Jääskeläinen outlines some risks involved in adopting Ericsson and Simon's framework in a wholesale manner. She is critical of the fact that TAPs are often used to investigate processes without any consideration for methodological validity. Highlighting the findings of three research projects in translation, she suggests that there might very well be an issue with the validity of TAPs. We are then presented with a proposal for a methodological study that would test the validity of Ericsson and Simon's framework. It is hoped that the proposed study comes to fruition, as the questions asked by Jääskeläinen are not only important, but essential, if research where thinking aloud is part of the methodological toolbox is to be credible and reliable.

For several years the PACTE Group (Process of Acquisition of Translation Competence and Evaluation) has been researching the nature of translation competence and its acquisition in a holistic and empirical-experimental way. They have published their findings along the way and, in so doing, have contributed significantly to our understanding of what translation competence is and how it is acquired. The article published in this volume focuses attention on the concepts of *Translation Project* and the *Dynamic Translation Index*, both of which are explained in detail. By comparing measurements between a group of professional translators and a group of language teachers, in both direct and inverse translation tasks, the PACTE Group reveals significant differences in translation competence between these two groups. The concept of a 'dynamic' approach to translation is found to be an important characteristic of translation competence. In addition, there is a close link between the 'dynamic' approach to translation and the acceptability of the final translated product. Both experimental groups are shown to have a 'dynamic' approach to translation. However, significant differences are found to exist in the acceptability of products, despite the similarity in approaches.

In 'Exploring translation competence acquisition: criteria of analysis put to the test' the TransComp team (Susanne Göpferich, Gerrit Bayer-Hohenwarter, Friederike Prassl and Johanna Stadlober) present an initial data analysis for their ambitious longitudinal study of translation competence acquisition. They argue in favour of longitudinal studies 'in the strictest sense of the term', where product and process are analysed for the same individuals at regular intervals during their training and later professional career. Their methods of data collection include think-aloud protocols, keystroke logging, screen recording, retrospective interviews and questionnaires. The TransComp project focuses on the analysis of three subcompetencies of translation-specific competence: (1) strategic competence, (2) translation routine activation competence and (3) tools and research competence. Strategic competence is analysed via product and process data. Similar to Angelone and Shreve (this volume), problem awareness is considered to be an essential component of strategic translation competence. Initial analyses indicate differences between professional and novice translators in problem awareness and solution. Tools and research competence is analysed via decision-making processes. Jungermann *et al.*'s (1998) typology of decision-making processes, which is based on the amount of cognitive effort involved in the decision process, is used for this analysis. Early analyses again suggest interesting differences between professionals and early novices in the types of decision-making strategies employed. Finally, tools and research competence is analysed in connection with translational creativity. The TransComp team draws here on creativity research (notably Guilford 1950), and their preliminary results suggest that there is a correlation between creativity and translation quality, and between creativity and high levels of competence. The results presented are preliminary in nature and are taken from a small sample of the TransComp corpus, but they signal that we can expect some very interesting findings about the acquisition of translation competence from this team in the future.

The topic of translation competence development is taken up again by Heloisa Pezza Cintrão, but this time the focus is not just on the novice, but the novice who has had little exposure to L2. Cintrão outlines the demand for translator training within language and literature programmes in the University of São Paulo, where students majoring in language and literature are often required to translate once they have graduated. Her question is whether it is possible to initiate the development of translation competence in students who have limited L2 capabilities. She adopts a corpus-based approach where process, product, interview and language competence data are collated over a period of four months. The process and product data are collated using Translog. Her study is comparative, using groups of professional bilinguals, language students with no exposure to translation training, and a control group of students who receive some training in the acquisition of translation competence. Cintrão observes interesting changes in the behaviour over time of her control group compared to the other two groups. The control group displays an increase in time dedicated to the translation drafting phase, and a positive correlation between this time increase and the 'functional appropriateness' of the translated product is suggested. Cintrão's exploratory study would suggest that the development of translation competence is possible even in novices with very limited L2 capabilities.

Angelone and Shreve present a product-oriented follow-up to an earlier process-oriented exploratory study on uncertainty management and metacognitive bundling. A three-stage model of problem-solving is proposed, where ideally the three stages of (1) problem recognition, (2) solution proposal and (3) solution evaluation are 'bundled' into triads. This classification is further sub-divided into Textual Level, Behavioural Focus and Translation Locus, thereby offering a theoretical granularity to the analysis of uncertainty management sequences in translation. They report on how the uncertainty management strategies of one professional translator and three translation students correlate with translation quality. Interesting differences between the professional translator's uncertainty management behaviour and that of the students are reported. The pinpointing of such differences is not only interesting, but also of considerable value for translation pedagogy, as it provides us with further confirmation that the development of awareness of the nature of problems is key to the development of expertise. The research also contributes to the theoretical and methodological frameworks for the analysis of uncertainty management in translation.

Christian Lachaud's contribution represents an ambitious journey from one discipline, psycholinguistics, into a related yet different discipline, translation studies. This type of journey is challenging because each discipline carries with it its current beliefs and ways of seeing and measuring things which are frequently unusual, if not unacceptable, to the other discipline. Yet each discipline, with eyes and ears wide open, could learn a lot from the other and this is why this contribution on using electroencephalography (EEG), eye tracking and keystroke logging simultaneously to measure cognitive load in transcoding deceptive cognates, non-cognates and true cognates is especially welcome. Going somewhat against the grain of accepted practice in translation studies, Lachaud carries out an experiment on the cognitive load in transcoding at the *word* level. The subjects in this experiment are also bilinguals, not translators. Nonetheless, this research breaks new ground because it effectively combines the three methods mentioned above, an accomplishment that is not to be underestimated, and it provides the groundwork for future research into the fascinating question of how useful 'prompting' might be for translators and for the translation process. Prompting is already in use for the production of online documentation and feedback systems, and Lachaud suggests that it could be successfully used to support, but not constrain, the translator's mental processes. Although Lachaud's article deals with the written word, the relevance of his field of investigation to interpreting processes should also be noted. For example, Shlesinger (2000: 5) highlights the relevance to interpreting research of cognitive psychology experiments on mental representations of meanings prior to full word recognition. Shreve and Angelone (2010: 10) state that '[t]o truly integrate translation process research and the cognitive sciences, it is almost certainly necessary to articulate the possible connections between the findings and models of psycholinguistics and neuroscience and those of translation studies'. Lachaud's article is an example of how such connections can be made.

Moving from the level of word back to the level of text, the topic of cognitive effort in translation directionality is tackled in Vincent Chieh-Ying Chang's paper. He draws on Kroll and Stewart's Revised Hierarchical Model, which predicts translation asymmetry, i.e. that translating from language A to language B is more cognitively demanding than the reverse direction. Chang highlights the fact that this model has only ever been tested at the word level, and therefore its applicability to text is as yet unexplored. Embracing this challenge, he implements an eye-tracking study to investigate the cognitive effort involved when translating to and from English and Mandarin Chinese. The research participants are all native speakers of Mandarin Chinese. Measurements of pupil diameter, fixation count, task time, fixation frequency and blink frequency are recorded and analysed in order to gauge the cognitive load in both translation directions. Chang's findings support the hypothesis that the predictions of the Revised Hierarchical Model are valid at a textual level. He highlights a number of interesting ways in which the research could be extended, and in particular applied to translation pedagogy.

In the article by Alves, Pagano and da Silva, the topic of reading modalities in and for translation is investigated through the eye-tracking lens. This topic is under-researched at present. Alves *et al.* seek to achieve two interesting objectives: one is to add to the small body of existing research on variations in cognitive load when reading modalities differ; the second is to try to replicate the findings of another eye-tracking study (Jakobsen and Jensen 2008) using the same texts and eye-tracking hardware but different participants and target languages. Alves *et al.* correctly point out that *replicability* in translation research has largely been ignored but is something that must be embraced if we are to move forward in understanding translation from a cognitive perspective. The assumption made was that as the reading task became more challenging, moving from reading for comprehension to reading for oral translation, evidence of increased cognitive processing would present itself in the eye-tracking data. Two participant groups are factored into the study, i.e. professional translators and translation students. Some of the findings are consistent with those of Jakobsen and Jensen (2008). However, some of the actual measurements, e.g. task time, were greater for Alves *et al.'s* cohort of participants than Jakobsen and Jensen's. These differences might be attributed to varying task instructions, or indeed to participant profile. The importance of reporting exact settings used, such as fixation filter settings, is highlighted by the authors if we are to be in a position to compare experimental results.

How do we translate metaphors? Do different translation strategies for metaphors require different levels of cognitive processing? These are some of the important questions Annette Sjørup asks in her article which describes her eye-tracking investigation of metaphor translation. Drawing on previous work, Sjørup presents three strategies for the translation of metaphor: use of an equivalent, replacement with another metaphor with the same meaning, or paraphrase. She postulates that paraphrase would require the greatest cognitive load and tests this assumption using the eye-tracking measurement Total Gaze Time. Sjørup uncovers some evidence for a link between the translation strategy chosen and the gaze time data. When gaze time for metaphors is compared with that of the rest of the text, differences across texts and individuals are observed. Sjørup also puts forward the theory that the cognitive effort invested in translating metaphors could be related to the frequency and applicability of the metaphorical image in the target text. This article reports early-stage research findings and foregrounds the eye-tracking measurement; future analysis of keyboard logging data and retrospective interviews is eagerly awaited.

Kristian Jensen combines keyboard logging and eye-tracking tools to investigate the distribution of attention between source text (ST) and target text (TT) during translation. A secondary aim of his study is to probe further the question of whether translation is a serial or parallel activity. With a group of 12 professional translators and 12 students translating from English (L2) into Danish (L1), he investigates the correlations between attention shifts and expertise, text complexity and segment type, i.e. whether attention is on the source text, target text or both ('parallel attention' in Jensen's terminology). Jensen's data demonstrate that both of his groups (professionals and students) paid more attention to the target text, regardless of the level of text complexity. He also finds evidence of parallel processing in both groups, though the extent of this is limited when compared with individual attention on the ST or TT. Differences between the mean source text segment duration for professionals and students lead Jensen to an interesting speculation about the efficiency of professional translators' behaviour when compared with student translators. The data on parallel attention lead him to another interesting speculation regarding an upper limit on cognitive processing.

What stands out in the collection of articles in this volume and in empirical investigations of the cognitive processes of translation in general, whether measured by means of TAPs, keyboard logging, descriptive analyses of the product, interviews or eye tracking, is that *individual variations* always present themselves. This is not unexpected, since we are human, and individual. Hansen (2010) makes an appeal for going beyond the triangulation of quantitative data produced via TAPs, keyboard logging, eye tracking etc. to a more 'integrative description of translation processes' which includes the 'life story' (values, emotions, memories) of the translator. This integrative description may well help us to comprehend the individual differences that appear to emerge with regularity. At the same time, we need to understand what is common in the translation process, which (sub-)tasks are more difficult than others, and what common strategies and processes exist among experts, so that we can build plausible models and viable theories to help us better understand the complex phenomenon that is translation. Searching for commonalities will require much larger group sizes than researchers have been able to cope with to date. The issues of common task assignments, participant profiling and replicability also need attention. We have begun to embrace these challenges.

Significant progress has thus been made in the exploration of translation as a cognitive activity. The papers included here represent a snapshot of the types of questions, issues, findings, methodologies etc. that currently occupy us. However, we are still in the early stages of that journey. Collaboration with other disciplines will undoubtedly help us make even greater strides.

Note

1 It will not go unnoticed that there are no contributions in this volume from the field of interpreting, due to a lack of response to the initial call for participation in the special panel at the IATIS 2009 conference.

Acknowledgements

A number of individuals deserve thanks for helping to make this volume become a reality: to Dr. Jeremy Munday and the publishers, Continuum, for being supportive of this idea; to all the contributors, for your great efforts and patience; and to the anonymous reviewers, thank you so much for contributing your time and expertise, which was greatly appreciated by the contributors and especially by me. I would also like to express my gratitude to IATIS and to the local organizers for the organization of the 2009 conference and to the speakers on the panel, all of whom contributed to its success.

References

Cronin, M. (2003), *Translation and Globalization*, London: Routledge.

Duchowski, A. (2003), *Eye-tracking methodology: theory and practice*, New York: Springer.

Ericsson, K.A. and H.A. Simon (1984/1993), *Protocol Analysis: Verbal Reports as Data*. Cambridge, MA.: MIT Press.

Fabbro, F., L. Gran, G. Basso and A. Bava (1990), 'Cerebral lateralization in simultaneous interpretation', *Brain and Language*, 39 (1), 69–89.

Göpferich, S., A.L. Jakobsen and I. Mees (eds) (2009), *Behind the mind: Methods, models and results in translation process research*, Copenhagen Studies in Language (37), Copenhagen: Samfundslitteratur.

Göpferich, S., A.L. Jakobsen and I. Mees (eds) (2008), *Looking at eyes: Eye-tracking studies of reading and translation processing*, Copenhagen Studies in Language (36), Copenhagen: Samfundslitteratur.

Hansen, G. (2010), 'Integrative description of translation processes'. In Shreve, M. Gregory and Erik Angelone (eds) *Translation and Cognition*, Amsterdam: John Benjamins, 189–212.

Hyönä, J. and A.M. Nurminen (2006), 'Do adult readers know how they read? Evidence from eye movement patterns and verbal reports', *British Journal of Psychology* 97, 31–50.

Jääskeläinen, R. (2000), 'Focus on methodology in think-aloud studies on translating'. In S. Tirkkonen-Condit and R. Jääskeläinen (eds), *Tapping and Mapping the Processes of Translation and Interpreting*, Amsterdam: John Benjamins, pp. 71–82.

Jackobsen, A.L. and K.T.H. Jensen (2008), 'Eye movement behaviour across four different types of reading task'. In S. Göpferich, A.L. Jakobsen and I. Mees (eds.), *Looking at eyes: Eye-tracking studies of reading and translation processing*, Copenhagen Studies in Language 36, Copenhagen: Samfundslitteratur, pp. 103–124.

Jackobsen, A.L. and L. Schou (1999), 'Translog documentation'. In G. Hansen (ed.) *Probing the process in translation: Methods and results*, Copenhagen Studies in Language (24), Copenhagen: Samfundslitteratur, pp.151–186.

Kaakinen, J., J. Hyönä and J. Keenan (2003), 'How prior knowledge, WMC, and relevance of information affect eye fixations in expository text', *Journal of Experimental Psychology: Learning, Memory and Cognition*, 29 (3), 447–457.

Krings, H.P. (2001), *Repairing Texts: Empirical Investigations of Machine Translation Post-Editing Processes*, Kent, Ohio: The Kent State University Press, edited/translated by G.S. Koby.

Kurz, I. (1994), 'A look into the 'black box': EEG probability mapping during mental simultaneous interpreting', In M. Snell-Hornby, F. Pöchhacker and K. Kaindl (eds), *Translation Studies: An Interdiscipline*, pp. 199–208.

Lazar, J., J. Feng and H. Hocheiser (2010), *Research Methods in Human-Computer Interaction*, Chichester: John Wiley.

Mees, I., F. Alves and S. Göpferich (eds) (2009), *Methodology, technology and innovation in translation process research: A tribute to Arnt Lykke Jakobsen*, Copenhagen Studies in Language (38), Copenhagen: Samfundslitteratur.

Moravcsik, J. and W. Kintsch (1995), 'Writing quality, reading skills, and domain knowledge as factors in text comprehension', In J. Henderson, M. Singer, and F. Ferreira (eds), *Reading and Language Processing*, New York, London: Psychology Press, pp. 232–246.

Moser-Mercer, B. (2000), 'Simultaneous interpreting: Cognitive potential and limitations', *Interpreting*, 5 (2), 83–94.

Muñoz Martín, R. (2010), 'On paradigms and cognitive translatology'. In Gregory M. Shreve and Erik Angelone (eds) *Translation and Cognition*, Amsterdam: John Benjamins, pp. 169–187.

O'Brien, S. (2009), 'Eye tracking in translation process research: methodological challenges and solutions'. In I. Mees, F. Alves and S. Göpferich (eds) *Methodology, Technology and Innovation in Translation Process Research: A tribute to Arnt Lykke Jakobsen*, Copenhagen Studies in Language 38, Copenhagen: Samfundslitteratur, pp. 251–266.

O'Brien, S. (2008), 'Processing fuzzy matches in translation memory tools: an eye-tracking analysis'.

In S. Göpferich, A.L. Jakobsen and I. Mees (eds) *Looking at Eyes: Eye-tracking studies of reading and translation processing*, Copenhagen Studies in Language 36, Copenhagen: Samfundslitteratur, pp. 79–102.

O'Brien, S. (2006), 'Eye tracking and translation memory matches'. In *Perspectives: Studies in Translatology*, 14(3), 185–205.

Radach, R., A. Kennedy, and K. Rayner (2004), *Eye movements and information processing during reading*. Hove: Psychology Press.

Rayner, K. (1998), 'Eye movements in reading and information processing: 20 years of research', *Psychological Bulletin* 124, 372–422.

Rinne, J., J. Tommola, M. Laine, B. Krause, D. Schmidt, V. Kaasinen, M. Teräs, H. Sipilä and M. Sunnari (2000), 'The translating brain: cerebral activation patterns during simultaneous interpreting', *Neuroscience Letters*, 294 (2), 85–88.

Shlesinger, M. (2000), 'Interpreting as a cognitive process'. In S. Tirkkonen-Condit, and R. Jääskeläinen (eds), *Tapping and Mapping the Processes of Translation and Interpreting*, Amsterdam: John Benjamins, pp. 3–15.

Shreve, G. and E. Angelone (eds) (2010), *Translation and cognition*, Amsterdam: John Benjamins.

Van Waes, L. and M. Leijten (2006), 'Logging writing processes with Inputlog'. In L. Van Waes, M. Leijten and C. Neuwirth (eds) and G. Rijlaarsdam (series ed.), *Studies in Writing: Vol. 17. Writing and Digital Media*, Oxford: Elsevier, pp. 158–166.

Back to Basics: Designing a Study to Determine the Validity and Reliability of Verbal Report Data on Translation Processes[1]

Riitta Jääskeläinen

Chapter Outline

Introduction

After the first exploratory studies into translation processes in the mid-1980s (Gerloff 1986; Krings 1986; Lörscher 1986) which used thinking aloud to elicit data, translation process research has made considerable progress. The number of process studies has steadily increased and the research designs have become more rigorous, the hypotheses more refined, and the variables more clearly defined. New methods of data elicitation have also been adopted, such as key logging (e.g. Jakobsen 1999, 2003), screen recordings (e.g. Ehrensberger-Dow and Perrin 2009) and eye tracking (e.g. Sharmin *et al.* 2008). Large projects have also allowed for an increase in the numbers of subjects investigated (see e.g. Hansen 1999; PACTE 2003; Barbosa and Neiva 2003; Ehrensberger-Dow and Perrin 2009; Göpferich and Jääskeläinen 2009).

Despite the progress made in some areas, some of the basic methodo-logical questions still remain unanswered. One such question is the validity and reliability of verbal reports, such as think-aloud protocols (TAPs), retrospective reports or dialogue protocols as sources of data on translation processes. The early TAP studies relied on the theoretical and methodological framework provided by cognitive psychology, mainly by Ericsson and Simon (1984/1993). However, adopting Ericsson and Simon's framework uncritically is not entirely unproblematic; for instance, the nature of tasks on which their framework is built is different from the nature of translating as a cognitive task. Although deplorably few studies have focused on methodology in translation process research, there is in fact some research evidence which challenges Ericsson and Simon's framework as far as translating is concerned (e.g. Jakobsen 2003; Krings 2001).

In this article I will first sum up Ericsson and Simon's framework and discuss its potential problems in relation to investigating translation processes. Then I will give an overview of the existing research in translation process research. Finally, I will outline a plan for a methodological study which will focus on determining the validity and reliability of verbal reports as sources of data on translation processes. The main objective of this paper is to provide a rough map of state of the art of process research in terms of methodology, and to sketch a plan for a systematic methodological study. At this point, several issues related to the practical implementation of the plan are still unclear and need to be determined later (Jääskeläinen 2009); therefore the outline proposed here represents a tentative research plan.

Ericsson and Simon's Framework

Ericsson and Simon's framework (1984/1993, 1987; see also Ericsson 2006) is based on the view of human cognition as information processing. According to Ericsson and Simon, subjects can report accurately on information which is attended to in working memory, i.e. consciously processed information. This rules out verbal reports on automated processing; as a result of practice, cognitive processing tends to become automated, hence unavailable for verbalization. Another hindrance to verbalization is high cognitive load; with extremely difficult tasks, all available resources tend to be used on task-related processing and none are left for verbalization. Furthermore, Ericsson and Simon postulate that the accuracy and completeness of verbal reporting is highest if the information attended to in working memory is verbally encoded. Ericsson and Simon divide verbally encoded or encodable information into three levels:

- Level 1: verbally encoded information ('talk aloud')
- Level 2: information that needs to be recoded into verbal code ('think aloud')
- Level 3: verbalizing selected information which is normally not attended to (e.g. answers to specific questions)

Based on an extensive survey of research evidence, Ericsson and Simon argue that thinking aloud does not change the course or structure of thought processes with the exception of a slight slowing-down effect, which results from recoding information into verbal code. In addition, retrospection is vulnerable to memory failure; therefore, it is best suited for relatively short tasks. Furthermore, immediate retrospection is recommended. Another means to overcome memory failure is to employ cued recall in which the subject is provided with some memory support; in translation process research, the playback function of key-logging software like *Translog* (Jakobsen and Schou 1999) can provide such support. However, Englund Dimitrova and Tiselius (2009) make an interesting point about using the subject's own translation as the cue: there is a risk that the subject will start commenting on his or her translation product instead of the process.

Ericsson and Simon also recommend task analysis prior to the experiment to identify the correct or plausible 'procedures, methods or knowledge available for producing the answers' (Ericsson and Simon 1987: 28). With translation this has proved to be difficult due to the different nature of the tasks involved. This will be elaborated below.

As mentioned above, there are some risks involved in adopting Ericsson and Simon's framework wholesale. First of all, the extent to which the knowledge required in translation is verbally encoded is not quite clear. Presumably there is more verbally encoded information involved in translating than in playing chess, for example. Still, it cannot be assumed that all the information is in verbally encoded form. If it were, we would come close to the idea of translating being a fairly mechanical code-switching operation, while the available research evidence shows that it is not. Instead, translators exploit a great deal of cultural, encyclopaedic, domain-specific and strategic knowledge (e.g. Englund Dimitrova 2005; Gerloff 1988; Jääskeläinen 1999; Künzli 2003; Tirkkonen-Condit 1992). The form in which cultural or domain-specific knowledge is stored or encoded is not totally clear, and the same applies to procedural and strategic knowledge. Such information figures centrally in the process of translation.

With regard to task analysis in translation, Ericsson and Simon (1987: 28) point out: 'Tasks like translating a particular sentence to a different language can be subjected to a similar task analysis, although the number of different acceptable translations will complicate the analysis.' The task analysis will become even more challenging when we are dealing with complete texts comprised of several sentences, which is the case in all process-oriented investigations. Ericsson and Simon also maintain that the task analysis would become considerably simpler if it can be assumed that 'the sentence is translated in strict left-to-right order' (1987: 28). This we cannot assume even with single sentences, let alone entire texts. It is obvious that the methodological framework proposed by Ericsson and Simon has not considered issues which are pertinent in translation. This task belongs to the domain of translation process research.

Secondly, the tasks investigated in cognitive psychology tend to be well-defined, which means that they have correct procedures and correct answers. This facilitates the task analysis to determine *a priori* potentially correct problem-solving strategies etc, while translating is clearly an ill-defined task with many different ways of proceeding and a number of correct answers. However, verbal reporting has been successfully used to study ill-defined problems in cognitive psychology, e.g. diagnosing X-ray pictures (Lesgold *et al.* 1988) or judicial decision-making (Lawrence 1988), which implies that the nature of the task need not stand in the way of using verbal reports as data.

Finally, research in cognitive psychology tends to be carried out in monolingual and mono-cultural settings, while research into translation processes always involves two languages and two cultures, and the entire body of research evidence could be characterized as multilingual and multicultural. This brings a whole set of new variables into the research mix, and this aspect has not been examined at all. In fact, there is evidence that with translating, Ericsson and Simon's framework does not really work as expected on the basis of their framework, which will be discussed further in the next section, Evidence from Process Studies.

Evidence from Previous Process Studies

When verbal report procedures, mainly TAPs, were introduced to translation studies, their theoretical underpinnings and conditions of elicitation were explained in some detail, drawing on cognitive psychology, second language acquisition (e.g. Faerch and Kasper 1986; Börsch 1986) as well as on writing research (e.g. Hayes and Flower 1980). Further methodological discussions mainly dealt with dialogue protocols (e.g. House 1988, 2000; Matrat 1995) and retrospection (e.g. Hansen 2006), which has become more popular, particularly together with the use of key-logging software. However, relatively few studies have focused specifically on methodology; instead, methodological issues have been touched upon as by-products of studies focusing on other research questions. Indeed, it seems that methodology has often been discussed in terms of justifying the method chosen for a particular piece of research by praising the method chosen while discrediting the other, which begs the fundamental questions of validity and reliability.

In what follows I will sum up some of the existing research evidence related to the validity and reliability of think-aloud and retrospection to highlight the need for further research. To my mind, validity becomes an issue with methods in which the situation is somehow manipulated and subjected to experimental control; we can legitimately ask whether the experimental situation changes the very process being investigated – are we still examining the task we set out to examine? As a result, validity is an issue with thinking aloud. The validity issue also relates to the think-aloud vs. dialogue discussion: without evidence to the contrary, I would argue that dialogue protocols, however rich and interesting, do not provide valid data on the task of translating on one's own. We are talking about two different processes (see also Krings 2001; Göpferich and Jääskeläinen 2009).

Reliability, in turn, concerns those methods in which the least amount of control can be exercised. As a result, we can question whether the data reflect the object of research accurately. Thus the reliability question concerns, for example, questionnaires or interviews which may be affected by people's tendency to make themselves look better, or try to provide the researcher with the answers or behaviour the informants assume the researcher wants. Reliability can also be compromised due to the limitations of human memory and recall. Consequently, despite the subjects' best intentions, memory distortions are a factor with retrospection.

To my knowledge, few studies have focused on methodology. In what follows, three studies – the results of which seem most relevant – will be discussed in more detail: (1) Krings' (2001) study of the post-editing processes of machine-translated texts that also looked at translation processes; (2) Jakobsen's (2003) study comparing the translation processes of nine subjects who translated texts with Translog; the subjects performed the translation tasks both with and without thinking aloud; and (3) Englund Dimitrova and Tiselius' (2009) study which explores retrospection as a method to elicit data on translation and simultaneous interpreting (SI).

As mentioned, Ericsson and Simon's framework predicts a slight slowing-down effect caused by thinking aloud, due to the processing time required for recoding information into verbal code. In Krings' (2001) study, the think-aloud (TA) condition slowed down the process by roughly 30 per cent. Similarly, Jakobsen (2003) points out that on average, think-aloud slowed down professional translators' processing considerably. Interestingly, these findings might suggest that, contrary to the assumptions in early process research (e.g. Krings 1986: 265–266), there may be less verbally encoded information involved in translation than has been assumed. In other words, the considerable slowing-down effect may result from the extensive application of information that is not verbally encoded, but needs to be recoded to allow verbalization.

Ericsson and Simon also maintain that thinking aloud does not change the course or structure of cognitive processes. However, with regard to translation, some changes have been observed. According to Krings (2001: 526), 'physical text production obviously takes place in smaller steps and/or with less linearity when the subjects have to think aloud.' Jakobsen (2003: 93) also found that thinking aloud increased the number of segments in professional translators' processing; in other words, thinking aloud made them work with smaller chunks of text. This points to a validity problem with thinking aloud – it might change the structure of the translation process. It can further be asked: does thinking aloud change the process to such an extent that it shows in the product (cf. Toury 1991)? For example, working with smaller chunks might affect coherence. To my knowledge there are no systematic studies focusing on the effect of think-aloud on the product. The pilot analysis comparing translations produced under TA and non-TA conditions which was carried out for my own dissertation (Jääskeläinen 1999) indicated that thinking aloud may make subjects reluctant to make large-scale lexical changes, like omissions or additions, while syntactic or textual changes were not affected by thinking aloud (only professional translators were willing to split or combine sentences). However, the non-TA data were gathered from translation students only, and therefore the results are not entirely comparable to those of my dissertation, in which the subjects were professional and non-professional translators (labelled as 'educated laymen').

According to Ericsson and Simon (1984/1993), the reliability of retrospection is compromised after more than an 8–10 second delay between task performance and retrospection. Obviously, for translation tasks of entire texts, this creates a problem: by the time subjects get to the end of the translation task, they are likely to have forgotten what they were thinking about at the beginning of the process. Instead, they will have to resort to speculating about what they must have been thinking about. Englund Dimitrova and Tiselius (2009) have started a study about using retrospection to elicit data on simultaneous interpreting (SI) and translation tasks. Six students of translation participated in the first stage of the project, three in a translation task, and three in a SI task. In the translation experiment, the subjects were asked to translate a text comprising 52 sentences, one sentence at a time, to avoid the problems caused by time delay. The source text was provided as the cue for retrospection. The first research report does not go into much detail about the accuracy or reliability of the resulting retrospective reports.

In sum, research evidence from translation process research suggests that there could be an issue with the validity of TAPs, while the reliability of retrospection may be compromised by time delay. The next step, which is long overdue (see Jääskeläinen 2000), is to determine to what extent, how, and why validity and reliability are compromised with verbal reports on translating.

In addition to the research discussed above, there are some other intriguing findings which highlight the need for a systematic methodological study. One of them deals with the ease or fluency of verbalizing. Some process researchers have reported that subjects do not produce many verbalizations (e.g. House 1988), while others have been satisfied with the amount of data acquired (e.g. Göpferich 2008; Jääskeläinen 1999).

Leaving aside the issues related to adequate experimental design (e.g. warm-up tasks and appropriate reminders), it has been reported for example, that German students of translation have had difficulties verbalizing (e.g. House 1988, 2000), and thinking aloud has been found to be an embarrassment to Danish professional translators (Jakobsen 2003). In contrast, silent Finns have been reported to be fluent verbalizers (e.g. Jääskeläinen 1999; Tirkkonen-Condit 1989) and similar findings were arrived at for

German speakers (e.g. Göpferich 2008) and British community translators (Fraser 1993). To explain this, it has been speculated that language-typological differences might play a role here – perhaps translating between Indo-European languages and the non-Indo-European Finnish requires more processing at the conscious level, resulting in more verbalizations? On the other hand, there are contradictory findings with Chinese – students in Hong Kong had difficulties in verbalizing (Li and Cheng 2007) while professional translators in Taiwan verbalized freely (Shih 2006). In addition to taking into account the two varieties of Chinese here, we should ask if cultural or social factors, such as respect for authority or preserving face, have an effect. In Li and Cheng's study, the experiments were administered by a teaching assistant; in Shih's study the experimenter was an outsider. The level of difficulty of the task may also contribute to the subjects' willingness or ability to verbalize. In Matrat's (1995) study comparing joint translating and thinking aloud, the source texts were paragraphs from Charles S. Pierce's *Logic as Semiotic: The Theory of Signs*. To me this represents a task likely to result in such a heavy cognitive load that it would silence even the most accomplished professional, let alone students. The type of trans-lation task might also offer an explanation: prototypical translation (i.e. translation which is relatively faithful to the source text while also being fluent target language) might require less processing at the conscious level than, say, translation tasks which require summarizing, adaptation or other rewriting procedures. Therefore the tasks in some of the Finnish studies (e.g. Jääskeläinen 1999; Tirkkonen-Condit 1989) requiring translational intervention may have been more conducive to verbalizing than the more prototypical tasks of other studies.

The above survey shows that the variables potentially affecting the fluency of verbalizing may have been overlooked in research. While some of the early studies lacked a proper warm-up task to train subjects to think aloud (e.g. House 1988; Jääskeläinen 1989), subsequent studies with a training session still provide contradictory findings (e.g. House 2000; Jääskeläinen 1999). However, the main problem with the fluency of verbalizing is that the actual amount of data elicited is usually not reported; furthermore, it is not specified how much verbalization is actually expected. In fact, we might be talking about the same amount of verbalization, but one researcher's glass is half full, while the other's is half empty, or some researchers might expect to hear the kind of information that is not available for verbalization under any condi-tions (cf. Krings 2001).

The research evidence discussed above shows that we need systematic methodological research which would help us identify the conditions and limitations of verbal reports on translation processes. Such research might also have something to offer to other fields of research; as was mentioned earlier, research in cognitive psychology tends to be carried out in monolingual and mono-cultural settings, and therefore examining the ways in which linguistic and cultural issues are intertwined in cognitive processing would seem like an ideal export product.

Finally, the choice of methodology always depends on the research aims and available resources as well as the researcher's philosophy of science, ranging from fundamental questions of ontology (how is the world and the human mind organized?), to epistemology (how can we gain information about the workings of the human mind?), to more personal views and attitudes. It is not possible to discuss these questions in detail here, but they will need more attention in the proposed methodological study.

Designing a Methodological Study

In this section I will sketch a research project which aims to determine the validity and reliability of verbal report data on translation processes. More specifically, the study outlined below deals with thinking aloud. Retrospection can be added to the research design at a later stage if necessary; however, at this point it seems reasonable to wait for further results from Englund Dimitrova and Tiselius' (2009) research project on retrospection. At the planning stage, not all the details of the project proposed here have been ironed out, but at least the considerations listed below should be taken into account. A more detailed project plan is under development (Jääskeläinen 2009).

To allow the examination of the potential language, or culture-specific, variables involved in translating and their effect on verbal reporting, the research project will involve a variety of related and unrelated language pairs. As a result, the project will be carried out as a joint international project consisting of language- and culture-specific sub-projects, with a carefully designed and uniform research design, including strict procedures for the setting of experiments and instructions given to the subjects. The experimental design and instructions will follow the recommendations provided by Ericsson and Simon's framework (1984/1993). In fact, the first step in planning the large-scale project is to survey existing translation process research to identify methodological shortcomings in previous research, such as insufficient or missing training of the subjects to think aloud (e.g. Jääskeläinen 1989; House 1988). Some of the main issues in designing the research project will be discussed below.

Selection of subjects

The subjects need to be selected on the basis of predetermined criteria. The subject pool may consist of both translation students and professional translators to examine whether one group is more affected by the TA condition than the other. The definition of 'professional translator' or 'expert translator' will need careful consideration in terms of the length of their work experience and qualifications (see Jääskeläinen, 2010). Similarly, with student subjects the required level of skill and experience must be considered, particularly due to different organization of translator training in different countries (e.g. as a BA or MA programme). The professionals' fields of specialization (i.e. the domains of their expertise) need to be taken into account as well, and the experimental translation tasks related to the professionals' domains: do they represent routine or non-routine tasks? This is likely to affect the amount of conscious vs. automated processing of the task. The same subjects will perform translation tasks in both TA and non-TA conditions to allow for the identification of the potential effects of think-aloud on their processing and to minimise the effect of personality differences.

Task analysis

As was mentioned earlier, the task analysis recommended by Ericsson and Simon (1987) has been seen as difficult in translation process research. Such a task analysis involves determining *a priori* a likely scenario of what will happen – in cognitive terms – in the process being investigated. With translation tasks, which are ill-defined problems, the analysis will inevitably deal with probabilities (e.g. which source text items are *likely* to require conscious problem-solving) rather than the correct procedures and answers typical of well-defined problems. However, the large-scale research projects (see e.g. PACTE 2009) have in fact dealt successfully with some aspects of the task analysis. Ericsson and Simon (1987: 28) outline the translation-relevant task analysis as follows:

- Of particular interest is the availability of linguistic rules as opposed to exceptions and idiomatic constructions.
- A description of the similarity of the two languages with respect to particular grammatical rules and specific lexical items is likely to be of major importance for assessing plausible cognitive representations and processes.
- Words with multiple lexical meanings are also likely to be particularly revealing with respect to the translation processes.

Although the above is suggested in connection with the idea of translating isolated sentences, preferably in a strict left-to-right order (see the section on 'Ericsson and Simon's Framework'), it does suggest a feasible scenario for task analysis in translation. To allow for the analysis of large amounts of process data, the PACTE project (2009) has identified 'Rich Points' in their source text in a series of pilot stages. These include linguistically, culturally and functionally challenging points, i.e. items which are expected to result in extensive processing activities. For the proposed methodological study, we would also need an analysis of other 'Points of Interest', i.e. presumably non-challenging points where the choice of translation variants is limited and little conscious thought expected, to determine whether thinking aloud raises into consciousness information that would not normally be attended to in working memory. Such instances would be evidence of validity problems.

The task analysis should be based on contrastive analyses of the language-pair involved to identify both challenging and non-challenging items in the source text (as suggested by Ericsson and Simon 1987) as well as exploratory and pilot studies to support the initial analysis. Contrastive analyses will provide the framework within which it is possible to determine 'plausible cognitive representations and processes' (Ericsson and Simon 1987: 28) in the experimental tasks, such as straightforward 1:1 correspondences (non-challenging items) or expressions which require problem-solving (challenging items) in the texts used in the experiment. This enables identification of instances in which think-aloud produces processing activities not expected on the basis of the task analysis, such as paying undue attention to choosing existing equivalents or the failure to pay attention to a challenging item. As a result, the source texts in the methodological study may have to be slightly manipulated to incorporate a number of 'Points of Interest' in it; in addition, we might need a pool of several texts to allow for language- and culture-specific variation. However, for the main part of the study, the texts must be the same in all the sub-projects of the large research project.

Type of translation task

The type of task should represent prototypical translation, at least in the first stage of the project. 'Prototypical translation' refers here to the type of translation task that aims to reproduce the source text content in fluent and idiomatic target language (for further discussion of prototypical translation, see e.g. Halverson 1999; Tirkkonen-Condit 1997). This choice is based on the assumption that prototypical translation represents a kind of default type of translation task, a kind of norm; perceived deviations from the prototype tend to be labelled as 'adaptation' or 'rewriting', not translation 'proper'. Other kinds of translation tasks, which require summarizing, popularizing and other more interventional procedures, will have to wait until we know more about what happens in the most basic kind of translation task, because it is likely that more intervention (or more deviation from the norm) may result in more conscious processing. The methodological aim would also justify sacrificing ecological validity to some extent, as the purpose is not to find out what happens in an authentic translation process, but to find out whether thinking aloud is a valid and reliable method to elicit data on translation processes.

Summary

This article has attempted to show that we need a systematic methodological study of using verbal reports, such as retrospection or think-aloud, in translation process research. Previous research has relied on the theoretical and methodological framework provided by cognitive psychology (Ericsson and Simon 1984/1993). Furthermore, verbal reporting is still being used in expertise research (for instance see Ericsson 2006). However, in translation studies there is research evidence indicating that our trust in Ericsson and Simon's framework might be to some extent misplaced. Both Krings (2001) and Jakobsen (2003) report considerable slowing down of processing speed and, more alarmingly, changes in the structure of the process, such as segmentation (size of translation unit). As a result, a methodological study would seem to be justified. The next step will include surveying the existing research evidence in translation process research and cognitive psychology to identify the issues which need to be addressed first in the planning and implementation of the research project proposed here.

Note

1 I am very grateful to the anonymous reviewer for their comments and suggestions which helped me revise the first draft and will help me to continue planning the methodological project.

References

Barbosa, H.G. and A.M.S. Neiva (2003), 'Using think-aloud protocols to investigate the translation process of foreign language learners and experienced translators'. In F. Alves. (ed.), *Triangulating Translation: Perspectives in Process Oriented Research*. Amsterdam & Philadelphia: John Benjamins. pp. 137–155.

Börsch, S. (1986), 'Introspective methods in research on interlingual and intercultural communication'. In J. House and S. Blum-Kulka (eds), *Interlingual and Intercultural Communication. Discourse and Cognition in Translation and Second Language Acquisition Studies*. Tübingen: Gunter Narr. pp.195–209.

Ehrensberger-Dow, M. and D. Perrin (2009), 'Capturing translation processes to access metalinguistic awareness'. *Across Languages and Cultures*, 10 (2). 275–288.

Englund Dimitrova, B. and E. Tiselius (2009), 'Exploring retrospection as a research method for studying the translation process and the interpreting process'. In F. Alves, S. Göpferich and I. Mees (eds), *Methodology, Technology and Innovation in Translation Process Research*. Copenhagen Studies in Language 38. Copenhagen: Samfundslitteratur. pp. 109–182.

Ericsson, K.A. (2006), 'Protocol analysis and expert thought: concurrent verbalizations of thinking during experts' performance on representative tasks'. In K.A. Ericsson, N. Charness, P.J. Feltovich and R.R. Hoffman (eds), *The Cambridge Handbook of Expertise and Expert Performance*. Cambridge: Cambridge University Press. pp. 223–242.

Ericsson, K.A. and H.A. Simon (1984/1993), *Protocol Analysis: Verbal Reports as Data*. Cambridge, MA.: MIT Press.

—— (1987), 'Verbal reports on thinking'. In C. Faerch and G. Kasper (eds), *Introspection in Second Language Research*. Clevedon: *Multilingual Matters*. pp. 24–53.

Faerch, C. and G. Kasper (1986), 'One learner – two languages: Investigating types of interlanguage knowledge'. In J. House and S. Blum-Kulka (eds), *Interlingual and Intercultural Communication. Discourse and Cognition in Translation and Second Language Acquisition Studies*. Tübingen: Gunter Narr. pp. 211–228.

Fraser, J. (1993), 'Public accounts: Using verbal protocols to investigate community translation'. *Applied Linguistics* 14 (4). 325–343.

Gerloff, P. (1986), 'Second language learners' reports on the interpretive process'. In J. House and S. Blum-Kulka (eds). *Interlingual and Intercultural Communication. Discourse and Cognition in Translation and Second Language Acquisition Studies*. Tübingen: Gunter Narr. pp. 243–262.

Göpferich, S. (2008), *Translationsprozessforschung: Stand – Methoden – Perspektiven*. Tübingen: Gunter Narr.

Göpferich, S. and R. Jääskeläinen (2009), 'Process research into the development of translation compe-tence: Where are we and where do we need to go?' *Across Languages and Cultures* 10 (2). 169–191.

Halverson, S. (1999), 'Conceptual work and the "translation" concept'. *Target* 11 (1). 1–31.

Hansen, G. (ed.) (1999), *Probing the Process in Translation: Methods and Results*, Copenhagen Studies in Language 24. Copenhagen: Samfundslitteratur.

—— (ed.) (2002), *Empirical Translation Studies. Process and Product*, Copenhagen Studies in Language 27. Copenhagen: Samfundslitteratur.

—— (2006), *Erfolgreich Übersetzen. Entdecken und Beheben von Störquellen*. Tübingen: Gunter Narr.

Hayes, J.R. and L.S. Flower (1980), 'Identifying the organisation of writing processes'. In L.W. Gregg and E.R. Steinberg (eds), *Cognitive Processes in Writing*. Hillsdale, N.J.: Lawrence Erlbaum Associates. pp. 3–30.

House, J. (1988), 'Talking to oneself or thinking with others? On using different thinking aloud methods in translation'. *Fremdsprachen lehren und lernen* 17. 84–98.

—— (2000), 'Consciousness and the strategic use of aids in translation'. In S. Tirkkonen- Condit and R. Jääskeläinen (eds), *Tapping and Mapping the Processes of Translation and Interpreting*. Amsterdam/ Philadelphia: John Benjamins. pp. 149–162.

Jääskeläinen, R. (1989), 'Translation assignment in professional vs. non-professional translation: a think-aloud protocol study'. In C. Séguinot (ed.), *The Translation Process*. Toronto: H. G. Publications. pp. 87–98.

—— (1999), *Tapping the Process: An Explorative Study of the Cognitive and Affective Factors Involved in Translating*. Joensuu: University of Joensuu.

—— (2000), 'Focus on methodology'. In S. Tirkkonen- Condit and R. Jääskeläinen (eds), *Tapping and Mapping the Processes of Translation and Interpreting*. Amsterdam/Philadelphia: John Benjamins. 149–162.

—— (2009), 'Methodology in translation process research: Designing a study to determine the validity and reliability of verbal reports as data on translation processes.' Unpublished research plan submitted to the Academy of Finland.

—— (2010), 'Are all professionals experts? Definitions of expertise and reinterpretation of research evidence in process studies'. In G. Shreve and E. Angelone (eds), *Translation and Cognition*. Amsterdam/Philadelphia: John Benjamins. pp. 213–228.

Jakobsen, A.L. (1999), 'Logging target text production with *Translog*'. In G. Hansen (ed.) *Probing the Process in Translation: Methods and Results*, Copenhagen Studies in Language 24. Copenhagen: Samfundslitteratur. pp. 9–20.

—— (2003), 'Effects of think aloud on translation speed, revision and segmentation'. In F. Alves (ed.), *Triangulating Translation. Perspectives in Process Oriented Research*. Amsterdam & Philadelphia: John Benjamins. pp. 69–95.

Jakobsen, A.L. and L. Schou (1999) 'Translog documentation'. In G. Hansen (ed.) *Probing the Process in Translation: Methods and Results*, Copenhagen Studies in Language 24. Copenhagen: Samfundslitteratur. Appendix, n.pag.

Krings, H.P. (1986), 'Translation problems and translation strategies of advanced German learners of French (L2)'. In J. House and S. Blum-Kulka (eds), *Interlingual and Intercultural Communication*.

Discourse and Cognition in Translation and Second Language Acquisition Studies. Tübingen: Gunter Narr. pp. 263–276.

———— (2001), *Repairing Texts. Empirical Investigations of Machine-translation Post-editing Processes.* Kent, OH.: Kent State University Press.

Künzli, A. (2003), Quelques stratégies et principes en traduction technique français-allemand et français-suédois (Forskningsrapporter 21). Stockholm: Stockholm University, Department of French, Italian and Classical Languages.

Lawrence, J.A. (1988), 'Expertise on the bench: modelling magistrates' judicial decision- making'. In M.T.H Chi, R. Glaser and M.J. Farr (eds), *The Nature of Expertise.* Hillsdale, N.J.: Lawrence Erlbaum Associates. pp. 229–260.

Lesgold, A., H. Rubinson, P. Feltovich, R. Glaser, D. Klopfer and Y. Wang (1988), 'Expertise in a complex skill: Diagnosing X-ray pictures'. In M.T.H. Chi, R. Glaser and M.J. Far (eds), *The Nature of Expertise.* Hillsdale, N.J.: Lawrence Erlbaum Associates. pp. 311–342.

Li, D. and M. Cheng (2007), 'Monologue vs. dialogue verbal reporting: Research subjects' perceptions'. *Journal of Translation Studies* 10 (1). 43–56.

Lörscher, W. (1986), 'Linguistic aspects of translation processes: Towards an analysis of translation performance'. In J. House and S. Blum-Kulka (eds), *Interlingual and Intercultural Communication. Discourse and Cognition in Translation and Second Language Acquisition Studies.* Tübingen: Gunter Narr. pp. 277–292.

Matrat, C.M. (1995), *Investigating the Translation Process: Thinking Aloud Versus Joint Activity.* Unpublished PhD thesis. Ann Arbor: University Microfilms International.

PACTE (2003), 'Building a translation competence model'. In F. Alves (ed.),*Triangulating Translation. Perspectives in Process Oriented Research.* Amsterdam & Philadelphia: John Benjamins. pp. 43–66.

—— (2009), 'Results of the validation of the PACTE translation competence model: acceptability and decision making'. *Across Languages and Cultures* 10 (2). 207–230.

Sharmin, S., O. Špakov, K.J. Räihä and A.L. Jakobsen (2008), 'Where on the screen do translation students look while translating, and for how long?'. In S. Göpferich, A.L. Jakobsen and I. Mees (eds), *Looking at Eyes. Eye-tracking studies of reading and translation processing,* Copenhagen Studies in Language 34. Copenhagen: Samfundslitteratur. pp. 31–52.

Shih, C.Y.Y. (2006), *Translators' Revision Processes: Global Revision Approaches and Strategic Revision Behaviours.* Unpublished PhD thesis, University of Newcastle-upon-Tyne, School of Modern Languages.

Tirkkonen-Condit, S. (1989), 'Professional vs. non-professional translation: A think-aloud protocol study'. In C. Séguinot (ed.) *The Translation Process.* Toronto: H.G. Publications. pp. 73–85.

—— (1992), 'The interaction of world knowledge and linguistic knowledge in the processes of translation: A think-aloud protocol study'. In B. Lewandowska-Tomaszczyk and M. Thelen (eds), *Translation and Meaning, Part 2.* Maastricht: Hogeschool Maastricht. pp. 433–440.

—— (1997), 'Towards a prototypical definition of translation'. In B. Lewandowska-Tomaszczyk and M. Thelen (eds), *Translation and Meaning, Part 4.* Maastricht: Hogeschool Maastricht. pp. 89–96.

Toury, G. (1991), 'Experimentation in translation studies: Achievements, prospects and some pitfalls'. In S. Tirkkonen-Condit (ed.), *Empirical Research on Translation and Intercultural Studies. Selected Papers of the TRANSIF Seminar, Savonlinna 1988.* Tübingen: Gunter Narr. pp. 45–66.

Results of the Validation of the PACTE Translation Competence Model: Translation Project and Dynamic Translation Index

2

PACTE GROUP
Allison Beeby, Mònica Fernández, Olivia Fox, Amparo Hurtado Albir (Principal researcher), Anna Kuznik, Wilhelm Neunzig, Patricia Rodríguez, Lupe Romero, Stefanie Wimmer

Chapter Outline

Introduction

The PACTE Group (Process of Acquisition of Translation Competence and Evaluation) has been carrying out holistic, empirical-experimental research into translation competence and its acquisition in written translation. Data have been collected on both the translation process and the translation product in inverse and direct translations involving six language combinations: English, French and German into and from Spanish and Catalan. The decision to include data on both inverse and direct translation was made in order to determine the characteristics of translation competence in relation to directionality.

The aim of this article is to present the results obtained relating to expert translators' dynamic concept of translation, and their dynamic approach to the translation of specific texts. We understand a 'dynamic' concept and approach to translation to be textual, communicative and functional as opposed to a 'static' concept and approach, which may be defined as linguistic and literal. Several theoretical models that have been proposed support this concept in Translation Studies, e.g. dynamic equivalence (Nida 1964); equivalence of meaning in the interpretive theory of translation (Seleskovitch 1968, Seleskovitch and Lederer 1984); functional equivalence (Reiss and Vermeer 1984, Nord 1991); and communicative translation (Hatim and Mason 1990).

Data have been obtained from two variables in our experiment on Translation Competence: (a) Translation Project, i.e. the way in which subjects approach the translation of a specific text and the units it comprises (procedural knowledge); and (b) 'Knowledge about Translation', i.e. subjects' implicit knowledge of the principles governing translation and other aspects of professional translation practice (declarative knowledge).

The methods used and the findings obtained for the variables Knowledge about Translation, Efficacy of the Process, Decision-making and Acceptability in our experiment on translation competence have been published in PACTE (2007a, 2007b, 2008, 2009).

In this article we present the results obtained for the variable Translation Project and their triangulation with those obtained for the variable Knowledge about Translation. The resulting Dynamic Translation Index is then triangulated with the indicator 'Acceptability' to determine the relationship between both.

Following a brief overview of the conceptual framework and methodology used in PACTE's research on translation competence, a description is given of the variable Translation Project and the results obtained from the indicators 'Dynamic Index' and 'Coefficient of Coherence'. Finally, data obtained for the variable Translation Project are triangulated with those of the variable 'Knowledge of Translation' to obtain the *Dynamic Translation Index.*

PACTE's Experimental Research on Translation Competence

The PACTE Group's empirical-experimental research project is divided into two phases:

- Phase 1 (completion date: 2010): the investigation of translation competence in professional translators, with the aim of developing a holistic model of translation competence which may subsequently be validated in a hypothetico-deductive study of professional translators.
- Phase 2 (running from 2010): the investigation of the process of acquisition of translation competence in trainee translators, with the aim of developing a holistic model of the acquisition of translation competence – based on the PACTE model of translation competence (PACTE 2003) – which may then be validated by a hypothetico-deductive study of trainee translators.

In the first phase of our research, expertise in translation was studied in an experiment comparing two groups of subjects pertaining to the same experimental universe (language professionals): 24 foreign-language teachers with no experience in translation, and 35 professional translators. Exploratory tests and a pilot study (PACTE 2002, 2005a, 2005b) preceded the final experiment.

It was necessary to carry out these studies since no holistic research had previously been carried out into what constitutes translation competence. Proposals related to the functioning of translation competence had been made by authors such as Wilss (1976), Bell (1991), Pym (1992), Kiraly (1995), Hurtado Albir (1996, 1999), and Hansen (1997). Other proposals made after the beginning of the PACTE project include: Risku (1998), Neubert (2000), Kelly (2005), Gonçalves (2005), Shreve (2006), and Alves & Gonçalves (2007). Some proposals are concerned with the specific functioning of translation competence in inverse translation (Beeby, 1996; Campbell, 1998). All of these models focus attention on the various components of translation competence but few attempts have been made to validate them from an empirical-experimental perspective (Gonçalves 2005, Alves & Gonçalves 2007, etc.).

The results obtained in the exploratory tests, pilot study and final experiment provide evidence of the competences specific to the professional profile of translators and serve as a basis for the second phase of our study: the process of acquisition of translation competence. This will be a longitudinal study involving repeated measurement.

Translation competence: definitions and theoretical model

The PACTE Group defines translation competence as the underlying system of knowledge required to translate. We believe that translation competence: (a) is expert knowledge; (b) is predominantly procedural knowledge, i.e. non-declarative; (c) comprises different inter-related sub-competences; and (d) includes a strategic component which is of particular importance.

In our model (cf. PACTE 2003), translation competence comprises five sub-competences as well as psycho-physiological components:

- **Bilingual sub-competence.** Predominantly procedural knowledge required to communicate in two languages. It comprises pragmatic, socio-linguistic, textual, grammatical and lexical knowledge.
- **Extra-linguistic sub-competence**. Predominantly declarative knowledge, both implicit and explicit. It comprises general world knowledge, domain-specific knowledge, bicultural and encyclopaedic knowledge.
- **Knowledge about translation**. Predominantly declarative knowledge, both implicit and explicit, about translation and aspects of the profession. It comprises knowledge about how translation functions and knowledge about professional translation practice.
- **Instrumental sub-competence**. Predominantly procedural knowledge related to the use of documentation resources and information and communication technologies applied to translation (dictionaries of all kinds, encyclopaedias, grammars, style books, parallel texts, electronic corpora, search engines, etc.).
- **Strategic sub-competence**. Procedural knowledge to guarantee the efficiency of the translation process and solve problems encountered. This sub-competence serves to control the translation process. Its function is to plan the process and carry out the translation project selecting the most appropriate method; evaluate the process and the partial results obtained in relation to the final purpose; activate the different sub-competences and compensate for any shortcomings; and identify translation problems and apply procedures to solve them.
- **Psycho-physiological components**. Different types of cognitive and attitudinal components and psycho-motor mechanisms, including cognitive components such as memory, perception, attention and emotion; attitudinal aspects such as intellectual curiosity, perseverance, rigour, the ability to think critically, etc.; abilities such as creativity, logical reasoning, analysis and synthesis, etc.

Translation competence, like all expert knowledge, is applicable to problem-solving. The solution of translation problems involves different cognitive operations within the translation process and requires constant decision-making on the part of the translator.[1] The expert translator thus possesses the ability to solve problems, which forms part of translation competence. We believe strategic competence to be the most important of all the sub-competences that interact during the translation process, since it serves to make decisions and to solve problems.

Since all bilinguals possess knowledge of two languages and may also possess extra-linguistic knowledge, we consider the sub-competences that are specific to translation competence to be: strategic competence; instrumental competence and knowledge of translation. Our research, therefore, focuses on these three competences.

Designing PACTE's research on translation competence

Our general hypothesis is that the degree of expertise in translation (i.e. translation competence) is reflected in both the process and the product of translation. Given that a high degree of expertise in translation may be expected in experienced translators, the definition of expertise for the purposes of our study is based on: (a) years of experience as a translator; (b) translation as a main source of income; and (c) experience in translating a wide range of texts. Our empirical and working hypotheses are based on the PACTE translation competence model (PACTE 2003).

The population from which our sample is taken is that of professionals working with foreign languages. From this population, two experimental groups were selected: professional translators and foreign-language teachers; 35 professional translators and 24 foreign-language teachers participated in the experiment on translation competence. A questionnaire was used to select subjects who fulfilled the criteria established. To ensure the absence of confounding variables, translators were not specialists in any particular field of translation (since specialisation in any specific field – literary, legal, audio-visual etc. – could distort results) and the period of their professional activity as translators was equivalent. Foreign-language teachers all had a minimum of five years' experience of teaching in the Spanish Ministry of Education's Modern Language School (*Escuela Oficial de Idiomas*). All subjects were required to be native speakers of Spanish and/or Catalan and to work in a professional capacity with German, French or English as their foreign language. Translators included in the study had an average of seven and a half (7.51) years of experience in translating, the average percentage of their income from translating was 86.43 per cent and their experience included translating a wide range of texts into their native language. Subjects were paid at market rates, simulating a real-life translation task.

Subjects performed the following tasks: (1) direct translation; (2) completion of a questionnaire about the problems encountered in the translation; (3) inverse translation; (4) completion of a questionnaire about the problems encountered in the translation; (5) completion of a questionnaire about translation knowledge; (6) participation in a retrospective interview.

Each of these tasks provided data for analysis. Further data were obtained from real time recordings of subjects' actions during the translation process using the software programs PROXY and Camtasia[2], and direct observation.

Variables

One independent variable and five dependent variables were selected for our study. The independent variable established was the degree of expertise in translation, defined in terms of years of experience in translating as the subject's main professional activity.

The dependent variables were: (a) Knowledge about Translation; (b) Efficacy of the Translation Process; (c) Decision-making; (d) Translation Project; and (e) Identification and Solution of Translation Problems. During the experiment a further variable 'Use of Instrumental Resources' was added.[3] Based on data obtained in the exploratory and pilot tests, a total of 18 indicators of the variables selected were identified (see Table 1). Of these, the most notable is the acceptability of subjects' translations, given that it reflects the quality of their translations, an important aspect of their translation competence. The indicator 'Acceptability' is used as a transversal indicator in conjunction with indicators of all the variables under study in order to determine the relationship that exists between the results obtained in these indicators and the quality of subjects' translations.

Table 1 summarizes the most important information relating to the dependent variables selected: conceptual definitions, indicators, data-collection instruments and data sources.

Table 1 Dependent variables (adapted from PACTE 2005a, 2005b)

KNOWLEDGE ABOUT TRANSLATION	
Related to the knowledge about translation sub-competence	
CONCEPTUAL DEFINITION	The subject's implicit knowledge about the principles of translation and aspects of the translation profession
INDICATORS	Dynamic index and coherence coefficient
INSTRUMENTS	Questionnaire on knowledge about translation
DATA SOURCE	Subjects' answers to the questionnaire

EFFICACY OF THE TRANSLATION PROCESS	
Related to the strategic sub-competence	
CONCEPTUAL DEFINITION	Optimum relationship between time taken to complete a translation task and the acceptability of the solution
INDICATORS	Total time taken; time taken at each stage of the translation process (orientation, development, revision[4]); acceptability
INSTRUMENTS	Translations, direct observation chart, PROXY and Camtasia recordings.
DATA SOURCE	Total time taken and time taken at each stage of the translation process in relation to the acceptable and partially acceptable results obtained

DECISION-MAKING	
This is the most complex variable. It provides data on subjects' procedural behaviour	
Related to strategic and instrumental sub-competences	
CONCEPTUAL DEFINITION	Decisions made during the translation process which involve the use of automatized and non-automatized cognitive resources (internal support) and the use of different sources of documentation (external support) (Alves, 1995, 1997)
INDICATORS	Sequences of actions; acceptability
INSTRUMENTS	Translations, direct observation charts, PROXY and Camtasia recordings
DATA SOURCE	Sequences of actions leading to results that are acceptable, partially acceptable and unacceptable in relation to Rich Points (specific source-text segments that contained translation problems; see Data Analysis below)

TRANSLATION PROJECT	
Related to the strategic sub-competence	
CONCEPTUAL DEFINITION	The subject's approach to the translation of a specific text and of the units it comprises
INDICATORS	Dynamic index in the overall translation project and that of each Rich Point; acceptability coherence between the overall translation project and that of each Rich Point
INSTRUMENTS	Translation problems questionnaire and retrospective interview
DATA SOURCE	Elements taken into account by the subject in relation to the translation brief

IDENTIFICATION AND SOLUTION OF TRANSLATION PROBLEMS	
Related to the strategic sub-competence	
CONCEPTUAL DEFINITON	Difficulties encountered by the subjects when carrying out a translation task
INDICATORS	Coefficient of perception of the overall difficulty of the text; subjects' identification of the Rich Points; characterisation of Rich Points identified by subjects; coefficient of subjects' satisfaction with the solution found for each Rich Point; type of internal support used to solve each Rich Point
INSTRUMENTS	Translation problems questionnaire and retrospective interview
DATA SOURCE	Problems identified and subjects' comments
USE OF INSTRUMENTAL RESOURCES	
Related to the instrumental competence	
CONCEPTUAL DEFINITION	Strategies used when consulting documentary resources in electronic format (webs, dictionaries and encyclopaedias in CD-ROM)
INDICATORS	Variety of resources, number of searches, time spent on searches (total and for each phase)
INSTRUMENTS	PROXY and Camtasia recordings, catalogue of searches
DATA SOURCE	Phase(s) of the search/es; time spent (initial/final); categories of resources (type, sub-type); number of resources (variety of searches); number of searches (quantity of searches)

Data Analysis

Triangulation of data

Data obtained have been triangulated as follows: i) comparing results for the different indicators of study variables; ii) comparing translators' and teachers' performance; iii) comparing their performance in direct and inverse translation; iv) comparing results for indicators of all variables and for Acceptability.

Analysis of data obtained for each Rich Point

Given that we consider translation to be a problem-solving process, the decision was made to focus data collection and analysis on specific source-text segments that contained translation problems. These we refer to as Rich Points. It should be noted that the decision to focus data collection on the selected Rich Points was also taken to facilitate the collection following Giegler's concept of 'scientific economy' (Giegler 1994) and triangulation of data (cf. PACTE 2007b, 2008, 2009).

The Rich Points selected were determined as a result of exploratory tests and a pilot study carried out prior to the final experiment (PACTE 2002, 2005a, 2005b). When identifying the Rich Points in each text, the following types of translation problems were taken into account:

- Linguistic problems: lexical (non-specialised) and morphosyntactic
- Textual problems: coherence, cohesion, text type and genre, and style
- Extralinguistic problems: cultural, encyclopaedic and subject-domain knowledge
- Problems of intentionality: difficulty in understanding information in the source text (speech acts, presuppositions, implicature, intertextual references)
- Problems relating to the translation brief and/or the target-text reader (affecting reformulation) which, from a functionalist point of view, would affect all Rich Points.

The texts selected for use in the experiment, together with five Rich Points identified in each, were trialled in the pilot study carried out in 2004 (reported in PACTE 2005a, 2005b). The Spanish source text used for inverse translation and the English source text used for direct translation are included in Appendix 1. The Rich Points selected are marked in each text.

Acceptability as a transversal indicator

Acceptability is related to the quality of the translation product. The quantitative and qualitative analysis of the data collected in our exploratory tests (PACTE 2002) and pilot study (PACTE 2005a, 2005b) confirmed the importance of this indicator in measuring subjects' expertise in translation. It is the only indicator that is used in conjunction with the specific indicators of each variable (see Table 1). In our research project, Acceptability is defined in terms of whether or not the solution effectively communicates (a) the meaning of the source text; (b) the function of the translation (within the context of the translation brief, the readers' expectations, genre conventions in the target culture); and (c) makes use of appropriate language.

Results (PACTE 2008, 2009) showed that the group of translators obtained more acceptable results in their translations than the group of foreign-language teachers, both in direct and inverse translation. The difference in the acceptability of the results obtained in both groups is much greater in direct translation (see Table 2).

Table 2 Acceptability scores for direct and inverse translation

'ACCEPTABILITY' IN DIRECT AND INVERSE TRANSLATION (PACTE 2008, 2009)		TRANSLATORS	TEACHERS
Direct translation	**Mean**	**0.73**	**0.49**
	Median	0.80	0.45
Inverse translation	Mean	0.52	0.48
	Median	0.50	0.40

Translation Project

As already mentioned, one of the study variables established in the PACTE Group's research on translation competence is Translation Project, defined as: 'The subject's approach to the translation of a specific text and of the units it comprises'. According to PACTE, a subject's translation project forms part of his/her strategic sub-competence and may therefore be considered to be procedural knowledge.

Instruments and indicators

The data obtained for this variable were collected using the translation problems questionnaire and the retrospective interview which focused on the Rich Points selected in each of the source texts for translation (cf. Appendix 2). The translation problems questionnaire includes a question concerning the subjects' overall translation project and another concerning the subjects' Translation Project for each of the Rich Points selected, i.e.:

- What were your priorities when translating the text? (Translation Project – overall)
- What were your priorities when solving it? (Translation Project – for each Rich Point)

When classifying subjects' responses to these two questions, two categories were established (the same two categories were used in our study of the variable Knowledge about Translation): (a) *dynamic*: communicative, functionalist, textual approach to translation; (b) *static*: linguistic and literal approach to translation.[5]

The indicators of the variable Translation Project are:

- Dynamic Index of Translation Project overall: the subjects' approach to the translation of a specific text.
- Dynamic Index of the Translation Project for Rich Points: how subjects approach the translation of the units of the text.
- Coefficient of coherence between the Translation Project overall and that of the Translation Project for Rich Points: consistency between the overall approach to the Translation Project and subjects' approach to the translation of each unit.

A scale of −1 to +1 was used to measure the Dynamic Index for both the Translation Project overall and the Translation Project for Rich Points: −1 (totally static); +1 (totally dynamic).

A scale of 0 to 1 was used to measure the Coefficient of coherence: 1 (totally consistent), whether or not the subject's approach to translation was static or dynamic; and 0 (totally inconsistent).

Dynamic Index of Translation Project overall

Translation Project overall: Dynamic responses
No significant differences were found in the responses obtained for the group of translators (85.71 per cent) and that of the foreign-language teachers (87.50 per cent) classified as *dynamic* in their approach to direct translation. In inverse translation, however, a slight difference is found between the percentage of translators (85.71 per cent) and foreign-language teachers (75 per cent) classified as *dynamic*.

Translation Project overall: 'Dynamic Index'
This index was calculated taking into account the responses to the Translation Project overall in both direct and inverse translation: −1 (all subjects whose translation project overall was *static* in both direct and inverse translation); 1 (all subjects whose translation projects overall was *dynamic* in both direct and inverse translation); and 0 (those subjects whose translation project overall differed between direct and inverse translation).

Regarding the Dynamic Index of the Translation Project overall (direct and inverse translation), no significant differences were found between translators and foreign-language teachers as regards their overall approach to the translation of a text, i.e. both groups' approach to their translation was *dynamic*. This may be attributed to the fact that both groups were language professionals and their aim, by default, was to communicate (see Table 3).[6]

Table 3 'Dynamic Index' of translation scores for translators and teachers

DYNAMIC INDEX OF TRANSLATION PROJECT OVERALL	TRANSLATORS	TEACHERS
Mean	**0.714**	**0.625**
Median	1.000	1.000
Minimum	−1.000	−1.000
Maximum	1.000	1.000
Std Dev	0.572	0.576

'Dynamic Index' of Translation Project for Rich Points

Translation Project for Rich Points: Dynamic responses

The percentage of dynamic responses to Translation Project was calculated for each Rich Point (RP). The results for direct translation were as follows:

- RP1. The title, which has a metaphoric aspect in all three texts (problem type: intentionality): translators 74.29 per cent and foreign-language teachers 50 per cent.
- RP2. A technical term: *keylogger // Download-Verzeichnis // édition de logiciels antivirus* (problem type: extralinguistic): translators 68.57 per cent and foreign-language teachers 54.17 per cent.
- RP3. Reference: *doubled ... surge // Schädling ... E-mail- Würmer ... Vorgängervariante // Le ver ... résurgence ... ses congénères* (problem type: textual): translators 54.29 per cent and foreign-language teachers 45.83 per cent.
- RP4. Elements in apposition present in all three texts, from which certain elements could be omitted: *a 'Trojan horse' program which could allow a hacker to take remote control of infected machines // Dateien-Tauchbörse Kazaa // Soumissions, des communications du virus* (problem type: textual and intentionality): translators 74.29 per cent and foreign-language teachers 50 per cent.
- RP5. A particularly Rich Point, presenting problems of comprehension and reformulation: *Cheltenham-based virus filtering firm // Tastatureingaben von PC-Nutzern nach Kreditkartennummern und Ähnlichem überwacht // Enregistrer les caractères tapés sur le clavier* (problem type: linguistic and intentionality): translators 85.71 per cent and foreign-language teachers 62.50 per cent.

It should be noted that:

1. The Rich Points that reflect the greatest difference between translators and teachers (i.e. where the translators' dynamic index was higher) are those

which involve problems of intentionality (RP1, RP4, RP5), problems that cannot be solved only by applying linguistic competence.
2. The Rich Point that reflects the smallest difference in the Dynamic Index obtained for both groups is RP3, a textual problem of reference which requires linguistic-textual knowledge for its solution.
3. RP3 (a textual problem) is the Rich Point for which the Dynamic Index in both groups is lowest.

If we consider the mean percentages obtained for the translation of all the Rich Points, it can be seen that the translators' approach to translation is clearly more dynamic than that of the foreign-language teachers (Table 4):

Table 4 Dynamic responses for Translation Project for Rich Points in direct translation task

DYNAMIC RESPONSES FOR TRANSLATION PROJECT FOR RICH POINTS, IN DIRECT TRANSLATION (%)	TRANSLATORS	TEACHERS
Mean	71.43	52.50
Minimum	54.29	45.83
Maximum	85.71	62.50
Std Dev	11.43	6.32

As for inverse translation, the results obtained for each Rich Point were as follows:

- RP1. *El Indiano . . . la fortuna del Americano* (problem type: extra-linguistic and textual): translators 74.29 per cent and foreign-language teachers 58.33 per cent.
- RP2. *gobierno alfonsino* (problem type: extra-linguistic): translators 80.00 per cent and foreign-language teachers 58.33 per cent.
- RP3. *desenfreno y dilapidación* (problem type: linguistic): translators 48.57 per cent and foreign-language teachers 45.83 per cent.
- RP4. *la geografía comarcal de Cataluña* (problem type: intentionality): translators 65.71 per cent and foreign-language teachers 45.83 per cent.
- RP5. *común . . . trona* (problem type: intentionality, textual and extra-linguistic): translators 74.29 per cent and foreign-language teachers 50.00 per cent.

We note that:

1. The Rich Points that reflect the greatest difference between translators and teachers (where the translators' dynamic index was higher) are those which involve extra-linguistic problems and problems of intentionality (RP2, RP5).

2. The Rich Point that reflects the smallest difference in the Dynamic Index obtained for both groups (RP3) is a linguistic problem.
3. RP3 is also the Rich Point for which the 'Dynamic Index' in both groups is lowest.

As regards the mean percentages obtained for inverse translation, as in direct translation, the group of translators shows a more dynamic approach to translation than the group of foreign-language teachers (Table 5):

Table 5 Dynamic responses for Translation Project for Rich Points in inverse translation task

DYNAMIC RESPONSES FOR TRANSLATION PROJECT FOR RICH POINTS, IN INVERSE TRANSLATION (%)	TRANSLATORS	TEACHERS
Mean	**68.57**	**51.67**
Minimum	48.57	45.83
Maximum	80.00	58.33
Std Dev	12.29	6.32

It may thus be concluded that there are significant differences between translators and teachers. Translators have a more dynamic translation project in both inverse and direct translation. The Rich Points for which results reflect the greatest difference between translators and teachers are those that present extra-linguistic problems and problems of intentionality, that is, those that cannot be solved by only using linguistic competence. On the other hand, those that present similar results in both groups of subjects are textual and linguistic problems. This may be explained by the fact that both groups share a common characteristic: they belong to the experimental population of language specialists. Finally, the Rich Points for which subjects' translation project is least dynamic are those that present problems that are linguistic and textual; this may be due to the fact that this type of problem requires a more static approach to translation, since solutions tend to be more fixed.

Translation Project for Rich Points: Dynamic Index

This index was calculated taking into account the number of subjects' dynamic responses to the Translation Project for each Rich Point, in both direct and inverse translation: 1 (more than 75 per cent were dynamic); 0 (26–74 per cent were dynamic); and −1 (25 per cent or less were dynamic).

The results obtained show that translators' approach to translation is more dynamic than that of foreign-language teachers. (Table 6):

Table 6 Dynamic Index of Translation Project for Rich Points

DYNAMIC INDEX OF TRANSLATION PROJECT FOR RICH POINTS	TRANSLATORS	TEACHERS
Mean	**0.571**	**0.208**
Minimum	−1.000	−1.000
Maximum	1.000	1.000
Std Dev	0.608	0.588

The Kruskal-Wallis Test shows that the difference in approach between translators and foreign-language teachers is significant

Table 7 Kruskal-Wallis test results

KRUSKAL-WALLIS TEST	
Chi-Square	5.6581
DF	1
p>Chi-Square	**0.0174**

Coherence Coefficient

When the coherence between subjects' approach to their translation project overall and their approach to the translation of each of the Rich Points established were examined, both experimental groups were found to be coherent in their approach to translation (Table 8):

Table 8 Coherence Coefficient of Translation Project

COHERENCE COEFFICIENT OF TRANSLATION PROJECT		TRANSLATORS	TEACHERS
Direct translation	**Mean**	**0.786**	**0.563**
	Median	1.000	0.500
	Minimum	0.000	0.000
	Maximum	1.000	1.000
	Std Dev	0.389	0.425
Inverse translation	**Mean**	**0.814**	**0.688**
	Median	1.000	0.750
	Minimum	0.000	0.000
	Maximum	1.000	1.000
	Std Dev	0.345	0.355

Table 8 shows that foreign-language teachers are coherent in both direct and inverse translation. However, the group of translators is more coherent than the group of teachers in both direct and inverse translation. Neither group behaves differently when translating into or out of the foreign language – they are equally coherent independent of directionality.

The Coherence Coefficient calculated for each group confirms (as evidenced in the variable Knowledge about Translation) that all subjects are coherent in their approach to translation. This would suggest that the selection of subjects for the experimental groups was appropriate.

Dynamic Translation Index and Expertise

Data obtained for the indicators of the variable Translation Project are related to those obtained for the variable Knowledge about Translation (PACTE 2008).

The variable Translation Project provides data concerning subjects' procedural knowledge and the variable Knowledge about Translation provides information about subjects' declarative knowledge. As mentioned, these two variables are defined as follows:

- Translation Project: The subject's approach to the translation of a specific text and the units it comprises; it forms part of the strategic subcompetence.
- Knowledge about Translation: The subject's implicit knowledge about the principles of translation and aspects of professional translation practice.

The categories *dynamic* and *static* were used to classify data from both variables, and the Dynamic Index and Coherence Coefficient calculated for each.

Data for the variable Knowledge about Translation were obtained from twenty-seven questions in the questionnaire administered to subjects (cf. PACTE 2008). Results show clear differences between the two experimental groups, with a significantly higher Dynamic Index for translators than for foreign-language teachers (Table 9):

Table 9 'Dynamic Index' of 'Knowledge about Translation'

DYNAMIC INDEX OF KNOWLEDGE ABOUT TRANSLATION	TRANSLATORS	TEACHERS
Mean	**0.273**	**0.088**
Median	0.200	0.150
Minimum	−0.200	−0.400
Maximum	0.900	0.625
Std Dev	0.204	0.261

In the PACTE Group's research on Translation Competence, three different types of Dynamic Index were calculated:

1. Dynamic Index of Knowledge about Translation
2. Dynamic Index of Translation Project overall (discussed above)
3. Dynamic Index of Translation Project for Rich Points (also discussed above)

These three indices together reflect subjects' consistency with regard to their concept of translation as a whole, and their approach to specific translation problems. This consistency is reflected in the Dynamic Translation Index which may then be triangulated with other indicators such as Acceptability, Sequence of Actions, etc.

Dynamic Index of Translation Project overall and Knowledge about Translation

In order to integrate these two indices, subjects were divided into three categories:

- *Static*: subjects whose dynamic index for Translation Project overall was classified as *static*, and whose dynamic index for Knowledge about Translation was also classified as *static*.
- *Inconsistent*: subjects whose dynamic index for Translation Project overall was classified as *static* and whose index for Knowledge about Translation was classified as *dynamic* or subjects whose dynamic index for Translation Project overall was classified as *dynamic* and whose index for Knowledge about Translation was classified as *static*.
- *Dynamic*: subjects whose dynamic index for Translation Project overall was classified as *dynamic* and whose index for Knowledge about Translation was also classified as *dynamic* (Table 10).

Table 10 Translation Project overall and Knowledge about Translation

TRANSLATION PROJECT OVERALL AND KNOWLEDGE OF TRANSLATION		TRANSLATORS	TEACHERS
Static	Mean	0.100	−0.125
	Median	0.100	−0.125
	Minimum	0.000	−0.125
	Maximum	0.200	−0.125
	Std Dev.	0.141	
	N	2	1
Inconsistent	Mean	0.188	−0.014
	Median	0.200	−0.100
	Minimum	0.000	−0.300
	Maximum	0.400	0.400
	Std Dev.	0.130	0.261
	N	6	7
Dynamic	Mean	0.305	0.145
	Median	0.300	0.200
	Minimum	−0.200	−0.400
	Maximum	0.900	0.625
	Std Dev.	0.213	0.256
	N	27	16

It was not possible to carry out a statistical test (Chi-square) of the results obtained for the categories *static* and *inconsistent,* given the very small number of subjects in each (fewer than eight). Significant differences were, however, found between translators and foreign-language teachers in the third category (*dynamic*). The translators classified as *dynamic* both for Translation Project overall and Knowledge about Translation were more 'dynamic' than the foreign-language teachers who were also classified as *dynamic* for both (see Table 11).[7]

Table 11 Kruskal-Wallis test results

KRUSKAL-WALLIS TEST	
Chi-Square	3.3156
DF	1
p	**0.0686**

Dynamic Index of Translation Project for Rich Points and Knowledge about Translation

Significant differences were found in the second (*inconsistent*) and third (*dynamic*) categories (Table 12):

Table 12 Translation Project for Rich Points and 'Knowledge about Translation' scores

TRANSLATION PROJECT FOR RICH POINTS AND 'KNOWLEDGE ABOUT TRANSLATION'		TRANSLATORS	TEACHERS
Static	Mean	0.200	−0.200
	Median	0.200	−0.200
	Minimum	0.200	−0.300
	Maximum	0.200	−0.100
	Std Dev.	0.000	0.141
	N	**2**	**2**
Inconsistent	Mean	0.245	0.153
	Median	0.200	0.200
	Minimum	0.000	−0.400
	Maximum	0.600	0.625
	Std Dev.	0.207	0.285
	N	**11**	**15**
Dynamic	Mean	0.293	0.032
	Median	0.300	0.000
	Minimum	−0.200	−0.200
	Maximum	0.900	0.250
	Std Dev.	0.214	0.164
	N	**22**	**7**

Translators classified as *dynamic* both for Translation Project for Rich Points and Knowledge about Translation were significantly more dynamic (see Table 13) than the foreign-language teachers who were also classified as *dynamic* for both. More foreign-language teachers were inconsistent than translators:

Table 13 Kruskal-Wallis test results

KRUSKAL-WALLIS TEST	
Chi-Square	7.6992
DF	1
p	**0.0055**

Dynamic Translation Index

The *Dynamic Translation Index* is the sum of three indices: the Dynamic Index of Knowledge about Translation + the Dynamic Index of Translation Project overall + the Dynamic Index of Translation Project for Rich Points. This index is not the average of these three indices, but the sum of all three (i.e. it can be greater than +1). Table 14 shows the results obtained for each of the experimental groups:

Table 14 Dynamic Translation Index scores

DYNAMIC TRANSLATION INDEX	TRANSLATORS	TEACHERS
Mean	**1.559**	**0.921**
Median	2.100	1.200
Minimum	−1.800	−1.300
Maximum	2.900	2.250
Std Dev.	1.087	0.968

The group of translators is significantly more dynamic (see Table 15) than the group of foreign-language teachers, both in their approach to and their concept of translation (procedural and declarative knowledge):

Table 15 Krusal-Wallis test results

KRUSKAL-WALLIS TEST	
Chi-Square	8.5309
DF	1
p	**0.0035**

Dynamic Translation Index and 'Acceptability'

As a result of the descriptive analysis of the relation between the Dynamic Translation Index and the Acceptability of subjects' translations in both experimental groups, an overall tendency was observed: both the Dynamic Translation Index and Acceptability were seen to move in the same direction, i.e. as one increased so did the other. There is thus a correlation between the Dynamic Translation Index and Acceptability. Although the Pearson-r correlation is low (0.44 for the foreign-language teachers and 0.34 for the translators), these figures do not detract from the interest of this finding. Only some of the acceptable solutions to translation problems are dynamic in origin (in concept and approach); others must be accounted for in terms of use of documentary resources, linguistic and extra-linguistic knowledge, etc. The fact that the percentage of translators' acceptable solutions of dynamic origin is lower than that of foreign-language teachers may be due to the fact that translators activate other sub-competences (strategic and instrumental) more often (see results for the variable 'Decision-making' in PACTE 2009).

Conclusions

We believe that the results obtained in our study show that a dynamic concept of, and approach to, translation is a characteristic of translation competence and determines the acceptability of translations.

A close relationship has been found between a dynamic concept of translation, a dynamic approach to the translation of a specific text, and a dynamic approach to the translation problems posed in the text (a relationship we refer to as the Dynamic Translation Index), and the acceptability of the solutions found to these problems. We believe that this relationship is one of the most important characteristics of expertise in translation.

Our experiment has shown that both language teachers and translators have an overall dynamic approach to the translation of a text. The reason for this lies, no doubt, in the fact that both groups are specialists in the use of language and are therefore aware of its communicative function. Results obtained to date, however, have shown that only expertise in translation enables subjects to convert this overall dynamic approach to the translation of a specific text into a dynamic approach to translation problems in a text, and acceptable solutions within a given context.

This finding supports theoretical models that have been proposed in the field of Translation Studies, such as that of Nida's dynamic equivalence (Nida 1964), Seleskovitch and Lederer's equivalence of meaning (Seleskovitch 1968, Seleskovitch and Lederer 1984), Reiss, Vermeer and Nord's functional equivalence (Reiss and Vermeer 1984, Nord 1991), and Hatim and Mason's communicative translation (Hatim an Mason 1990).

PACTE is currently triangulating the results obtained for the variable Translation Project, described in this article, with results obtained for the indicators of the variables Identification and Resolution of Problems and Use of Instrumental Resources. Our aim is to determine whether a dynamic concept and approach to translation affects subjects' identification and conceptualization of the nature of translation problems, and their use of instrumental resources. This will be the last step in the validation of our translation competence model.

How and when translator trainees acquire a dynamic concept of, and approach to, translation will be an important aspect of our future investigation of the process of acquisition of translation competence. Our hypothesis is that progression from a *static* to a *dynamic* concept of translation is a key element in the move from novice knowledge (pre-translation competence) to expertise in translation (translation competence).

Notes

1 As Krings (1986) reports, when analysing the translation process, these problems may be detected through subjects' behaviour : pauses; use of strategies; omissions; corrections, etc.

2 PROXY is a program (compatible with Windows) designed for the remote control of computers and users connected to a network. Camtasia records the subject's actions on the computer in real time and stores these recordings for subsequent study and data collection.

3 This was done because a large amount of data were collected on the use of instrumental resources by translators, and the indicators of the variables associated with the instrumental sub-competence (Decision-Making and Identification and Solution of Translation Problems) could not provide a sufficiently detailed analysis of the data obtained.

4 Based on the distinction made by Jakobsen 2002.

5 For example, 'so that the reader can understand it'; 'so that it sounds natural' (*dynamic*); 'it's the way they say it in French', 'leave it as it is' (*static*).

6 Although both groups showed the same dynamic approach to their overall translation project, this was not necessarily reflected in the solutions they found to specific translation problems. Taking into account the Acceptability of results obtained (cf. Table 2), the results obtained by translators were much more acceptable than those obtained by the foreign-language teachers in direct translation. The acceptability of the solutions provided by translators was 0.73 (on a scale of 0-1) and that of the foreign-language teachers 0.49. In inverse translation, the acceptability of the solutions found by translators was 0.52 while that of the group of foreign-language teachers was 0.48. Thus although the foreign-language teachers' approach to translation overall was dynamic, their solutions to specific translation problems were not as acceptable as those of translators. The explanation for this lies in the teachers' lack of expertise in converting this dynamic approach to translation into acceptable translation solutions.

7 A probability level of 0.1 may be interpreted in this type of study to be within the limits of significance.

References

Alves, F. (1995), *Zwischen Schweigen und Sprechen: Wie bildet sich eine transkulturelle Brücke? Eine Analyse von Übersetzungsvorgängen zwischen portugiesischen und brasilianischen Übersetzern.* Hamburg: Dr. Kovac.

—— (1997), 'A formação de tradutores a partir de uma abordagem cognitiva: reflexões de um projeto de ensin'. *TradTerm. Revista do Centro Interdepartamental de Tradução e Terminologia*, 4 (2). 19–40.

Alves, F. and J.L. Gonçalves (2007), 'Modelling translator's competence: relevance and expertise under scrutiny'. In Y. Gambier, M. Shlesinger and R. Stolze (eds), *Translation Studies: Doubts and Directions. Selected papers from the IV Congress of the European Society for Translation Studies.* Amsterdam: John Benjamins. pp. 41–55.

Beeby, A. (1996), *Teaching Translation from Spanish to English.* Ottawa: University of Ottawa Press.

Bell, R.T. (1991), *Translation and Translating.* London: Longman.

Campbell, S. (1998), *Translation into the Second Language.* London: Longman.

Giegler, H. (1994), 'Test und Testtheorie'. In R. Asanger and G. Wenninger (eds), *Wörterbuch der Psychologie.* Weinheim: Psychologie Verlag Union. pp. 782–789.

Gonçalves, J.L. (2005), 'O desenvolvimiento da competência do tradutor: em busca de parâmetros cognitivos'. In F. Alves, C. Magalhães and A. Pagano (orgs.), *Competência em tradução: cognição e discurso.* Belo Horizonte: Editora da UFMG. pp. 59–90.

Hansen, G. (1997), 'Success in translation: perspectives. *Studies in Translatology*, 5, (2), 201–10.

Hatim, B. and Mason, I. (1990), *Discourse and the Translator.* London: Longman.

Hurtado Albir, A. (1996), 'La enseñanza de la traducción directa 'general'. Objetivos de aprendizaje y metodología'. In A. Hurtado Albir (ed.), *La enseñanza de la traducción*, Col. Estudis sobre la traducció 3. Castellón: Universitat Jaume I.

—— (ed.). (1999), *Enseñar a traducir. Metodología en la formación de traductores e intérpretes.* Madrid: Edelsa.

Jakobsen, A. (2002), 'Orientation, segmentation, and revision in translation'. In G. Hansen (ed.), *Empirical Translation Studies: Process and Product. Copenhagen Studies in Language.* Copenhagen: Samfundslitteratur. pp. 191–204.

Kelly, D. (2005), *A Handbook for Translator Trainers.* Manchester: St Jerome.

Kiraly, D. (1995), *Pathways to Translation. Pedagogy and Process.* Kent: Kent State University Press.

Krings, H.P. (1986), *Was in den Köpfen von Übersetzern vorgeht. Eine empirische Untersuchung zur Struktur des Übersetzungsprozesses an fortgeschrittenen Französischlernern.* Tübingen: Narr.

Neubert, A. (2000). 'Competence in language, in languages, and in translation'. In C. Schäffner and B. Adab (eds), *Developing Translation Competence.* Amsterdam: John Benjamins. pp. 3–18.

Nida, E.A. (1964), *Toward a Science of Translating, with Special Reference to Principles and Procedures Involved in Bible Translating.* Leiden: E.J. Brill.

Nord, C.(1991), *Text analysis in Translation.* Amsterdam: Rodopi.

PACTE. (2002), 'Exploratory tests in a study of translation competence'. *Conference Interpretation and Translation*, 4 (2). 41–69.

—— (2003), 'Building a Translation Competence Model'. In F. Alves (ed.), *Triangulating Translation: Perspectives in Process Oriented Research*. Amsterdam: John Benjamins. pp. 43–66.

—— (2005a), 'Primeros resultados de un experimento sobre la Competencia Traductora'. In *Actas del II Congreso Internacional de la AIETI. Información y documentación*. Madrid: Publicaciones de la Universidad Pontificia Comillas. pp. 573–587.

—— (2005b), 'Investigating translation competence: Conceptual and methodological issues'. *Meta*, 50 (2). 609–619.

—— (2007a), 'Zum Wesen der Übersetzungskompetenz. Grundlagen für die experimentelle Validierung eines Ük-Modells'. In G. Wotjak (ed.), *Quo vadis Translatologie? Ein halbes Jahrhundert universitärer Ausbildung von Dolmetschern und Übersetzern in Leipzig. Rückschau, Zwischenbilanz und Perspektiven aus der Außensicht*. Berlin: Frank & Timme. pp. 327–432.

—— (2007b), 'Une recherche empirique expérimentale sur la compétence en traduction'. In D. Gouadec (ed.) *Actes du Colloque International: Quelle formation pour le traducteur?* Paris: La Maison du dictionnaire. pp. 95–116.

—— (2008), 'First results of a translation competence experiment: Knowledge of translation and efficacy of the translation process'. In J. Kearns (ed.), *Translator and Interpreter Training. Issues, Methods and Debates*. London: Continuum. pp. 104–126.

—— (2009), 'Results of the validation of the PACTE Translation Competence model: Acceptability and Decision-making'. *Across Language and Cultures*, 10 (2). 207–230.

Pym, A. (2003), 'Redefining translation competence in an electronic age: in defence of a minimalist approach', *Meta*, 48 (4). 481–97.

Reiss, K. and J. Vermeer (1984), *Grundlegung einer Allgemeinen Translationstheorie*. Tübingen: Niemeyer.

Risku, H. (1998), *Translatorische Kompetenz. Kognitive Grundlagen des Übersetzens als Expertentätigkeit*. Tübingen: Stauffenburg.

Seleskovitch, D. (1968), *L'interprète dans les conférences internationales. Problèmes de langage et de communication*. Paris: Minard

Seleskovitch, D. and M. Lederer (1984), *Interpréter pour traduire*, Col. Traductologie 1. Paris: Didier Érudition.

Shreve, G.M. (2006), 'The deliberate practice: translation and expertise', *Journal of Translation Studies*, 9 (1). 27–42.

Wilss, W. (1976), 'Perspectives and limitations of a didactic framework for the teaching of translation'. In R.W. Brislin (ed.), *Translation Applications and Research*. New York: Gardner. pp. 117–37.

Appendix 1: Texts[1]

DIRECT TRANSLATION TEXT

---

1 Email virus strikes in new form

Computer users were warned last night to be on the lookout for an email virus that can steal confidential information and allow hackers to take control of infected machines. The virus, a new variant of the BugBear email worm that infected tens of thousands of computers around the world last October, began to spread rapidly from Australia to Europe and the USA at around 8am yesterday. According to MessageLabs, a **5Cheltenham-based virus filtering firm** which reported about 30,000 infected messages in 115 countries, the **3propagation rate** of BugBear.B almost **3doubled** every hour throughout the morning. There was also a huge **3surge** as US users came online. Like its predecessor, the variant spreads by sending itself as an attachment to every address in an infected machine's email address book. To disguise where it came from, it uses different subject headings. As well as searching for anti-virus software and disabling it, BugBear.B installs a **2keylogger** to record what the user types, which may allow hackers to record confidential information such as credit card details and passwords. It also installs a **4"Trojan horse" program which could allow a hacker to take remote control of infected machines**. [...]

The Guardian – Friday, June 6, 2003

RP1: The title (problem type: intentionality)
– *Wurm in der leitung*
– *Bugbear.b, le virus informatique qui lit par – dessus l'épaule de ses victimes*
RP2: A technical term (problem type: extralinguistic)
– *Download-Verzeichnis*
– *Édition de logiciels antivirus*
RP3: Reference (problem type: textual)   .
– *Schädling / E-Mail Würmer / Vorgängervariante*

---

1 For the purposes of direct translation, parallel texts in English, French and German on the subject of computer viruses were used: 'E-mail virus strikes in new form' (*The Guardian*, June 6, 2003), 'Wurm in der Leitung' (*Frankfurter Allgemeine Zeitung*, June 14, 2003) and 'Bugbear.B, le virus informatique qui lit par-dessus l'épaule de ses victimes' (*Le Monde*, June 13, 2003).

– *Le ver / résurgence / ses congénères*

RP4: Elements in apposition (problem type: textual and intentionality)

– *Dateien-Tauchbörse Kazaa*

– *Soumissions, des communications du virus*

RP5: A particularly rich point (problem type: linguistic and intentionality)

– *Tastatureingaben von PC-Nutzern nach Kreditkartennummern und Ähnlichem überwacht*

– *Enregistrer les caractères tapés sur le clavier*

INVERSE TRANSLATION TEXT

La Plana Novella

La Plana Novella es una antigua heredad adquirida por el **1Indiano** Pere Domenech i Grau en 1885 que se encuentra en una pequeña planicie en el centro del Parc Natural del Garraf y pertenece al municipio de Olivella. La Finca fue declarada colonia agrícola 10 años más tarde por el **2gobierno alfonsino**, pero de aquella época perdura una leyenda de **3desenfreno y dilapidación** que hizo desaparecer la **1fortuna del americano**. El estilo arquitectónico del Palacete es ecléctico, es decir que mezcla diferentes estilos. **4La geografía comarcal de Cataluña** lo califica de "Castillo de Bambalinas" como si fuese un decorado de teatro. Sin ningún tipo de duda la construcción estilísticamente más original de Palau Novella es el lavadero gaudiniano, pero una de las piezas más características y llamativas del Palau es el **5común**, conocido como **5"la trona"**.

http://www.laplananovella.

RP1: *El Indiano … la fortuna del americano* (problem type: extralinguistic and textual)

RP2: gobierno *alfonsino* (problem type: extralinguistic)

RP3: *desenfreno y dilapidación* (problem type: linguistic)

RP4: *la geografía comarcal de Cataluña* (problem type: intentionality)

RP5: *común… trona* (problem type: intentionality, textual and extralinguistic).

Appendix 2: Questionnaire on Problems of Translation

1. How difficult do you think this text is to translate?

   On the scale between 'very easy' and' very difficult', put a cross on the line of squares below to show how difficult you think it would be to translate this text

   Translation of this   Translation of this

   text is very easy   text is very difficult

   ☐☐☐☐☐☐☐☐☐☐☐☐☐☐☐☐☐☐☐☐☐☐☐☐☐☐☐☐☐☐☐☐☐☐☐

2. **What are the general characteristics of the text that make you think so?**

3. **What were your priorities when translating the text?**

4. **What were the main problems you found when translating this text? Name 5 and answer the following questions about each.**

   Problem 1:   Why was it a problem?
   ....

   What were your priorities when solving it?

   Explain as clearly as possible what you did to solve it

   Are you satisfied with the solution? ☐ Yes ☐ No Why?

Exploring Translation Competence Acquisition: Criteria of Analysis Put to the Test

Susanne Göpferich, Gerrit Bayer-Hohenwarter, Friederike Prassl, Johanna Stadlober

3

Chapter Outline

Introduction[1]

How translation competence develops or is acquired has been of interest to Translation Studies for several decades. Most investigations conducted to answer this question follow a contrastive design. Two or more groups of participants, assumed to differ in their competence levels (typically translation students vs. professional translators), have to accomplish a translation task, from which product and/or process data are collected and then compared (for a survey of such investigations and their results, see Göpferich 2008: 168 ff.). The methods employed for data collection are verbal reports (think-aloud, cued or uncued retrospection), keystroke logging, questionnaires and interviews. In recent studies (Dragsted and Hansen 2008; Dragsted 2010), a combination of keystroke logging (to monitor the writing processes) and eye tracking (to capture the reading and comprehension processes) were used to gain insight into the coordination of comprehension and production in translation, again in a contrastive paradigm. The contrastive paradigm can also be found in expertise studies conducted in cognitive psychology, in which the development of expertise (viewed as the highest level of competence that can be achieved) has been analysed in various domains, such as playing chess or driving taxis (cf. Ericsson and Smith 1991). Although contrastive studies shed light on the differences between groups of participants with different competence levels, they leave us in the dark as to what exactly happens in between, i.e., they do not provide us with insights into the development of translation competence in its continuity. For this purpose, longitudinal studies in the strictest sense of the term are needed, i.e., longitudinal studies involving the analysis of translation products and processes of the *same* individuals *at regular intervals* during their training and later professional career.

To the best of our knowledge, the only two studies that fulfil these requirements are the CTP project (Capturing Translation Processes) conducted at Zurich University of Applied Sciences (Ehrensberger-Dow and Perrin 2009)[2] and the TransComp project conducted at the University of Graz (Göpferich 2009a). One reason for the scarcity of longitudinal studies may be the fact that they are extremely cumbersome and time-consuming.

As far as translation competence is concerned, there seems to be consent among translation scholars that it is composed of several sub-competencies. What sub-competencies have to be taken into account, and how they can be defined, is still a matter of debate (see, for example, PACTE 2000; 2002; 2003; 2005; Pym 2003; Shreve 1997; Wilss 1992). There is no doubt, however, that at least the following three competencies play a decisive role: communicative competence in the source language and the target language, domain competence, and tools and research competence (see the TransComp translation competence model below). Furthermore, there is general agreement that translation competence involves more than the sum total of these three – and perhaps other – sub-competencies.

The next two sections describe the translation competence model that forms the frame of reference for TransComp, and the PACTE Group's model of translation competence acquisition.[3] TransComp explores the development of translation competence in 12 students of translation over a period of three years and compares it with that of 10 professional translators. The methods of data collection employed are think-aloud, keystroke logging with Translog (Jakobsen/Schou 1999), screen recording with Camtasia Studio, webcam records, and short retrospective interviews and questionnaires (for the questionnaires, see Göpferich 2008: 257 ff.). The goals of the study are to gain insights into the development of translation competence in its continuity, to refine the models of translation competence and translation competence acquisition presented in the literature so far, and to use the empirical findings to improve translation didactics.

The TransComp Translation Competence Model

The TransComp translation competence model (see Göpferich 2008: 155 ff.; 2009a) has been developed on the basis of Hönig's (1991; 1995) model of an

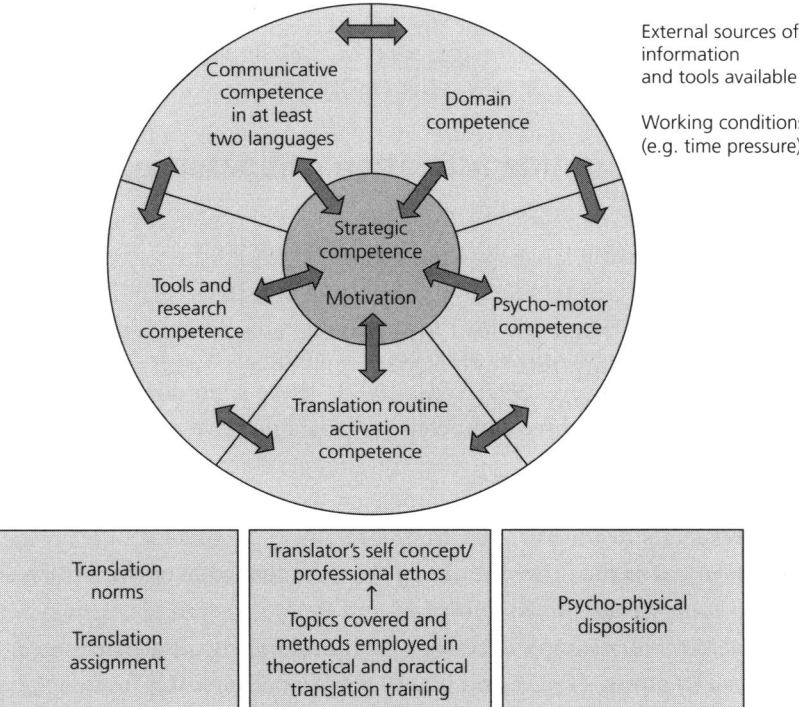

Figure 1 The TransComp translation competence model
(Göpferich 2008: 155 ff.; 2009a)

ideal translation process, the translation competence model of the PACTE Group (PACTE 2002; 2005: 610; 2007: 331; 2009) and our own experience in translation didactics.

As illustrated in Figure 1, a distinction is made between six sub-competencies, of which three are considered to represent the main translation-specific competencies in which translation competence differs from the competence of bilinguals with no specific training in translation. These three subcompetencies will be described below. For a complete description of the model, see Göpferich (2008: 155 ff.; 2009a).

1. Tools and research competence

This component comprises the ability to use translation-specific conventional and electronic tools, from reference works such as dictionaries and encyclopaedias (either printed or electronic), term banks and other databases, parallel texts, search engines and corpora, to the use of word processors, terminology and translation management systems as well as machine translation systems. It corresponds to the PACTE Group's 'instrumental sub-competence', a term we did not adopt because of the polysemy of 'instrumental', which could lead to misunderstandings, such as 'serving as a means'.

2. Translation routine activation competence

This competence comprises the knowledge and the abilities to recall and apply certain – mostly language-pair-specific – standard transfer operations (or shifts), as they can be found in contrastive overviews such as Friederich (1987), and which frequently lead to acceptable target-language equivalents. In Hönig's terminology, this competence could be described as the ability to activate productive micro-strategies.

3. Strategic competence

This corresponds to the PACTE Group's 'strategic competence' and controls the employment of the other sub-competencies mentioned above. As a meta-cognitive competence, it sets priorities and defines hierarchies between the individual sub-competencies, leads to the development of a macro-strategy in the sense of Hönig (1995), and ideally subjects all decisions to this macro-strategy (cf. the narrower definition of a 'strategic approach' in the section 'Analysing tools and research competence').

Modelling Translation Competence Acquisition

If modelling translation competence is a difficult endeavour, modelling translation competence acquisition presents an even greater challenge. Apart from a recent proposal by Bergen (2009), whose model combines translation competence acquisition with second-language acquisition, the only existing model of translation competence acquisition is that of the PACTE Group (PACTE 2000: 104). Their acquisition model is based on their own competence model, which we, however, propose to replace by our model presented above because the PACTE model does not take account of translation-routine activation, which, as our results will show, has important explanatory power in the description of translation competence acquisition (see 'Analysing translation routine activation competence'). According to the PACTE model, the acquisition of translation competence involves the development of the individual sub-competencies and in addition to this the development of the integrative competence to fall back on the individual competencies and to prioritize them depending on the respective assignment and communicative situation (integration of the sub-competencies). The development of these competencies and their integration not only involve the accumulation of declarative knowledge, but above all the restructuring of existing knowledge (PACTE 2000). According to the PACTE Group, this integration and restructuring is only made possible by a learning competence with specific learning strategies.

The Experimental Design of TransComp

The participants in the TransComp project are 12 undergraduate students of translation, recruited at the beginning of their first semester, and 10 professional translators. The number of professional translators is smaller because the project focuses on the students' development of translation competence and the data from professional translators serve the purpose of comparison only. The most crucial selection criteria for the student participants were 'very good' or 'good' grades in their final secondary school examinations in German (L1) and English (their L2). English also had to be the first foreign language they chose for their Translation Studies programme.

The 12 student participants were divided into two groups of six, the 10 professional translators into two groups of five. All students had to translate ten English texts of approximately 200 to 300 words each (eight extracts from popular-science texts and two extracts from operating instructions for household appliances) into German, according to the scheme in Table 1. An example of such a text (the popular-science text B2) can be found in Appendix 1.

Table 1 Translation scheme[5]

	GROUP A (6 STUDENTS)	GROUP B (6 STUDENTS)
Beginning of 1st semester	Text A1, Text A2, Text A3	Text B1, Text B2, Text B3
Beginning of 2nd semester	Text A4, Text A5	Text B4, Text B5
	Text B1 (1 semester's lag)	Text A1 (1 semester's lag)
Beginning of 3rd semester	Text B2 (2 semesters' lag)	Text A2 (2 semesters' lag)
Beginning of 4th semester	Text B3 (3 semesters' lag)	Text A3 (3 semesters' lag)
Beginning of 5th semester	Text B4 (3 semesters' lag)	Text A4 (3 semesters' lag)
Beginning of 6th semester	Text B5 (4 semesters' lag)[5]	Text A5 (4 semesters' lag)
End of 6th semester	Text A1 (6 semesters' lag)	Text B1 (6 semesters' lag)

The scheme allows us to check for progress over longer periods. It also takes into account that progress may proceed in steps, with varying improvement speeds over the whole period.

All the texts were translated only once by each student, except for Text A1 and Text B1, which will be re-translated after three years when the learning effect can be assumed to have become highly attenuated, i.e. when the students can be assumed to have more or less forgotten how they had translated it three years before. Nevertheless it must be acknowledged that students may still be able to remember certain aspects of the original translation.

The professional translators translate the same texts according to the scheme in Table 2.

Table 2 Translation scheme (professional translators)

GROUP A (5 PROFESSIONAL TRANSLATORS)	GROUP B (5 PROFESSIONAL TRANSLATORS)
Text A1, Text A2, Text A3, Text A4, Text A5	Text B1, Text B2, Text B3, Text B4, Text B5

The source texts (STs) selected present a range of different translation problems: lexical, syntactic, pragmatic, text-linguistic, culture-specific, creativity-demanding and comprehensibility-related problems caused by defects in the ST. Their comprehension, however, does not require any specialized knowledge. They were chosen primarily because, as their prior use in translation courses had shown, they are relatively easy to understand, but difficult to transfer into the target language.[6] These texts have to be translated in Translog 2006, which registers all keystrokes, mouse clicks, and the time intervals between them. To guarantee ecological validity, the participants are allowed to use the internet as well as any other electronic and conventional resources they wish. Consultation of electronic resources is registered using the screen-recording software Camtasia Studio; use of conventional resources is documented by observers. These sit in the background behind the participants during the experiments in order to minimize the sense of being observed and to create a situation which does not invite the participants to communicate with the observers.

During the experiments, the participants have to think aloud in the strictest sense of the term, i.e. they are requested to verbalize everything that goes on in their minds without justifying this or giving any additional explanations (level 1 and 2 verbalizations according to Ericsson and Simon 1999: 79). They were trained for this in a trial session prior to the first test wave (for reasons why think-aloud was preferred to cued retrospection, see Göpferich 2009a). The think-aloud is transcribed using XML (for a detailed description of the transcription conventions used, see Göpferich 2010b).

Immediately after each translation, the participants complete a questionnaire on how they felt during the translation process, on the problems they encountered, the strategies they employed to solve them, the estimated degree of text difficulty, and the extent to which they were satisfied with their solutions (for the questionnaire, see Göpferich 2008: 257 ff.). After this, short retrospective interviews are conducted.

Although retrospective verbalization, in contrast to think-aloud (concurrent verbalization), has the advantage of not interfering with the translation process, think-aloud is used as a primary source of information because '[f]or tasks of longer duration, the validity of think-aloud reports appears to be higher than that of retrospective reports' (Ericsson and Simon 1999: xxii). However, here we have to take into account that the professionals' think-aloud cannot be compared with that of the student translators in all respects for at least the following two reasons. Findings from expertise studies lead us to assume that (1) in professional translators more processes are automatized and thus not accessible for verbalization, and (2) professionals consider more potentially translation-relevant factors in their translation processes, which may lead to higher cognitive load and thus reduce the memory capacity available for additional concurrent verbalization (cf. Ericsson and Smith 1991; Hansen 2006). Since our participants translate into their L1, i.e., the same language in which they are thinking aloud, interferences are assumed to be smaller than in studies where the language in which the participants' think-aloud differs from the target language.

In addition to their translation products and translation processes, the participants' self-concepts as translators are analysed by means of a questionnaire (for the questionnaire, see Göpferich 2008: 264 ff.).

The results will be triangulated, set in relation to the quality of the participants' translation products, and used to correct, optimize and refine our provisional translation competence model (Fig. 1) and the translation competence acquisition model of the PACTE Group (2003: 60).

The quality of the translations, for which precise assignments were formulated and handed out to the participants (see Appendix 1), is assessed according to functional principles in a consensus-oriented process (for more details of the assessment procedure, see 'Analysing strategic competence').

Data Analysis: Criteria and Operationalization

TransComp concentrates on the following components of translation competence: (1) strategic competence, (2) translation routine activation competence and (3) tools and research competence (cf. the objectives in PACTE 2005: 611). These sub-competencies, which form the dependent variables in our study, have been chosen because we assume that they represent the main translation-specific competencies. The term *translation-specific* is used here to refer to competencies which do not automatically result from bilingualism and therefore cannot be assumed to have developed in bilingual persons with no specific training in translation.

By requiring our students to have good or very good grades in their final secondary school examinations in German and English, we aim to ensure that their communicative competence in these languages can be considered a controlled variable. However, clearly the impact of individual activities, such as visits abroad, and personal factors, such as their intelligence, are beyond the control of this study and may also play a role. The same applies to the participants' psychomotor competence. By selecting STs whose comprehension does not require any domain-specific knowledge, we hope to have ensured that the participants' domain competence can also be regarded as a more or less controlled variable.

Since we will work closely with our participants for three years, we expect to be able to learn something about their psycho-physical disposition, which may also have an impact on their development. During the entire study, the participants' development will be analysed against the background of the controlled theoretical and practical input of their translation training, which is assumed to shape each individual's translator self-concept and professional ethos.

To analyse the development of the three sub-competencies mentioned above, numerous criteria may be relevant, even criteria that may not be covered by the theoretical model used as a starting point. In this respect, working with think-aloud has the advantage that it offers the possibility of collecting data in an unstructured way, i.e. without bias from our theoretical model (see Krings 2001: 218), and unexpected criteria are able to emerge. Therefore as a first step we will analyse our corpus using the criteria described below. In the course of our analyses, further criteria are expected to emerge, and these will then be added.

Analysing strategic competence

Starting from the assumption that strategic competence becomes salient when problems occur and need to be solved,[7] we first analyze the transcripts for problems that occurred during the translation process.[8] For this analysis, we use an adapted version of the primary and secondary problem indicators suggested by Krings (1986). For a detailed description of these indicators and their application, see Göpferich (2010a). After having identified the problematic items in the translation process, we pursue both a product- and a process-oriented approach for further data analysis.

In the product-oriented approach, the target texts (TTs) of all participants are analysed and assessed for correctness. First, all errors that occurred in the TTs are classified into the primarily (but not exclusively) linguistic categories which are listed and explained in the error classification scheme in Appendix 2. Second, all errors are weighted following functional principles on a three-level scale (−0.5 / −1 / −1.5) depending on the degree to which they impair the TT's communicative function. This assessment is carried out by three raters who hold a university degree in Translation Studies. Where discrepancies in their assessments occur, these are discussed among the three raters until consensus is achieved.

One of the aims pursued by the process-oriented approach is to investigate whether, and to what extent, the participants proceeded in a strategic manner. The term *strategic* is used in our study to refer to processes in which a participant was aware of, or systematically developed an awareness of, the criteria that a specific TT section has to fulfil in order to be an adequate correspondent for the respective ST unit. Proceeding in a strategic manner can thus be regarded as the opposite of guessing, to which participants frequently resort when they are not aware of the criteria to be fulfilled by an adequate TT version. The degree to which participants proceed in a strategic manner, and thus avoid guessing, is regarded as one indicator of strategic competence (see also the analysis of decision-making processes described in 'Analysing tools and research competence'). This indicator, however, must always be considered against the background of the adequacy and acceptability of the translation product. Therefore process-oriented analyses are combined with the product-oriented analyses mentioned above.

Furthermore, we assume that problem awareness is a prerequisite for strategic competence. Problem awareness is revealed in a number of phenomena in our data, such as low numbers or the absence of translation errors, the number of translation problems solved and the number of translation errors reflected upon. A translation error is counted as reflected upon if the participant had generated translation alternatives for the respective ST unit (either in the translation process protocol (TPP)[9], in the key-logging file, or the retrospective questionnaire), had negatively evaluated the erroneous version, uttered or shown doubt[10] about it (in the TPP or the questionnaire) or had consciously decided not to translate a part of the ST which should have been translated.

Since the degree to which each participant proceeded in a strategic manner cannot be analysed for the whole translation process due to the complexity of this analysis (see below) and practical constraints, we restrict our analyses for strategic behaviour (in contrast to the analyses for translation problems and translation errors) to a number of translation segments in each ST which are representative of the repertoire of different potential translation problems mentioned in 'The Experimental Design of TransComp' above.

An exploratory investigation of part of the TransComp corpus was conducted on the translations of an operating instructions text (Text A3) by six novices at the beginning of their first semester and by five professional translators (reported in Göpferich 2010a), and the translations of a popular-science text (Text B2) by five novices and five professional translators.[11] This investigation used the procedure of analysis described above. Table 3 gives an overview of the results obtained.

Table 3 Translation errors and translation problems

	NOVICES	PROFESSIONAL TRANSLATORS
Text A3		
Total translation errors	18.9	12.4
Percentage of reflected translation errors	38.1 %	31.5 %
'Subjective' translation problems	36.3	16.6
Percentage of solved translation problems	67.5 %	69.1 %
Text B2		
Total translation errors	32.2	21.6
Percentage of reflected translation errors	32.9 %	30.8 %
'Subjective' translation problems	34.0	23.6
Percentage of solved translation problems	43.5 %	61.9 %

The analysis revealed that the professional translators on average had one third fewer errors in their TTs (12.4 errors in Text A3; 21.6 errors in Text B2) than the novices (18.9 errors in Text A3; 32.2 errors in Text B2), and had at least one third fewer 'subjective' translation problems (Text A3: 16.6 professionals vs. 36.3 novices; Text B2: 23.6 professionals vs. 34.0 novices). Interestingly, however, the novices' percentage of reflected translation errors hardly differed from the professionals' (Text A3: 31.5 per cent professionals vs. 38.1 per cent novices; Text B2: 30.8 per cent professionals vs. 32.9 per cent novices). Nor was there a difference in the percentage of solved translation problems in Text A3 (69.1 per cent professionals vs. 67.5 per cent novices), whereas in Text B2, the professionals solved one third more translation problems than the novices (61.9 per cent professionals vs. 43.5 per cent novices). The question why there was no difference here for text A3 but a clear difference for text B2 cannot yet be answered. However, it may be possible to suggest reasons once the data from the other experiments have been analysed.

It would be wrong to interpret the almost equal percentages of reflected translation errors in both groups of participants and for both texts as indicating equal degrees of problem awareness in both groups, because here we have to take into account that the total number of translation errors these percentages refer to are about one third lower for the professionals than for

Table 4 Strategies relating to the problem-solving paths for rendering the item 'control switch' in text A3 (operating instructions for hand mixer)

SUBJECT	FINAL TT VERSION	ALTERNATIVES CONSIDERED (INCLUDING SUGGESTIONS FOUND IN DICTIONARIES)	PROBLEM-SOLVING PATH
Professional KEG	Schalter D (acceptable)	Hauptschalter Sicherheitsschalter	utters the goal to designate the switch according to its function (+) to find out the switch's function, wants to have the mixer at his disposal (+) concludes from the co-text (probably from 'With the control switch (D) on 0, the attachments can be removed …') that it must be an ON/OFF-switch *(Hauptschalter)*, so that the function is clear and the comprehension problem solved (+); rendering, however, is postponed. discovers the information 'Speeds selected with control switch' in the co-text provided which did not have to be translated, and correctly concludes that there is only one switch, which he then calls just *Schalter* (switch), which solves the production problem (+)
Novice KNI	Haupt-schalter D (acceptable)	Kontrollknopf Hauptschalter Bedienungs schalter Steuerschalter	searching for a common German term for *control switch*, she spontaneously associates *Kontrollknopf* and *Hauptschalter*, of which she prefers *Hauptschalter* (0) looks up *control switch* in the bilingual online dictionary *Leo*, in which she reads various potential equivalents, among them *Hauptschalter*, by which she feels confirmed in her preferences although this designation does not sound good in her opinion (−) ignores her personal preferences arguing that the fact that something sounds good or not is not a relevant criterion here (+)

the novices. The fact that the professionals make fewer mistakes can already be regarded as an indicator of their higher problem-solving competence. Nevertheless, it is interesting that in both groups and for both texts about one third of the errors are reflected. Further research is needed in order to be able to suggest confidently possible reasons for this.

It also becomes apparent that the professional translators are better problem solvers from an analysis of the extent to which they proceeded in a strategic manner. In Göpferich (2010a), the problem-solving paths for three text sections from text A3, which turned out to be 'subjective' translation problems for most participants, were analysed qualitatively. Table 4 gives an example of how these problem-solving paths were analysed.

In the fourth column of Table 4, which summarizes the participants' problem-solving paths as they become obvious in their TPPs, + signs indicate useful and goal-oriented measures and decisions, – signs indicate measures which are not useful, and 0 signs indicate decisions for which it cannot be determined whether they were goal-oriented, i.e. positive (+), or not, i.e. negative (−). As can be seen from Table 4, both participants, the professional translator KEG and the novice KNI, rendered the term *control switch* correctly. The professional translator KEG, however, followed a strategic problem-solving path (+ signs only), whereas the novice KNI shows hardly any awareness of the criteria by means of which an acceptable solution can be identified. Her solution may just have been correct by chance. In Göpferich (2010a), the problem-solving paths for the three subjective translation problems in text A3 mentioned above are documented for all participants in the same manner as shown in the example in Table 4. They clearly show the tendency for the professionals to proceed in a *strategic* manner in the sense defined above in more cases and to a higher extent than the novices, as expected. To objectify further the results of our analyses, we attempted to quantify them by counting the + signs, − signs and 0 signs. However, this was in practice unfeasible because the participants need different numbers of steps to come to a conclusion, and not every step leaves a trace in the TPPs, so that the results are not comparable on a purely numerical basis. From a qualitative perspective, however, the professionals' more strategic approaches are immediately apparent as the comparison in Table 4 illustrates.

The fact that the novices frequently experienced problems with the same ST sections as the professionals (as in the example in Table 4) indicates that they already have problem awareness but, as the analysis of their problem-solving paths shows, lack the competence to solve these problems in a systematic manner, i.e. a manner guided by objective criteria. This assumption is corroborated by the observation that the professionals rarely returned to a translation problem once they had reflected upon it, whereas the novices frequently did. These returns to unsolved or unsatisfactorily solved translation problems may have different reasons. Translators may sometimes wisely postpone making a final decision to reach a higher understanding of the translation problem or scene first (cf. Tirkkonen-Condit's [1997: 79] concept of tolerance of ambiguity). In the context of the operating instructions text, however, the novices' high return rate seems more likely to suggest an inefficient problem-solving procedure, characterized by a lack of awareness of the criteria the potential TT versions have to fulfil. This is because the novices still continue to postpone the final solution of translation problems once they have already read the entire text and cannot expect to get more information from the context on which to base their decisions.

Analysing tools and research competence

As defined above, tools and research competence includes the ability to use reference resources. All consultations of reference resources are embedded in decision-making processes. Such decision-making processes start when uncertainty or doubt occur during ST reception and/or TT production and end when the final TT version is written down. It is only within this larger frame of observation that factors which trigger research processes become visible and that their outcomes can be assessed. Thus it was decided to embark on the investigation of *tools and research competence* by an analysis of decision-making processes.

In translation, decisions can sometimes be taken without consulting external resources; sometimes they are not possible without them. In some cases, decisions can be made without any conscious reflection; in other cases, long chains of knowledge retrieval from one's long-term memory (internal support) and/or knowledge integration from external resources (external support) are required. Starting from the assumption that the way in which decisions are made during translation may shed light on translation competence and especially, but not exclusively, on research competence, a number of text segments from the TransComp corpus were analysed for the types of decision made when translating them (see Prassl 2010). For this purpose, Jungermann *et al.*'s (1998: 29 ff.) typology of decision-making processes was used (see also Svenson 1990 and 1996, on which Jungermann *et al.*'s typology is based). This typology is based on criteria related to the amount of cognitive investment involved in decision processes, such as consciousness, concentration and the awareness that new information is needed. The indicators Jungermann *et al.* propose for these phenomena had to be specified for our purposes to be traceable in our data. The typology differentiates between four types of decisions: routinized[12] decisions, stereotype decisions, reflected decisions and constructed decisions. These four decision-making types are defined as follows: *Routinized* decision-making processes occur when a single TT equivalent is retrieved automatically, i.e. unconsciously, in a pattern-matching process, needing no further evaluation.[13] *Stereotype* decisions occur when more than one TT equivalent is available immediately and there is no indication that evaluation is guided by rational criteria, i.e. this type of decision is based on scheme-activation, which requires judgements on a holistic, possibly emotional, but not on a cognitively controlled level. *Reflected* decision-making may also begin with automatically retrieved options but, if the spontaneous process is disturbed, options have to be generated consciously using an internal or external search followed by cognitively controlled evaluation. If, towards the end of the reflected decision-making process, answers deemed necessary to complete the decision have not been found and consequently the translator has to resort to guessing to come to a conclusion, *constructed* decisions are made.

Table 5 gives an overview of the characteristics of these four types of decision-making processes, taking into account whether knowledge retrieval and evaluation of options (if the latter occurs at all) are conscious, or unconscious.[14]

Table 5 Typology of decision-making processes

	ROUTINIZED DECISIONS	STEREOTYPE DECISIONS	REFLECTED DECISIONS	CONSTRUCTED DECISIONS
retrieval of options	unconscious	unconscious	unconscious or conscious	conscious
evaluation of options	—	no indication of rational criteria in TPPs	conscious	conscious and with remaining doubt

In an exploratory study, this classification of decision-making processes was applied to the analysis of the decision-making processes involved in the translation of five segments of the popular-science text B2 from the TransComp corpus by five novices at the beginning of their first semester and five professionals. Table 6 gives an overview of the distribution of the four decision-making types for both groups of participants, and also indicates the numbers and percentages of decisions in each category which were successful.

Table 6 Distribution and success of decision-making processes. The numbers in parentheses indicate the number of successful decisions out of the total number of decisions in the respective category given first. The percentages refer to the total number of decisions made in each participant group, and the percentages in parentheses only to the successful ones.

ROUTINIZED DECISIONS		STEREOTYPE DECISIONS		REFLECTED DECISIONS		CONSTRUCTED DECISIONS		TOTAL	
Prof.	Stud.	Prof.	Stud.	Prof.	Stud.	Prof.	Stud.	Prof.	Stud.
11 (4)	4 (0)	2 (1)	0 (0)	11 (8)	20 (2)	1 (0)	1 (0)	25 (13)	25 (2)
44 %	16 %	8 %		44 %	80 %	4 %	4 %	100 %	100 %
(36.36 %)	(0 %)	(50 %)		(72.72 %)	(10 %)	(0 %)	(0 %)	(52 %)	(8 %)

As can be seen from Table 6, professional translators resort to routinized and stereotype decisions, the two decision-making types with relatively low cognitive involvement, in more than 50 per cent (52 per cent) of all cases, whereas students only do so in 16 per cent of cases. This could indicate that decision making places much more cognitive strain on students than on professional translators. In spite of their high cognitive involvement, only 8 per cent of the students' decision-making processes were successful and none of their routinized decisions led to an acceptable result. The professional translators' success rates increase as they move from routinized decisions (36.36 per cent), to stereotype decisions (50 per cent)[15], to reflected decisions (72.72 per cent), i.e. the more cognitive effort they invest, the more successful their decisions become. For the novices, no such tendency can be observed. Although 84 per cent of their decision-making processes are either reflected or constructed, they have a success rate of only 8 per cent. This may suggest that novices, in contrast to professionals, do not proceed in a strategic manner as defined in 'Analysing Strategic Competence' above, i.e. lack the ability to use or develop situation-specific criteria to apply in the evaluation processes. To improve their ability to proceed in a strategic manner, they need an awareness of the criteria a TT version has to fulfil. Although the professional translators' total success rate (52 per cent of all decision-making processes) is much higher than that of the students (only 8 per cent), it still does not indicate translational expertise. Their poorer results in routinized and stereotype decisions as compared to reflected decisions suggest that the professionals sometimes succumbed to over-routinization and would have needed a conscious problem-solving mode in more cases.

Analysing translation routine activation competence

The participants' translation routine activation competence is analysed in connection with their translational creativity (cf. Bayer-Hohenwarter 2010). Here we have assumed that proficient translators show a cognitively efficient balance of flexible problem-solving (which requires creativity, the opposite of translation routine) and routinized reflex (an indicator of translation routine activation competence). The ability to switch between a more routinized, automatized and eventually reflex-based mode of translation behaviour (routine) and a flexible, cognitively demanding problem-solving mode is considered one aspect of strategic competence in the TransComp translation competence model.

How are creativity and translation routine measured? The creativity dimensions that are taken into account are acceptability, flexibility, novelty (originality) and fluency (see Figure 2 below). Generally speaking, acceptability is conceived as skopos-adequacy; flexibility, as the ability to depart from the ST structure; novelty, as the rareness or uniqueness of translation solutions; and fluency, as the ability to produce TT solutions rapidly. The decision for these dimensions was based on the widely accepted postulates in creativity research (e.g., Guilford 1950) that firstly, truly creative work must be acceptable and novel, and secondly, that flexibility, fluency and novelty are the prototypical creativity dimensions linked to 'divergent thinking'. On a lower level, a large number of potential indicators seemed to be suited to being assigned to these individual dimensions. The indicators which seemed to be most revealing and easiest to measure were chosen (see Figure 2) and the operationalization criteria were specified (see Bayer-Hohenwarter 2010 for more details). Among the most important indicators are *creative (primary and secondary) shifts*, the core types of which are *abstraction, modification* and *concretisation*.[16]

To measure creativity, one bonus point is awarded for each instance of phenomena in the translation processes and/or the translation products which can be regarded as an indicator of creativity. A full description of these indicators is beyond the scope of this paper but is provided in Bayer-Hohenwarter (2009 and 2010). Some of these indicators, such as creative search strategies, imagination and all indicators of fluency are only found at the process level of analysis, i.e. they can only be detected by an analysis of the TPPs. Others, such as acceptability and novelty, are only found at the product level of analysis, i.e., in the TTs. Some indicators of flexibility, such as primary

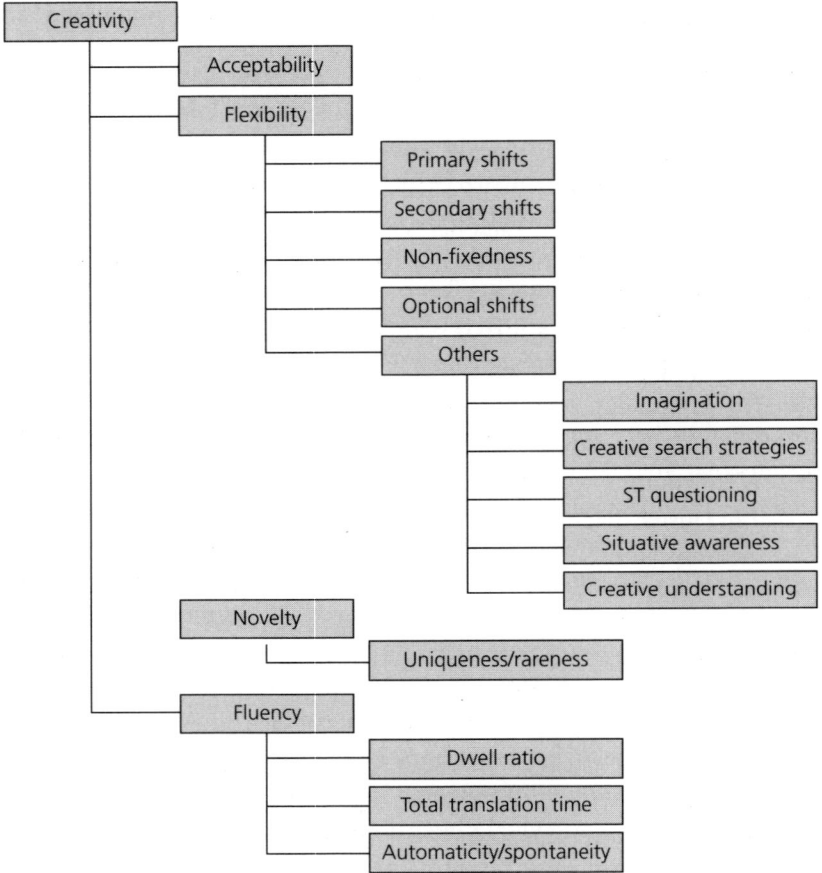

Figure 2 Overview of creativity dimensions and indicators

and secondary shifts and non-fixedness, are found at both levels of analysis. The relevant phenomena for which bonus points are awarded are thus related to aspects of behaviour (process level) and to creative aspects of TTs (product level) as determined according to the operationalization criteria specified in Bayer-Hohenwarter (2009 and 2010).

Next, total scores for every single dimension (acceptability, novelty, flexibility, fluency) are calculated. To make the scores comparable across participants and units of analysis, the bonus (and minus) points are not simply added up across dimensions. This is not possible because each indicator and each unit of analysis has a different potential for creative solutions. Instead, for each indicator and unit of analysis, the highest acceptability, flexibility, novelty and fluency scores obtained by the participants who translated it are determined. The highest score in each of these dimensions for each unit of analysis corresponds to 100 per cent; the lower scores are transformed into lower percentages accordingly.

Secondly, an overall creativity (OC) score is calculated. To do so, the percentages for the individual dimensions acceptability, flexibility, novelty and fluency are added up for each participant and each unit of analysis, and these are again transformed into percentages between 0 and 100 per cent according to the procedure specified above. This OC score *including fluency* reflects a comprehensive view of creativity in line with Guilford's dimensions of divergent thinking. Additionally, the percentages for OC *without fluency* are calculated and set in relation to the percentages for fluency for each participant. The OC score without fluency reflects a narrower view of creativity as opposed to routine, which is associated with fluency. These relations are visualised in cluster diagrams which we call 'creativity/routine profiles'. They indicate the translator's switch competence (see Figures 3 and 4 below).

In an exploratory study, this complex procedure of analysis was applied to the translations of four units of analysis (two creativity-demanding units and two routine units – see Figures 3 and 4) by four first-semester students, three third-semester students, and five professional translators. The preliminary results provide some support for the assumption that there is a correlation between the creativity scores and the quality of the translations. Furthermore, the results give some indication that more competent translators will show higher creativity scores, especially with creativity-demanding units, and higher routine (fluency) scores with routine units (see the creativity/routine profiles in Figures 3 and 4 below). At the same time, however, translators who are more competent also show higher routine scores for the creativity-demanding units, whereas the students' results for creativity and routine are more mutually exclusive, i.e. high fluency values tend to result in low creativity results and vice versa. What appears as a contradiction at first can be explained if we assume that expertise shows in the ability to be creative with a low level of cognitive involvement. This is what high creativity scores combined with relatively high routine scores show.

Only when the professional translators found a routine unit difficult was their behaviour similar to that expected for creativity-demanding units (see Fig. 3). Overall, for routine units, they showed high routine scores and relatively high creativity scores (see Fig. 4). The students' behaviour, when confronted with routine units, however, resembled more the behaviour

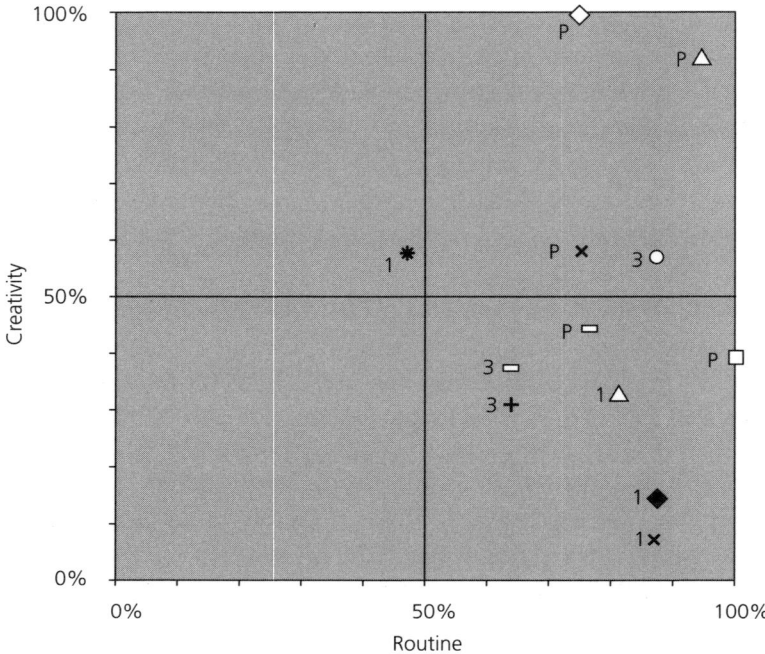

Figure 3 Creativity/routine profile for the two creativity-demanding units 'When you get *within ten feet of him*, he [the dog] will begin to wag his tail.' and 'If you stop and pat him, he will *almost jump out of his skin* to show you how much he likes you.' from Source Text B2. Foci of analysis in italics. 1 = student at the beginning of first semester; 3 = student at the beginning of third semester; P = professional translator.

expected from professional translators, but resulted in more inadequate translations (Bayer-Hohenwarter 2010).

Summary, Outlook to Further Research and Implications for Translation Didactics

Although the results of the exploratory analyses presented in this article are based on a modest sample from the TransComp corpus, tendencies can be observed which suggest that the criteria applied may indeed provide insights into the *development* of translation competence. Professional translators appear to make fewer errors, have fewer problems, translate faster, and,

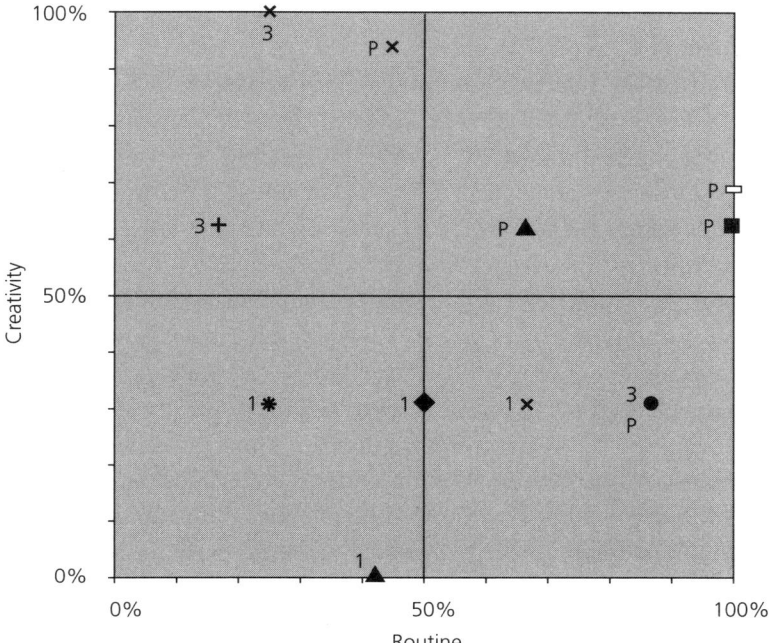

Figure 4 Creativity/routine profile for the two routine units 'You may meet him [the dog] tomorrow *coming down the street.*' and '*Did you ever stop to think that* a dog is the only animal that doesn't have to work for a living?' from Source Text B2. Foci of analysis in italics. 1 = student at the beginning of first semester; 3 = student at the beginning of third semester; P = professional translator.

more interestingly, proceed in a more strategic manner, with fewer returns to unsolved or unsatisfactorily solved problems. They are more creative, work more efficiently with less cognitive involvement, and know better than students when to switch from a routine mode to a problem-solving mode.

Extending these analyses to larger parts of the corpus and to all test waves will reveal whether, and at what stages in their BA programme, the students' translation sub-competencies, and their interaction, will show significant improvements (or deteriorations) and how these are related to the content and methods they have been exposed to in their BA programme.

In this article, the analysis of the participants' tools and research competence was limited to one aspect of this competence, their decision making. This analysis will be extended in future studies to include criteria such as which reference resources (monolingual dictionaries, bilingual dictionaries, parallel texts, etc.) are consulted, whether they are consulted before the participants have any primary equivalent association or only after that, and whether search items are predominantly used in the source language or the target language.

For translation didactics, our preliminary results have several implications. Firstly, as the analysis for the strategies used in our participants' problem-solving paths showed, novices frequently seem to be unaware of the criteria that an acceptable TT correspondent of a ST unit has to fulfil. This has a negative impact on their evaluation competence, which, in Pym's (2003) minimalist model of translation competence, is one of the two central abilities which make up translation competence (the other one could be termed associative competence). For successful and efficient evaluation processes, translators need criteria. To support students in developing evaluation competence, they should be encouraged to make lists of the criteria to be fulfilled by the TT correspondents they are looking for before they start searching for actual solutions. Making students aware of such criteria is more important than providing them with a whole range of possible solutions.

Requesting students to verbalize such criteria, even in cases in which they tend to resort to routinized decisions, may also help them to avoid the negative effects of over-routinization by encouraging them to make more reflected decisions. In reflected decisions, an awareness of the criteria to be met can be expected to increase the students' success rates, which amounted to only 10 per cent, compared with 72.2 per cent for the professionals, who showed an awareness of the criteria to be fulfilled. With regard to translation routine activation competence, creating more awareness of the criteria to be met may also have a positive effect on their switch competence, which helps them to decide when to switch from a routine mode to a problem-solving mode.

Conversely, for students who show awareness of the criteria to be met but cannot think of any way to produce an adequate TT due to lack of resourcefulness, the deliberate use of creative shifts can help them to find alternative paths of thinking and thereby improve their associative competence (cf. Pym 2003).

Notes

1 The research reported in this article forms part of the TransComp project, for which funding by the Austrian Science Fund (FWF) is acknowledged (project No. P20908–G03, September 2008–August 2011).

2   Hansen (see especially Hansen 2006) has also conducted investigations which, especially if her follow-up study is taken into account, can be called longitudinal. Although the same participants may have been involved in more than one experimental wave (this, for example, applies to the participants who also took part in the follow-up study after several years of professional work experience), some (or even many?) of her participants changed. Therefore, the term 'longitudinal study *in the strictest sense* of the term' does not apply here.

3   For a more detailed description of the existing translation competence and translation competence acquisition models, see Göpferich (2008: Ch. 6).

4   Unfortunately, we will not have data for a time lag of five semesters because this would have involved distributing two additional texts for translation to the participants at the beginning of their first semester, which was not feasible due to time and staff constraints.

5   'Lag' indications show the time elapsed from the moment the relevant text was translated by one group to the moment the same text was translated by the other group or re-translated by the same group as in the case of Text A1 and Text B1.

6   This estimation of the texts' difficulty was confirmed in the retrospective interviews we conducted with our participants.

7   This does not imply that translators use strategic competence *only* when they encounter actual problems. However, when problems occur, strategic competence is required to solve them in a reliable way.

8   We make a distinction between 'objective' problems, i.e. ST segments that we expected to cause difficulties for our participants, and 'subjective' problems, i.e. difficulties that the participants actually encountered and that we identified using Krings' problem indicators. Here we refer to 'subjective' translation problems. Cf. Nord (1997: 64), who also differentiates between 'objective' *problems* and subjective *difficulties*: '[T]ranslation *problems* are here considered to be objective or at least intersubjective; they are not to be equalled with translation *difficulties*, which are subjective difficulties that a particular translator or trainee encounters in a translation process because of deficient linguistic, cultural or translational competence or because they do not have appropriate documentation. Translation problems will always remain problems, even when a translator has learnt how to deal with them rapidly and effectively.'

9   We do not use the term *think-aloud protocol* here because the transcripts do not only contain what was said during the translation process, but also other actions such as the consultation of dictionaries and the adjustment of the headset. For this reason, the term *translation process protocols* is deemed more appropriate.

10   An indicator of doubt is, for example, checking the TT version by means of external resources.

11   We chose these two texts (the operating instructions text A3 and the popular-science text B2) because we wanted to test our criteria of analysis on two different genres, and these texts were among the first in our longitudinal study for which we had a complete data set and which will not be re-translated by the participants at the end of their sixth semester, so that we do not have to keep the results secret.

12   The term *routinized* (in contrast to *routine*) emphasizes the *process* of routine acquisition, the prerequisite for future routinized decisions.

13 Making routinized decisions is not part of translation routine activation competence. This competence only includes the ability to associate standard equivalents. Whether these can actually be used in a specific translation situation has to be decided upon by the translator. An appropriate decision here requires strategic competence.

14 From eye-tracking studies, we know that conscious processes may be taking place without the participant verbalizing or being able to verbalize anything (cf. the eye-mind hypothesis of Just and Carpenter 1980). Since gaze data are not available to us, we cannot determine whether a process was conscious or unconscious if no verbalization occurred. In such cases, we avoid the term 'unconscious' and replace it by 'no indication of rational criteria in the TPPs' (see Table 5). We are fully aware that cases in which participants made decisions consciously without verbalizing it may lead to a distortion of our results. Whether they have a significant effect will have to be determined by analysing a larger part of our corpus, and investigating whether there are any tendencies observable in our participants' decision-making behaviour from the beginning of their training until their graduation.

15 As can be been in Table 6, this refers to only one decision out of two and needs verification in a larger corpus.

16 *Abstraction* refers to cases in which translators use more vague, general or abstract TT solutions as compared with the ST. *Modification* refers to shifts that are considered to be at the same level of abstraction (e.g. express a ST metaphor with a different TT metaphor without the image becoming more abstract or concrete). *Concretization* refers to instances in which the TT evokes a more explicit, more detailed and more precise idea or image than the ST.

References

Bayer-Hohenwarter, G. (2009), 'Translational creativity: how to measure the unmeasurable'. In S. Göpferich, A.L. Jakobsen and I.M. Mees (eds), *Behind the Mind: Methods, Models and Results in Translation Process Research*. Copenhagen Studies in Language 37. Copenhagen: Samfundslitteratur. pp. 39–59.

—— (2010), 'Comparing translational creativity scores of students and professionals: flexible problem-solving and/or routinised reflex?' In S. Göpferich, F. Alves and I.M. Mees (eds), *New Approaches in Translation Process Research*. Copenhagen Studies in Language 39. Copenhagen: Samfundslitteratur. pp. 83–111.

Bergen, D. (2009), 'The role of metacognition and cognitive conflict in the development of translation competence'. *Across Languages and Cultures*, 10 (2). 231–250.

Dragsted, B. (2010), 'Coordination of reading and writing processes in translation: an eye on uncharted territory'. In G. Shreve and E. Angelone (eds). *Translation and Cognition*. Amsterdam, Philadelphia: John Benjamins. pp. 41–62.

Dragsted, B. and I.G. Hansen (2008), 'Comprehension and production in translation: A pilot study on segmentation and the coordination of reading and writing processes'. In S. Göpferich, A.L. Jakobsen and I.M. Mees (eds), *Looking at Eyes. Eye-Tracking Studies of Reading and*

Translation Processes. Copenhagen Studies in Language 36. Copenhagen: Samfundslitteratur. pp. 9–29.

Ehrensberger-Dow, M. and D. Perrin, (2009), 'Capturing translation processes to access metalinguistic awareness'. *Across Languages and Cultures*, 10 (2). 275–288.

Ericsson, K.A. and H.A. Simon, (1999), *Protocol Analysis: Verbal Reports as Data* (revised edition). Cambridge (Mass.), London (England): MIT Press.

Ericsson, K.A. and J. Smith, (1991), 'Prospects and limits of the empirical study of expertise: an introduction'. In K.A. Ericsson and J. Smith (eds), *Towards a General Theory of Expertise: Prospects and Limits*. Cambridge etc.: Cambridge University Press. pp. 1–38.

Friederich, W. (1987), *Technik des Übersetzens. Englisch und Deutsch*. 4th ed. München: Hueber.

Göpferich, S. (1995), *Textsorten in Naturwissenschaften und Technik: Pragmatische Typologie – Konstrastierung – Translation*. (Forum für Fachsprachen-Forschung 27). Tübingen: Narr.

—— (2008), *Translationsprozessforschung: Stand – Methoden – Perspektiven*. (Translationswissenschaft 4): Tübingen: Narr.

—— (2009a), 'Towards a model of translation competence and its acquisition: the longitudinal study *TransComp*'. In S. Göpferich, A.L. Jakobsen and I.M. Mees (eds), *Behind the Mind: Methods, Models and Results in Translation Process Research*. Copenhagen Studies in Language 37. Copenhagen: Samfundslitteratur. pp. 11–37.

—— (2009b), 'Adding value to data in translation process research: the TransComp Asset Management System'. In I.M. Mees, F. Alves and S. Göpferich (eds), *Methodology, Technology and Innovation in Translation Process Research. A Tribute to Arnt Lykke Jakobsen*. Copenhagen Studies in Language 38. Copenhagen: Samfundslitteratur. pp. 159–182.

—— (2010a), 'The translation of instructive texts from a cognitive perspective: Translation novices and professionals compared'. In S. Göpferich, F. Alves and I.M. Mees (eds), *New Approaches in Translation Process Research*. Copenhagen Studies in Language 39. Copenhagen: Samfundslitteratur. pp. 5–52.

—— 2010b, 'Data documentation and data accessibility in translation process research'. *The Translator*, Vol. 16, No. 1. 93–124.

Göpferich, S., G. Bayer-Hohenwarter and H. Stigler (2008 ff.), *TransComp: The Development of Translation Competence*. Graz: University of Graz, http://gams.uni-graz.at/container:tc/ (6 June 2009).

Guilford, J.P. (1950), 'Creativity'. *American Psychologist*, 5, 444–454.

Hansen, G. (2006), *Erfolgreich Übersetzen: Entdecken und Beheben von Störquellen*. (Translationswissenschaft 3). Tübingen: Narr.

Hönig, H.G. (1991), 'Holmes' 'Mapping Theory' and the landscape of mental translation processes'. In K. van Leuven-Zwart and T. Naajkens (eds), *Translation Studies: The State of the Art. Proceedings from the First James S. Holmes Symposium on Translation Studies*. Amsterdam: Rodopi. pp. 77–89.

—— (1995), *Konstruktives Übersetzen*. Tübingen: Stauffenburg.

Jakobsen, A.L. and L. Schou (1999), 'Translog Documentation Version 1.0'. In G. Hansen (ed.), *Probing the Process of Translation: Methods and Results*. Copenhagen Studies in Language 24. Copenhagen: Samfundslitteratur, Appendix.

Jungermann, H., H.-R., Pfister and K. Fischer (1998), *Die Psychologie der Entscheidung*. Heidelberg, Berlin: Spektrum.

Just, M.J. and P.A. Carpenter, (1980), 'A theory of reading: from eye fixation to comprehension'. *Psychological Review*, 87.4. 329–354.

Krings, H.P. (1986), *Was in den Köpfen von Übersetzern vorgeht. Eine empirische Untersuchung zur Struktur des Übersetzungsprozesses bei fortgeschrittenen Französischlernern*. Tübingen: Narr.

—— (2001), *Repairing Texts: Empirical Investigations of Machine Translation Post-Editing Processes*. Kent (Ohio), London: Kent State University Press.

Kußmaul, P. (1995), *Training the Translator*. (Benjamins Translation Library 10). Amsterdam, Philadelphia: John Benjamins.

Nord, C. (1997), *Translating as a Purposeful Activity: Functionalist Approaches Explained*. Manchester: St. Jerome.

PACTE (2000), 'Acquiring translation competence: hypotheses and methodological problems in a research project'. In A. Beeby, S. Ensinger and M. Presas (eds), *Investigating Translation*. Amsterdam, Philadelphia: John Benjamins. pp. 99–106.

—— (2002), 'Exploratory texts in a study of translation competence'. *Conference Interpretation and Translation* 4 (4). 41–69.

—— (2003), 'Building a translation competence model'. In Alves, F. (ed.), *Triangulating Translation*. Amsterdam, Philadelphia: John Benjamins. pp. 43–66.

—— (2005), 'Investigating translation competence: conceptual and methodological issues.' *Meta*, 50 (2). 609–619.

—— (2007), 'Zum Wesen der Übersetzungskompetenz – Grundlagen für die experimentelle Validierung eines Ük-Modells'. In G. Wotjak (ed.), *Quo vadis Translatologie? Ein halbes Jahrhundert universitäre Ausbildung von Dolmetschern und Übersetzern in Leipzig. Rückschau, Zwischenbilanz und Perspektiven aus der Außensicht*. Berlin: Frank & Timme. pp. 327–342.

—— (2009), 'Results of the validation of the PACTE translation competence model: acceptability and decision making.' *Across Languages and Cultures*, 10 (2). 207–230.

Prassl, F. (2010), 'Translators' decision-making processes in research and knowledge integration'. In S. Göpferich, F. Alves and I.M. Mees (eds), *New Approaches in Translation Process Research*. Copenhagen Studies in Language 39. Copenhagen: Samfundslitteratur. pp. 57–81.

Pym, A. (2003), 'Redefining translation competence in an electronic age. In defence of a minimalist approach'. *Meta* 48 (4). 481–497.

Shreve, G.M. (1997), 'Cognition and the evolution of translation competence'. In J.H. Danks, G.M. Shreve, S.B. Fountain and M.K. McBeath (eds), *Cognitive Processes in Translation and Interpreting*. Thousand Oaks: Sage Publications. pp. 120–136.

Svenson, O. (1990), 'Some propositions for the classification of decision situations'. In K. Borcherding, O.I. Larichev and D.M. Messik (eds), *Contemporary Issues in Decision Making*. Amsterdam: North-Holland. pp. 17–32.

—— (1996), 'Decision making and the search for fundamental psychological regularities: What can be learned from a process perspective?' *Organizational Behavior and Human Decision Processes* 65. 252–267.

Tirkkonen-Condit, S. (1997), 'Who verbalises what: A linguistic analysis of TAP texts'. *Target* 9 (1). 69–84.

Wilss, W. (1992), *Übersetzungsfertigkeit. Annäherungen an einen komplexen Begriff.* Tübingen: Narr.

Appendix 1: Example of a source text used

Source text B2 with assignment

Übersetzungsauftrag:

Der Text „Do this and you'll be welcome anywhere" ist entnommen aus dem Buch *How to Win Friends & Influence People* von Dale Carnegie (New York, London, Toronto, Sydney: Pocket Books, S. 53). Auf dem Umschlag des Buches, das erstmals bereits 1936 erschien und seither ununterbrochen in immer neuen Auflagen im Handel erhältlich ist, kann man Folgendes lesen:

"CELEBRATING 70 YEARS IN PRINT
THE FIRST—AND STILL THE BEST—BOOK OF ITS KIND—TO LEAD YOU TO SUCCESS
YOU CAN GO AFTER THE JOB YOU WANT—AND GET IT!
YOU CAN TAKE THE JOB YOU HAVE—AND IMPROVE IT!
YOU CAN TAKE ANY SITUATION YOU'RE IN—AND MAKE IT WORK FOR *YOU*!

Dale Carnegie's rock-solid, time-tested advice has carried countless people up the ladder of success in their business and personal lives. One of the most groundbreaking guidebooks of all time, HOW TO WIN FRIENDS & INFLUENCE PEOPLE will teach you:

- THE SIX WAYS TO MAKE PEOPLE LIKE YOU
- THE TWELVE WAYS TO WIN PEOPLE TO YOUR WAY OF THINKING
- THE NINE WAYS TO CHANGE PEOPLE WITHOUT AROUSING RESENTMENT

… and much, much more. Learn to live well and prosper with HOW TO WIN FRIENDS & INFLUENCE PEOPLE – a must-read for the twenty-first century.
MORE THAN 15,000,000 COPIES SOLD!"

Bitte übersetzen Sie den Text für die deutsche Version des Bestsellers.

Do this and you'll be welcome anywhere

Why read this book to find out how to win friends? Why not study the technique of the greatest winner of friends the world has every known? Who is he? You may meet him tomorrow coming down the street. When you get within ten feet of him, he will begin to wag his tail. If you stop and pat him, he will almost jump out of his skin to show you how much he likes you. And you know that behind this show of affection on his part, there are no ulterior motives: he doesn't want to sell you any real estate, and he doesn't want to marry you.

Did you ever stop to think that a dog is the only animal that doesn't have to work for a living? A hen has to lay eggs; a cow has to give milk; and a canary has to sing. But a dog makes his living by giving you nothing but love.

When I was five years old, my father bought a little yellow-haired pup for fifty cents. He was the light and joy of my childhood. Every afternoon about four-thirty, he would sit in the front yard with his beautiful eyes staring steadfastly at the path, and as soon as he heard my voice or saw me swinging my dinner pail through the buck brush, he was off like a shot, racing breathlessly up the hill to greet me with leaps of joy and barks of sheer ecstasy.

Appendix 2: Error classification scheme

ERROR CATEGORY	DESCRIPTION/EXAMPLE
Formal errors	
Punctuation	missing or wrong punctuation mark
Spelling	spelling mistake which is not an obvious typo (e.g. *Tauchen Sie das Gehäuse ihres Gerätes nie unter Wasser.*)
Formatting	line break where there should be none (the participants were not required to do any other formatting in the text)
Lexical errors	
Semantic errors	use of words and phrases which do not express the intended meaning either denotatively or connotatively; use of expressions which do not exist; omission of relevant information; wrong register on the word level
Collocation	wrong collocation (e.g. *schnelle Geschwindigkeit* instead of *hohe Geschwindigkeit*)

ERROR CATEGORY	DESCRIPTION/EXAMPLE
Blending	error caused by melting together parts of linguistic units or constructions which enter working memory simultaneously
Preposition	use of a wrong preposition; use of a prepositional phrase instead of a genitive (e.g. *von seinem Vater* instead of *seines Vaters*)
Grammatical errors	
Tense	use of wrong tense
Case, number, agreement	use of wrong case or grammatical number, mostly after prepositions or in appositions; agreement error
Mode	wrong mode, e.g. in indirect speech
Syntax	syntactical error; constructions which are hard to understand due to their length, long parentheses, etc.
Article	use of an article where there should be none; use of a definite article where an indefinite article should be used, etc.
Modality/illocution	wrong illocutionary indicator, such as *sollte* (recommendation) instead of *muss* (instruction)
Infinitive (Inf.)	grammatically wrong use of an infinitive construction (e.g. *Das Wetter war zu schlecht, um schwimmen zu gehen.*)
Text-level errors	
Text coherence	incoherent text segments, e.g. logically wrong connection of clauses and sentences by the use of semantically inappropriate conjunctions; use of wrong pronouns; missing second part of correlative (two-part) conjunctions
Functional sentence perspective	wrong topic-comment structure (theme/rheme)
Rhetoric	loss of communicative emphasis or effect (e.g. replacing a poem by a mere description of its content)
Other	
Idiomaticity/genre conventions	unidiomatic expression which does not lead to a change of meaning but may make the text hard to understand and betray that it is a translation in a negative sense; use of expressions which do not conform to genre conventions (e.g. *Das Bild ist kein Zufallstreffer.* instead of *Das Bild ist kein Schnappschuss.* and *Anfangend mit Namen* as a title.)
Cultural specificity	missing adaptation to the target culture or missing cultural neutralization

Development of Translation Competence in Novices: a Corpus Design and Key-Logging Analysis[1]

4

Heloísa Pezza Cintrão

Chapter Outline

Introduction

What thoughts and actions take place when somebody is producing a translation? Are there patterns that allow for the construction of models of the translation process or of translation competence, i.e. what we need to know to carry out a translation efficiently? Are there patterns that allow us to distinguish between different levels in the development of translation competence (TC)?

The eighties saw the first efforts to answer questions like these using empirical methods. More precisely, data acquired by recording people's actions and their reports on their thoughts and actions while translating were examined (e.g. Krings 1986, Gerloff 1987, Jääskeläinen 1989). These empirical studies have been carried out in various situations, generally in the form of experimental studies, i.e. by controlling some of the variables involved, such as the subjects' professional experience (for a literature review on research between 1982 and 2000, see Orozco 2000).

Empirical-experimental studies of this kind are now a few decades old. However, there is still a scarcity of data which can help us to know more about how someone becomes an expert translator. What is the nature of this thing that is called 'development of TC' by Chesterman (2000), 'acquisition of TC', by the PACTE Group (e.g. 2005), Orozco (2000) and Göpferich (2009), or 'evolution of TC', by Shreve (1997)? Toury (1995), Shreve (1997) and Chesterman (2000) have presented some interesting insights on this learning process, but empirical data are still lacking. Some projects with the aim of producing large-scale empirical data are underway at this moment, for instance, that conducted by the PACTE Group (e.g. 2005) and more recently the *TransComp* project, carried out by Göpferich (2009).

In this paper, a corpus for studying some aspects of the development of TC will be presented and analysed. The corpus collection was part of my doctoral research between 2002 and 2006.

Context

The experiment reported here focused on an introductory translation module devised for Brazilian students majoring in Spanish who were still at the initial phase of their foreign language learning, in the Language and Literature course at the University of São Paulo. The context is not, therefore, a bachelor's degree in translation. Nevertheless, we know that these graduates will work not only as language or literature teachers but quite often as translators as well. Moreover, some informal surveys have shown that they usually have expectations about what the university has to offer in terms of translator training. These important reasons led to the setting up of a translation training project in 2004 within the Department of Modern Languages, with the aim of offering a set of five optional modules in translation for each modern language.

The profile of the undergraduates in Spanish is that most of them only start learning Spanish as a foreign language in the university. The modules in translation practice were intended to be offered one per semester, starting as late as possible, taking into consideration the level the students would have attained in their Language and Literature studies. Since the foreign language modules only start in the third semester, after a whole year in which students take more general courses such as Introduction to Linguistics, the sequencing meant that the students for the first of these modules would have just finished a basic level of studies in the Spanish language. This raised the problem of what would be the minimum level of mastery of the second language for the students enrolling on these optional modules. This problem was especially critical for the first module.

Course Design: Models, Assumptions and Hypothesis

Our more general hypothesis in this study was that it was possible to offer students with this profile an introductory module in translation practice which could efficiently initiate the development of important aspects of TC.

One supporting argument is that TC is qualitatively different from bilingual competence as it is composed of a set of other sub-competences. The TC model proposed by the PACTE Group distinguishes the following sub-competences: bilingual, extra-linguistic, translation knowledge, instrumental and strategic, apart from pycho-physiological components 'that are cognitive and behavioural (memory, attention span, perseverance, critical mind, etc.) and psychomotor mechanisms' (PACTE 2005: 610). These sub-competences interact, and this TC model assumes that it is *strategic sub-competence* that plays a major role:

> . . . it is responsible for solving problems and the efficiency of the process. It intervenes by planning the process in relation to the translation project, evaluating the process and partial results obtained, activating the different sub-competencies and compensating for deficiencies, identifying translation problems and applying procedures to solve them. (*idem*)

In relation to bilingual sub-competence, the difficulty for these Brazilian undergraduates was the low level of mastery in only one language of their language combination. In the first translation module, if we worked on written translations into the mother tongue, it would limit the problem to reading comprehension in Spanish, the language which they had not yet mastered to an advanced level. Instrumental sub-competence is defined by PACTE as being 'made up of knowledge related to the use of documentation sources and information technologies applied to translation', and careful work on this sub-competence, combined with text-analysis directed at translation, could perhaps help to overcome the difficulties in reading comprehension, and at the same time contribute to developing research skills, as an important part of strategic sub-competence, i.e. how to identify the nature of comprehension difficulties and problems in a source text and apply procedures to solve them. Moreover, reading comprehension is precisely the language skill in which the proximity between Portuguese and Spanish may most facilitate and accelerate the language acquisition process.

Last but not least, many studies that compared students with translators have pointed out that students and beginners, as well as lay-people in general, often have a limited idea of translation. Consequently they tend to translate concentrating substantially on the isolated word and the meaning of the words in the source text (Toury 1995), and they do not take the functionality of the language and the new context in which the translation will be placed into account (Jääskeläinen 1989). So there is a narrow mental schema concerning translation that negatively interferes with the process and with the quality of the final product (Shreve 1997). This mental schema seems to correspond to the *knowledge about translation sub-competence*, defined by PACTE (2005) as comprising 'knowledge of the principles that guide translation (processes, methods and procedures, etc.) and the profession (types of translation briefs, users, etc.)'. There does not seem to be much reason to suppose that this mental schema, which guides the choice of strategies and many of the decisions on how to translate (strategic sub-competence), is dependent on the level of competence in the second language.

Thus our specific hypothesis was that it would be possible to work on the introductory module so that strategic sub-competence could activate other sub-competences, such as instrumental sub-competence, knowledge about translation and even the proficiency of these students in their first language, in order to compensate for their linguistic deficiencies in the second language.

To organize an introductory module for this purpose, the Chesterman model of the development of TC seemed to be helpful. Chesterman (2000) proposes five stages in the development of TC, based on a model of the growth of any expert knowledge: novice, advanced beginner, competence stage, proficiency, expertise. According to this developmental model, expert translator processing is highly automatic and intuitive, but the function of rationality, consciousness and analytical thinking is dominant at first, and at the novice stage 'certain rules and concepts have to be learned consciously' (p. 80). These concepts and rules have to be 'the most basic' (p. 80) as well as 'relevant to the skill in question' (p. 77). They are what Chesterman calls 'conceptual tools'. His choice of conceptual tools includes a set of translation strategies (and/or methods and/or procedures) which are *overtly presented* at the first stages of translator training. Their initial understanding is exercised in different ways: the trainer explicitly points out examples of each strategy with the aid of a translation plus its source text, the trainees are asked to examine a translation alongside its original and identify the strategies that have been used (I will call this 'translation case analysis' in both cases), and exercises are devised to train the students in the active use of the strategies.

Drawing on the previous considerations, the assumption was that the ability to achieve functional appropriateness is one of the most important components of strategic sub-competence, and that it depends heavily on the mental schema or beliefs of the subjects as to what translation is about.

Thus despite the fact that there is some controversy concerning the convenience of explicitly presenting theory in introductory courses,[2] I opted for a course format that brought together practical activities in translation or translation case analyses with the explicit presentation of a repertoire of theoretical concepts, in line with what Chesterman calls 'conceptual tools'. Functional, pragmatic and cognitive views on translation were an important part in the conceptual toolkit, besides linguistic and textual procedures. Elements from the *Skopos theory* (Reiss and Vemeer 1984), notions of situational dimensions (House 1981), and translation procedures (Vinay and Darbelnet 1958), among others, were presented and discussed alongside translation practice and analyses. A careful selection of texts was made so that various types of translation problems could emerge. A detailed account of the procedures in the classes, with the presentation of each text used, can be found in Cintrão 2006.

The aim in the presentation of these concepts was not that the students memorized them or were able to define or even name them at the end of the module, but only that they would have an overall idea of the range of variables that come into play in translation, and their relevance in identifying the nature of the different translation problems encountered, as well as the usefulness of the concepts and models as criteria for decision making, or as textual procedures, or as cognitive strategies in problem solving. In fact all of them, combined, were supposed to function in a unique way so as to modify the students' mental maps about translation.

In other words, declarative input (knowledge about translation) was intended to result in procedural output (changes in the strategic sub-competence), with discernible indicators in the translation product and process. At the product level, the indicator should be primarily an improved functionality of the translation solutions offered. For the process, I did not have a previous hypothesis, and in this aspect the study could be said to be only descriptive and exploratory.

Data Collection and Corpus Composition

Rationale

A longitudinal corpus of translations was collected in a synchronized manner during this introductory module, which lasted twenty-eight hours and was offered over four months to eight Brazilian undergraduates in the Spanish Language and Literature course at the University of São Paulo, who volunteered for the experiment.

These four months are too short a period if the point of reference were to be the time supposedly needed for a translation student to achieve a relatively high level of TC (say, in a four-year university degree in translation). In fact, the corpus was collected within the time constraints of the doctoral research, and allows for observing aspects of the development of TC only at the novice stage, in the particular pedagogical situation described.

Although four months is too brief a period for a longitudinal corpus of TC acquisition, we believe that the data analyses that it allows can contribute to the incipient empirical research on the development of TC in at least two ways. First, it can reveal something about the learning process in translation at the novice stage. Second, in methodological terms, this study can contribute to the debates and proposals on the collection of corpora for studying the development of TC, and test ways in which these data can be analysed.

Source texts and translation tasks

Because the corpus was compiled to observe a kind of developmental process, the bulk of it is longitudinal, that is, composed of data collected at different moments over time. A corpus of this kind must allow for observation of the evolution of the subjects' manner of translating as time goes by, ideally gathering data from the same subjects at different moments during their learning process.

The four translations for the longitudinal corpus were taken from children's stories by the Argentinean writer María Elena Walsh, which varied between two and three pages in length (Table 1). All of them were translated from the foreign language, Spanish, into the mother tongue, Portuguese.

The translations were synchronized with three different stages in the course. The subjects did T1 before the start of the course, T2 in the middle of the course, T3 when the course had finished, and T4 a few days after T3. T4 was a re-translation of the source text that had been translated in T1, carried out four months after T1 had been undertaken. Consequently the students' memory of the source text was not very recent. The re-translation was done without the students knowing that they were going back to translate a text that they had already worked on; they also had no access to the first translation completed. All four translations were done outside of class and were never discussed during the classes.

Table 1 Translations for the longitudinal corpus

CODE	SOURCE TEXTS (CHILDREN'S STORIES BY WALSH)	CHARACTERS (WITH SPACES)	DIRECTION (SP > PT)	MOMENTS
T1	'Historia de una Princesa'	5,028	L2 > L1	before the course
T2	'El patio'	3,262	L2 > L1	middle of the course
T3	'La Luna y la Vaca'	4,170	L2 > L1	after the course
T4	'Historia de una Princesa'	5,028	L2 > L1	a few days after T3

These children's stories were considered comparable (similar text type, same author, similar length), do not have specialized language and present various kinds of translation problems, including fragments with rhymes, play on words and cultural references. In the case of the latter fragments, the translator has to choose between retaining the linguistic meaning or to attend to textual or functional aspects related to the purpose (*Skopos*) of the translation. The decisions made in the translation of these fragments were converted in our indicators of functional appropriateness in a first data analysis. However, the various types of problems in these stories allow for further exploratory studies.

Subjects

Data were collected from twenty-one subjects, distributed among the main group and two control groups. The control groups were put together with the intention of isolating the 'competence in the foreign language' variable and the 'training in translation' variable.

The *main student group* (SM) was composed of eight volunteers. When the first translation was carried out, they were finishing their second semester of Spanish Language studies. They took the introductory translation module.

The *control student group* (SC) contained seven students with the same profile as the main group, but they did not receive any kind of training in translation during the months of the data collection. This group was chosen to allow a comparison of the behaviour of students who were just following language and literature studies in that period.

The *bilingual control group* (B) or group of language professionals was made up of six volunteers who had graduated from a Spanish Language and Literature course. Five of them had finished their Master's degree and all had experience teaching Spanish as a Foreign Language. They were considered to be experts in the field of language (linguistic, textual and literary knowledge), but not professional translators. Their professional experience with translation varied within the group, but translation was not their main source of income. This group was our parameter for the translation behaviour of proficient bilingual subjects. Because they were volunteers and each section of data collection was very time-consuming, it would have been difficult to ask them to do the four translation tasks and two complementary tasks of four hours each. In addition, their bilingual competence could be assumed to be at a stable stage and there was no reason to suppose that their behaviour in translation would vary significantly over four months. Thus they only did the first translation (T1).

Corpus collection and composition

For each translation, the subjects came for scheduled individual sessions of four hours each, and worked with no time constraints, always in the same office within the Faculty building, on the same computer, using Translog 2000, a program that registers key strokes in real time.

An interview was recorded immediately after each translation was finished, in which the subjects explained the reasons for their pauses, corrections, and decisions made, as registered by Translog, following the methodology adopted by Alves and Magalhães (2004).

Table 2 Outline of the corpus

COMPLEMENTARY DATA	SM (8)	SC (7)	B (6)	TOTAL
Subjects' profile form	8	7	6	21
Permission for the use of data	8	7	6	21
Questionnaire about concepts of translation	8	7	5	20
TXT file of the reading task in L1	8	7	5	20
LOG file of the reading task in L1	8	7	5	20
TXT file of the essay in L2	8	7	5	20
LOG file of the essay in L2	8	7	5	20
Brief questionnaire about the essay in L2	8	7	5	20
TRANSLATION PRODUCT AND PROCESS DATA				
TXT file of T1 (story 'Historia de una Princesa')	8	7	6	21
LOG file of T1	8	7	6	21
Transcription of the interview for T1 (retrospective protocol)	8	7	6	21
TXT file of T2 (story 'El patio')	8	7	–	15
LOG file of T2	8	7	–	15
Transcription of the interview for T2 (retrospective protocol)	8	7	–	15
TXT file of T3 (story 'La Luna y la Vaca')	8	7	–	15
LOG file of T3	8	7	–	15
Transcription of the interview for T3 (retrospective protocol)	8	7	–	15
TXT file of T4 (story 'Historia de una Princesa')	8	7	–	15
LOG file of T4	8	7	–	15
Transcription of the interview for T4 (retrospective protocol)	8	7	–	15

TRANSLATION DATA BY TYPE	T1	T2	T3	T4	TOTAL
TXT translation files (product data)	21	15	15	15	66
LOG files (process data by Translog 2000)	21	15	15	15	66
Interviews/Retrospective verbal reports (process data)	21	15	15	15	16

Thus the translation corpus proper includes 66 files of translations in TXT format, which provide mainly product data, plus 66 LOG files from these translations generated by Translog, which provide process data, such as pauses, and allow for measurements of total time and of the translation phases (orientation, drafting and revision), plus 66 recorded interviews on the translations, providing qualitative process data (a corpus outline is given in Table 2).

The corpus is composed also of complementary data. All the subjects filled out a profile, answered a questionnaire in order to probe their ideas concerning translation, wrote an essay in Spanish (L2) and carried out a text interpretation in Portuguese (L1). These writing and reading tasks lasted four hours each and were also done in individual sections, using Translog.

As we had in mind the use of the corpus for exploratory analyses, these different kinds of data were gathered in order to allow for the cross-referencing of their information – in particular performance in reading and writing, and ideas about translation – with the performance in translating. Unfortunately, one of the bilinguals did not complete these additional tasks. The subjects in the main group also answered a questionnaire about the course after it had finished. The questionnaires and the instructions read aloud to the subjects in reading, writing and translation tasks can be found in Cintrão 2006.

The reference material available was controlled, the subjects having the same consultation resources at their disposition. For each task, they were provided with a broad set of hard copy bilingual and monolingual dictionaries and with some grammars (always the same set). They also had access to the internet.

Data Analyses

In this section, the aim is to report on analyses of time measurements allowed by the Translog log files (process data): total time, drafting and revision phases (as proposed by Jakobsen 2002). This was an exploratory study. A previous product data analysis will be briefly described because I am interested in correlating the results with those of the process data analysis. A detailed account of the methodological procedures for this product analysis is available in Cintrão, 2006 (in Portuguese) and 2010 (in English).

In the graphs and tables, the group of language professionals is indicated by B (bilinguals), the main and control student groups by SM and SC, respectively, and by only an S when all students are being considered together.

Sensitivity to functional problems and quality of their solutions

In this product analysis, the aim was to test the hypotheses for the introductory module described above. Thus the performance was observed from the point of view of some functional aspects.

The translations of eighteen passages from the stories translated before and after the introductory module were selectively observed (ten passages in the source text for T1 and T4, 'Historia de una Princesa', and eight passages for the source text of T3, 'La Luna y la Vaca'). In these passages, semantic equivalence with the source text and appropriateness to the target context conflicted. The subjects needed to choose which one to prioritize, taking into consideration the target audience of Brazilian children for whom they were told to translate. This aspect was focused on because the ability to prioritize stylistic and functional dimensions when making decisions was assumed to be an aspect of the strategic sub-competence that had considerable independence from bilingual competence, being more dependent on the translator's concept of translation, as explained above.

The first analysis took into account whether the subjects had made any attempt to prioritize the functional appropriateness instead of the semantic equivalence with the source text. For each of the eighteen passages, a score of 1 was given to attempts to prioritize functional appropriateness and a score of 0 for the absence of this attempt. Secondly, scores between 0 and 3 were used to evaluate the quality of the solutions given for these functional problems (details in Cintrão 2006).

For the binary analysis in 'Historia de una Princesa' (T1 and T4), for instance, the sum of the scores for each of the ten passages resulted in a total score between 0 and 10 (or 0 per cent and 100 per cent) for each subject. This allowed an average percentage score for each group in each task. Thus the groups with a different number of subjects could be compared, as well as the performance of the same group in different translation tasks.

In T1, the translation done before the start of the training, the bilinguals had an average score (70 per cent) that was considerably higher than the students' score (37 per cent and 38 per cent) for the binary analysis (priority to functional appropriateness, Graph 1). As for the quality of the solutions for the selected passages, the bilingual group also showed a higher performance (49 per cent) when compared to the students' performance (20 per cent and 21 per cent) in T1 (Graph 2).

In the second translation of '*Historia de una Princesa*' (T4), after four months had passed, both student groups showed improvement in their average score for giving priority to functional appropriateness (Graph 1), but the improvement in the main group was more marked (control group – SC: 37 per cent > 57 per cent; main group – SM: 38 per cent > 68 per cent). Nevertheless, in the translation of '*La Luna y la Vaca*' (T3), produced a few days before T4, the control group yielded a poorer performance in the binary score (Graph 1) in relation to T1, while in contrast, the group that took the classes also showed an improvement in the translation of a new children's story (SC: 37 per cent > 32 per cent; SM: 38 per cent > 59 per cent).

Something led the group that had not taken any translation training to improve their performance when they translated the same story again, four months later (T4). The residual memory and/or the experience of three previous translations (T1, T2, T3) and/or the reflective work of explaining the problems and the criteria for finding solutions during the interview are possible reasons. However, the control group showed themselves to be incapable of transferring this improvement when working with a new story with problems of a similar nature (T3), a few days before.

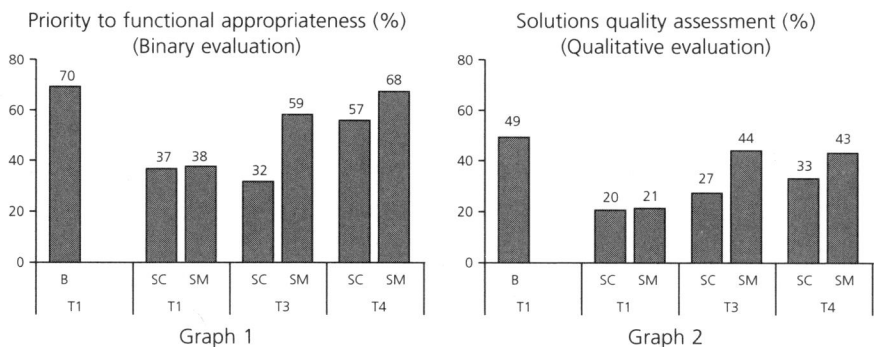

Graph 1   Graph 2

In the analysis of the quality of the solutions (Graph 2), both groups improved over time and the improvement of the main group is considerably more marked.

In both analyses, by the time they translated T3 and T4, the students who took the short module in translation were very close to the results of the bilingual subjects, which appears to confirm that this important functional aspect of the strategic sub-competence really has considerable independence from bilingual competence, at least in the sense that it can be improved before the subjects have mastered the foreign language to an advanced level.

Total time, drafting and revision time for T1

Some time measurements were observed which compared the bilinguals with the fifteen students for the translation done before the start of the training (T1).

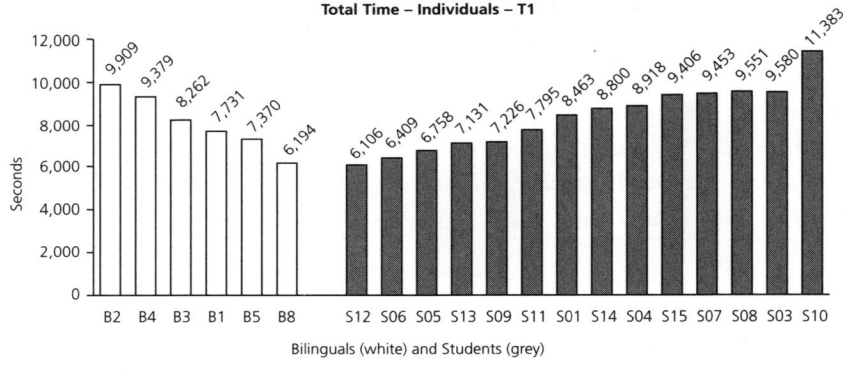

[Graph 3 – Total time for T1 (seconds)]

For the total time in seconds, the surprising result was that, in this first translation, most of the students were not slower than the bilinguals. Some were faster than most of the bilinguals (Graph 3) and the averages for the groups were not significantly different (see average time and standard deviation in Table 3), though the students needed to rely heavily on the consultation of dictionaries because of their deficiencies in knowledge of the foreign language.

Table 3 Averages for total time (in seconds)

	BILINGUALS	STUDENTS	DIFFERENCE	FASTER
Total time	8,141	7,543	548	Bilinguals
Standard deviation	1,358	1,504		

Table 4 Average typing speed (seconds/100 characters)

BILINGUALS	STUDENTS	DIFFERENCE	DIFFERENCE %	FASTER
98.8	125.6	26.8	21.34 %	Bilinguals

However, the allocation of time to drafting and revision by students and bilinguals was different. Bilinguals were faster both in measurements of typing speed (Table 4) as in the time they used for the first draft of the translation (drafting phase). They took longer in the revision, both in absolute time and percentage of the total time (see groups' averages in Graphs 4 and 5).

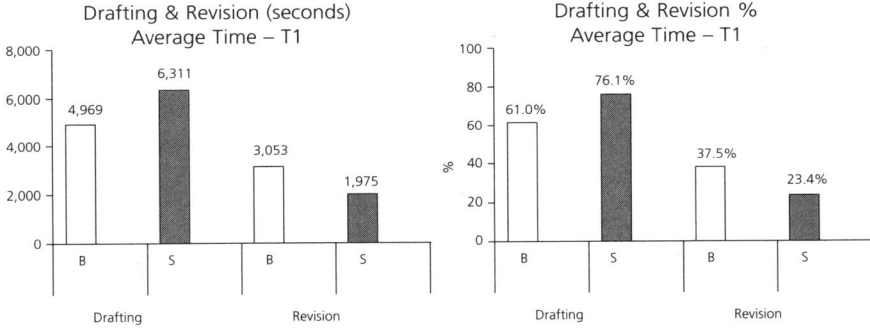

[Graphs 4 and 5 – Drafting and revision average time per group – T1]

These results show some similarity with the findings of a study by Jakobsen (2002), comparing the allocation of time by final-year translation students and professional translators, despite the different profiles of our subjects.

The strength of the correlation of the drafting and revision times with the product analysis scores was then calculated separately within the group of six bilinguals and within the group of the fifteen students, using Pearson's correlation coefficient (Tables 5 and 6). For both negative and positive values, a correlation between 0.1 and 0.3 is usually interpreted as weak (W), between 0.3 and 0.5 as medium (M), and between 0.5 and 1 as strong (S).

Table 5 Drafting and performance scores (T1)

	DRAFTING			
	STUDENTS (15 SUBJECTS)		BILINGUALS (6 SUBJECTS)	
	ABSOLUTE TIME	PERCENTAGE	ABSOLUTE TIME	PERCENTAGE
Sensitivity scores	−0.21 (W)	−0.43 (M)	−0.42 (M)	−0.62 (S)
Quality scores	−0.24 (W)	−0.47 (M)	−0.27 (W)	−0.33 (M)

Table 6 Revision and performance scores (T1)

	REVISION			
	STUDENTS (15 SUBJECTS)		BILINGUALS (6 SUBJECTS)	
	ABSOLUTE TIME	PERCENTAGE	ABSOLUTE TIME	PERCENTAGE
Sensitivity scores	0.41 (M)	0.38 (M)	0.64 (S)	0.61 (S)
Quality scores	0.47 (M)	0.44 (M)	0.36 (M)	0.33 (M)

The number of eight subjects in the bilingual group is too small to make generalizations; however, for both groups the figures suggest some correlation between the distribution of time between drafting and revision and the scores obtained for functional sensitivity and quality. For the subjects that combined less drafting time and more revision time, there tended to be better scores for sensitivity to the functional problems observed (binary scores) and better scores for the quality of the solutions proposed (Table 7).

Table 7 Correlational trend between phases and functional scores

DRAFTING TIME ⊙	+	REVISION TIME ⊙	=	FUNCTIONAL ⊙ APPROPRIATENESS

Longitudinal time measurements

The third analysis consisted of observing how the measurements of total time, drafting and revision progressed throughout the longitudinal corpus.

A general trend wherein the students dedicated a lower percentage of time to the revision (RV) and a higher percentage to the drafting (DF) phase than the bilinguals can be seen in Graph 6 (in the graphs, OR=orientation phase).

In order to allow for a comparison of the absolute time in seconds between

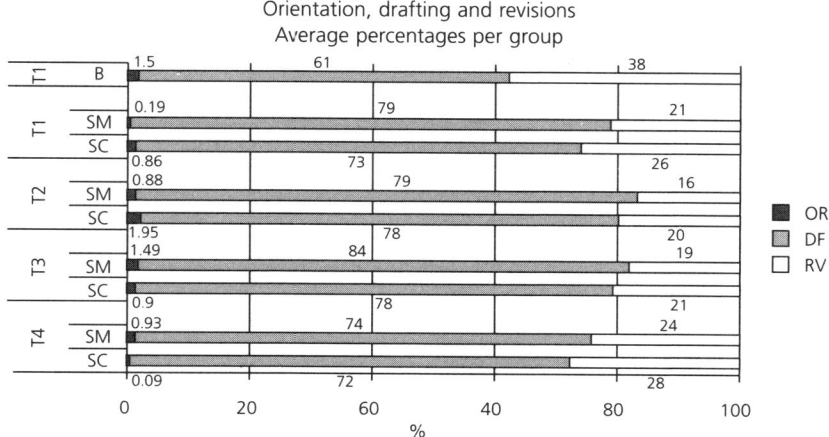

[Graph 6 – Translation phases per group and task]

the three texts of different lengths, a calculation was done using the seconds for each thousand characters of text (Graph 7).

Looking at the longitudinal progression of time with these absolute numbers, the group of students who took part in the course increased their total time (TT). They did so mainly because the absolute time dedicated to the drafting phase (DF) increased (Graph 7). This increase is more visible between T1 and T2, and slowly drops off in the subsequent translations (T3 and T4).

This suggests that the students in the main group began to work in a more reflective way after T1. From the interviews, it can be seen, for example, that they attempted to better exploit the different consultative materials available.

Considering the averages in absolute numbers (Graph 8), the two groups of students increased their total translation time (TT) throughout these few months, but this increase is more substantial for the group that took the course (SM).

This suggests that a more reflective attitude in the novice phase is independent of formal training, though the training seemed to intensify it. Something similar happened for the time dedicated to the drafting phase (DF).

In the revision phase (RV), there is a smooth rise in the time used by the main group (SM) from T1 to T4, while for the control group (SC), the absolute revision time drops subtly.

Bilinguals – T1

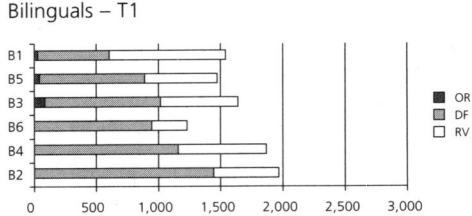

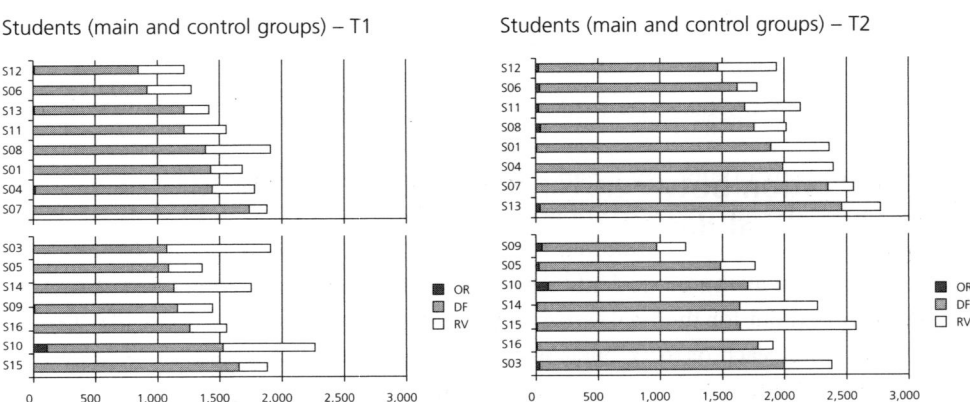

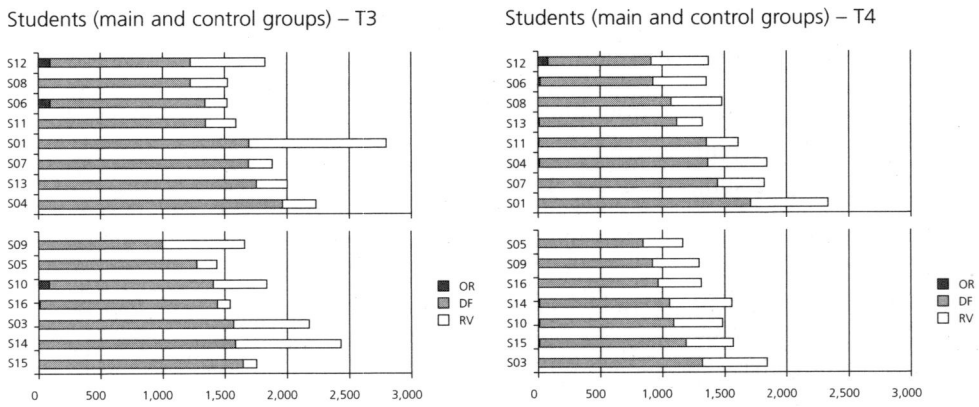

Graph 7 – Translation phases per group and task (seconds / 1000 characters)[3]

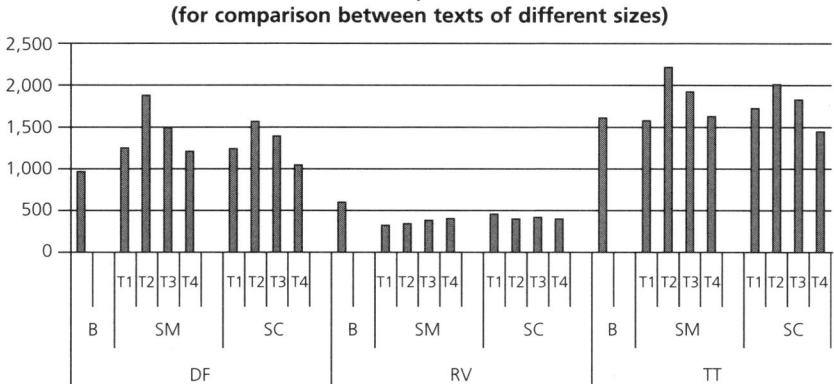

[Graph 8 – Averages over time (seconds / 1000 characters)]

Correlation between time and functionality for longitudinal data

Correlational analyses between time measurements and functional scores were also carried out for the final translations T3 and T4, using Pearson's coefficient.

This time, each of the groups of students was observed separately. The result was particularly interesting for T3: the increase in the absolute time dedicated to the drafting phase in T3 resulted in an improvement in the functional appropriateness achieved by the students who underwent the training, but correlated with a worsening in this product level for the students in the control group (Graph 9).

Final Remarks

The findings obtained from these analyses should only be considered as the basis for hypotheses to be tested in further studies. One reason is that the number of subjects in the groups would need to be greater in order to make generalizations. The correlation rates, for example, may be significantly altered in some cases when subjects with deviating behaviour are excluded. Nevertheless, there is some evidence of the following: After some preliminary practice in translation the two student groups increased the time allocated to the drafting phase and the total translation time, especially from T1 to T2, but also comparing T1 with T3. If restricted to the main group, this could only indicate that the type of educational intervention encouraged an intensification

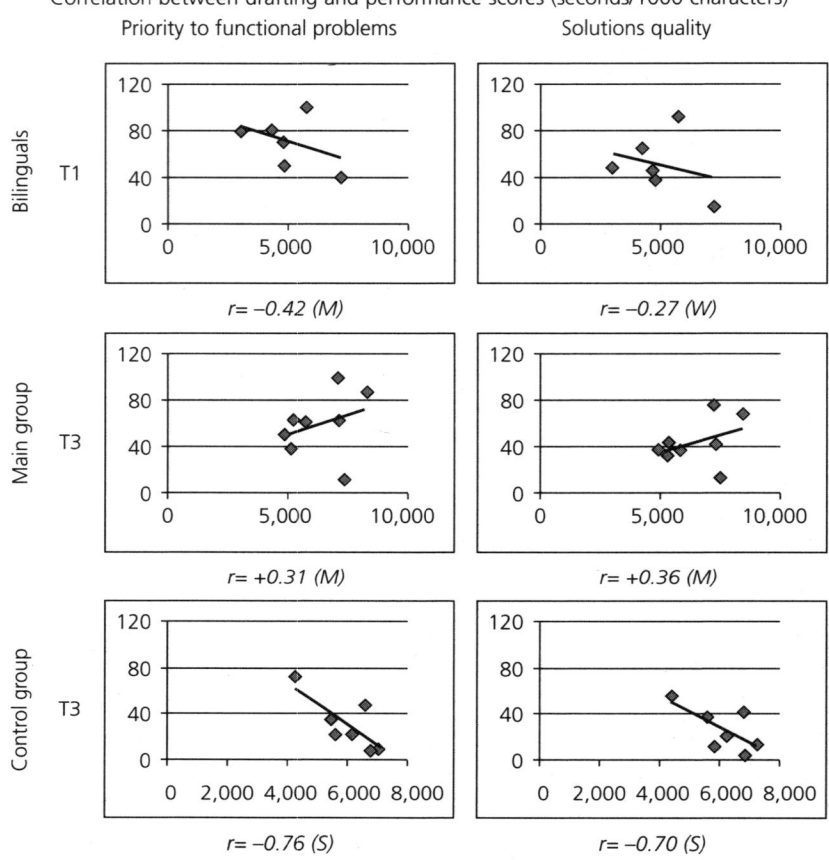

Correlation between drafting and performance scores (seconds/1000 characters)

[Graph 9 – Drafting and scores (scatter graphs and Pearson coefficients)]

of reflective behaviour, as would be expected given the theoretical and analytical component of the training. But since the group who had not undergone any formal training also increased the time allocated for the drafting phase, it seems reasonable to suppose that the novice stage is really characterized by being more reflective, as Chesterman (2000) suggests, with or without the 'conceptual tools'. Translating becomes slower in the drafting phase, initially going in the opposite direction of the allocation of time by professionals.

Process studies comparing beginners or students with professional translators can be used as parameters to infer the competences needed to translate. This could allow us 'to collect the significant differences, and to organize those differences in terms of a set of learning objectives or competencies' (Pym 2009: 136). However, Chesterman's model and the results of this exploratory study suggest that we cannot take for granted a linear development in which the learners gradually get closer to professionals' behaviour. At some stages, this development may go in the opposite direction, as in the case of these learners who, with or without training, showed an increase in the absolute time dedicated to the drafting phase, instead of getting closer to the professionals' allocation of time described by Jakobsen (2002), which is characterized by a decrease in time dedicated to drafting and an increase in the revision time. This would emphasize the importance of describing the development of translation competence in its different stages.

Furthermore, in T3, for the group that underwent training, the increase in time allocated to the drafting phase showed a positive correlation with functional appropriateness at the product level, while for the control group this correlation was negative. This suggests that the conceptual tools had some benefits in relation to the product quality. Methodologically, it also shows that to establish a correlation between process and product is fundamental: longitudinal behaviour that was apparently similar for each group in the use of time (process) led to opposite characteristics in the product.

The corpus described can be broadened in different ways: e.g. collecting translations for these same stories made by professional translators, replicating the collection of the corpus for the introductory module, and compiling a new corpus for students undergoing other types of pedagogical intervention.

In its present form, the corpus can still be used in exploratory studies focusing on other features of translation and to probe other methodologies of analysis, e.g. for observing pauses, the type of revisions carried out for linguistic product analyses, for linguistic product analyses, or to propose criteria for overall quality assessment.

In conclusion, if considered as tentative descriptions and the basis for hypotheses to be tested, the findings seem to offer contributions to the studies on the development of TC, and future explorations of this corpus, even taking into account its limitations, may provide useful insights and methodologies of analysis, especially when considering that this type of longitudinal study is still rare.

Notes

1 The first version of this paper was translated by Sarah Johnson. The final version was revised by John Warrener.

2   See, for instance, the stance taken by Hurtado (1996: 37 note 9).

3   Students main group in Graph 7 = the first set of subjects (S01, S04, S06, S07, S08, S11, S12, S13). Within each group, subjects are displayed following a growing order of duration of the drafting phase.

References

Alves, F. and C. Magalhães, (2004), 'Using small corpora to tap and map the process-product interface in translation'. *TradTerm*, 10. 179–212.

Cintrão, H.P. (2006), *Colocar Lupas, Transcriar Mapas [Magnifying Glasses Modifying Maps]*, PhD Thesis. São Paulo: FFLCH – Universidade de São Paulo. Available at <http://www.teses.usp.br/teses/disponiveis/8/8145/tde-08082007-145636/>

Cintrão, H.P. (2010), 'Magnifying glasses modifying maps. A role for translation theory in introductory courses'. In D. Gile, G. Hansen and N. Pokorn (eds), *Why Translation Studies Matter*. Amsterdam/Philadelphia: John Benjamins. pp. 167–182.

Chesterman, A. (2000), 'Teaching strategies for emancipatory translation'. In C. Schäffner and B. Adab (eds), *Developing Translation Competence*. Amsterdam/ Philadelphia: John Benjamins. pp. 77–89.

Gerloff, P. (1987), 'Identifying the unit of analysis in translation: some uses of think-aloud protocol data'. In C. Færch and G. Kasper (eds), *Introspection in Second Language Research*. Philadelphia: Multilingual Matters. pp. 135–158.

Göpferich, S. (2009), 'Towards a model of translation competence and its acquisition: the longitudinal study *TransComp*'. In S. Göpferich, A.L. Jakobsen and I.M. Mees (eds), *Behind the Mind*. Copenhagen Studies in Language 37. Copenhagen: Samfundslitteratur. pp. 11–37.

House, J. ([1977] 1981), *A Model for Translation Quality Assessment*. Tübingen: Narr.

Hurtado, A. (1996), 'La enseñanza de la traducción directa general' ['Teaching "general" translation into L1']. In A. Hurtado (ed.), *La Enseñanza de la Traducción*. Castelló de la Plana: Universitat Jaume I. pp. 31–55.

Jääskeläinen, R. (1989), 'Translation assignment in professional vs. non-professional translation: a think-aloud protocol study'. In C. Séguinot (ed.), *The Translation Process*. Toronto: H. G. pp. 87–98.

Jakobsen, A.L. (2002), 'Translation drafting by professional translators and by translation students'. In G. Hansen (ed.), *Empirical Translation Studies*. Copenhagen: Samfundslitteratur'. pp. 191–204.

Krings, H.P. (1986), 'Translation problems and translation strategies of advanced German learners of French (L2)'. In J. House and S. Blum-Kulka (eds), *Interlingual and Intercultural Communication*. Tübingen: Narr. pp. 263–276.

Orozco, M. (2000), *Instrumentos de Medida de la Adquisición de la Competencia Traductora [Instruments for Measuring the Acquisition of Translation Competence]*. PhD thesis. Barcelona: FTI – Universidad Autónoma de Barcelona.

PACTE (2005), 'Investigating translation competence: conceptual and methodological issues'. *Meta*, 50 (2). 609–619.

Pym, A. (2009), 'Using process studies in translator training: self-discovery through lousy experiments'. Available at <http://www.tinet.cat/~apym/on-line/training/2009_lousy_experiments.pdf>. Accessed January 2010.

Reiß, K. and H.J. Vermeer, ([1984] 1996), *Fundamentos para una Teoría Funcional de la Traducción.* [*Fundamentals for a Functional Translation Theory*], transl. S. García Reina, C. Martín de León and H. Witte. Madrid: Akal.

Shreve, G.M. (1997), 'Cognition and the evolution of translation competence'. In J.H. Danks, G.M. Shreve, S. B. Fountain and M.K. McBeath (eds), *Cognitive Processes in Translation and Interpreting.* Thousand Oaks: Sage. pp. 120–136.

Toury, G. (1995), 'A bilingual speaker becomes a translator: a tentative developmental model'. In *Descriptive Translation Studies and Beyond.* Amsterdam/Philadelphia: John Benjamins. pp. 241–258.

Vinay, J.P. and J. Darbelnet (1958), *Stylistique comparée du français et de l'anglais.* Paris: Didier.

Uncertainty Management, Metacognitive Bundling in Problem-solving and Translation Quality

5

Erik Angelone and Gregory M. Shreve

Chapter Outline

Introduction

Uncertainty is broadly defined as a cognitive state of indecision, marked by a distinct class of behaviours potentially occurring during the translation process. Uncertainty behaviours are visible and can generally be determined by analysis to be relevant to some aspect of the cognitive problem-solving processes at the core of the translation activity. The behaviours emerge as 'interruptions' in the translation process, related to the inability to make particular translation decisions, and can be regarded as potentially inherent in all translation activity.

Observable indicators of uncertainty, such as extended pauses, deletions, revisions, or other editing actions, as well as direct or indirect articulation, including, for instance, hedges on quantity or quality, tend to arise when the translator reaches what Angelone (2010) has termed a *problem nexus*. A nexus is the confluence of a given textual property and level (lexis, term, collocation, phrase, syntax, sentence, macro-level feature[1]) and some sort of deficit in cognitive resources: a lack in the declarative or procedural knowledge the translator possesses.

Using think-aloud protocols, examples of such uncertainty behaviours can be seen in translator articulations: 'I don't know this word in English' (direct articulation), 'Is this a correct collocation in English?' (indirect articulation), and 'This word order doesn't sound quite right' (directly articulated qualitative hedge). Verbal articulations associated with uncertainty and problem-solving have also been described by Tirkkonen-Condit (2000). One could argue that uncertainty behaviours may potentially include a variety of other non-articulated phenomena as well, such as revising already generated target text, and online information search and retrieval of various kinds. Studies by Englund Dimitrova (2005) and Jakobsen (2002), for instance, have found patterns of revision in novice translators that are suggestive of a connection between revision and uncertainty. A 2005 PACTE study of the use of internal and external support by novice and professional translators also suggests an association between uncertainty and specific information-seeking behaviours.

When encountering a problem nexus, the translator will ideally engage in *uncertainty management* (UCM), the application of conscious strategies for reducing uncertainty by solving the problems of comprehension, transfer or production that arise at these junctures, and bringing the current translation activity to a successful conclusion (Tirkkonen-Condit 2000). The stock of such strategies, their efficacy, and the ability to determine when and how to apply them successfully appear to vary with expertise (Angelone 2010). Thus, the quality of uncertainty management should express itself in measures of translation quality. Error analysis, for instance, should reveal correlations between the efficacy of uncertainty management and the number of errors in translations produced by professional and novice translators.

The current paper is a product-oriented follow-up to Angelone's earlier process-oriented exploratory study of metacognition and uncertainty management in translation problem solving (2010). After introducing the central concepts of uncertainty and uncertainty management and proposing a three-stage model of problem-solving, the paper reports on how the uncertainty management strategies of one professional translator and three translation students correlate with translation quality.

Metacognition, Monitoring and Problem-solving Metacognitive Bundles

Metacognition can be defined broadly as the conscious, volitional, strategic control over complex cognitive tasks (Shreve 2009). It is highly associated with expertise, particularly the ability to utilize *monitoring*, a component of metacognition that involves the ability to self-reflect and provide internal feedback on and control over the progress of a problem-solving sequence (cf. Shreve 2009 for a discussion of metacognition and monitoring in translation). Some translation scholars have proposed that highly-developed monitoring skills are a determining factor of translation expertise (cf. Sirén and Hakkarainen 2002; Shreve 2006).

Monitoring and uncertainty management are inextricably linked. Fraser (2000: 11) determined that professionals generally exhibit greater tolerance for ambiguity and uncertainty than non-professionals. This may be not only because they have more effective mechanisms for managing uncertainty, but also because they are more aware of that capacity and more able to guide the problem resolution process through self-reflection and self-regulation. A number of other recent studies focusing on uncertainty management (Tirkkonen-Condit 2005; Asadi and Séguinot 2005; Hansen 2003; Fraser 2000) have also emphasized the importance of monitoring in the UCM process. Hansen's research (2003: 26), in particular, suggests that professional translators have a greater monitoring capacity for purposes of self-feedback.

In this current study, we use a three-stage behavioural model (Angelone 2010) that describes the problem-solving sub-processes of uncertainty management that occur at a problem nexus. This model decomposes the problem-solving activity into 1) *problem recognition* (PR), which involves direct or indirect knowledge assessment, 2) *solution proposal* (SP), which involves strategy planning and the generation of solution options, and 3) *solution evaluation* (SE), which involves monitoring translation outcomes for evaluation purposes. All of these sub-processes can be shown to be highly associated with metacognition, and the final stage is characterized expressly by monitoring.

These three uncertainty management components are ideally 'bundled' into triads in a generally linear fashion, with initial problem recognition followed by subsequent solution proposal, in turn followed by solution evaluation. From a problem-solving perspective, a translation could be seen as a temporal chain of such bundles. Table 1, an excerpt from a think-aloud/screen-recording protocol obtained from Angelone's earlier study (2010), illustrates the bundled nature of a professional translator's (DE-EN) articulated uncertainty management behaviour at a problem nexus:

Table 1 The bundled nature of uncertainty management

	ARTICULATION	TEXTUAL LEVEL	BEHAVIOURAL LEVEL
1	'tanken Sie Energie … hmm'	collocation	problem recognition
2	'rejuvenate? … recover?'	collocation	solution proposal
3	'recharge your batteries?'	collocation	solution proposal
4	'there we go … recharge your batteries'	collocation	solution evaluation
5	'that's pretty close'	collocation	solution evaluation
6	'Nordsee … that is the North Sea isn't it?'	term	problem recognition
7	…		

Rows 1–5 represent a problem recognition-solution proposal-solution evaluation *bundle*, a set of related cognitive stages (marked in this case by specific articulated uncertainty indicators) through which the translator cycles to manage the uncertainty associated with the collocation *'Energie tanken'* (EN: recharge [your] batteries). The bundle can be seen as a *cognitive translation unit*, commencing with a problem recognition indicator at row 1 and concluding prior to row 6, where a second, distinct problem recognition indicator (also an articulation) signals the initiation of a second bundle addressing transfer uncertainty pertaining to a proper noun.

The transition from one bundle to another, moving from the solution evaluation stage of one cognitive unit to the problem recognition stage of the next, is recognizable only by behavioural indicators that indicate that the translator has moved on, having reached a so-called *tipping point* in the temporal course of the bundle (Shreve, personal communication, April 29, 2009). The tipping point is a theoretical concept describing a change in state, where the translator makes a decision to exit from one problem-solving bundle at a particular nexus and initiate another. Exit from a bundle may be by successful resolution of the problem, but also by recognition of failure, or even postponement of solution (Shreve 2006).

Angelone (2010) classified any sequence of problem-solving stages that initiated with a problem recognition indicator and concluded with the transition from a solution evaluation to a new problem recognition indicator as a metacognitive UCM bundle. These bundles are ideally uninterrupted or coherent. However, if a new problem recognition indicator emerged prior to the completion of the solution proposal or solution evaluation stages of the current sequence, the sequence was considered 'interrupted' or 'non-bundled' (even if the translator later 'jumps back' or returns to resolve an earlier problem). Examples of interrupted sequences would be, for instance, problem recognition with no subsequent solution proposal or evaluation (as is the case when solution is postponed), or articulation of recognition followed by one or more solution proposals, but no subsequent solution evaluation (potentially indicative of an inability to decide on a solution, or of a weak solution).

The analysis of behaviours observed during the progress of the chain of UCM bundles comprising a translation can be supported by adopting a more detailed classification scheme. The purpose of the classification is to achieve a certain theoretical granularity in the analysis of uncertainty management sequences. We have already identified behavioural stages associated with problem-solving (problem recognition, solution proposal, solution evaluation), and to this we can add categories for textual level and translation locus. Textual level attempts to site the problem-solving behaviour at a particular location of difficulty in the text, while translation locus attempts to allocate the problem-solving to a particular gross stage of the overall translation activity. In other words, at a problem nexus, uncertainty management behaviour involves a particular kind of translation issue, a specific textual property and a particular stage in problem-solving. Table 2 summarizes the parameters of the classificatory scheme adopted for this study.

Table 2 Uncertainty management classification parameters

PARAMETER	CLASSIFICATIONS
Textual level	lexis, term, collocation, phrase, syntax, sentence, macro-level
Behavioural focus	problem recognition, solution proposal, solution evaluation
Translation locus	comprehension, transfer, production

Using these parameters, an analysis of the protocol excerpt presented in Table 1 shows that the translator is engaging in uncertainty management at the collocation level of the text and cycles through the triadic bundle of behavioural foci. We have not indicated the translation locus in the figure, though we could classify it as transfer.

It should be noted that the PACTE Group (2005) has employed the related concept of *rich points* in its studies of translation competence and what they have called 'decision-taking'. A rich point is an element or segment of the source text representing a potential focus of problem-solving activity. Each rich point is classified by the PACTE Group as to problem type, and its 'relevant characteristics' described (2005: 7). Our classification of the parameters associated with a problem nexus is similar to the PACTE Group's analysis of rich points, in that both attempt to identify the relevant problem-solving characteristics of a textual segment. However, rich points are apparently pre-selected and then used to analyse subsequent translation products, while our UCM classification occurs after the translation is completed and applied to segments associated with indicators of uncertainty management such as the articulations mentioned earlier.

In our classification and analysis of uncertainty management at a problem nexus, we rely heavily on concepts associated with metacognition. We have argued that metacognitive activity should be heavily associated with the triad of behavioural foci that begins with problem recognition and concludes with solution evaluation. Much of the literature on metacognition holds that metacognition comes online as a result of problem-solving activity, and Shreve (2009) has explicitly argued that the metacognition that occurs in translation is almost exclusively activated as a result of the cognitive problems posed by the characteristics of the translation situation. Other scholars have also explicitly associated metacognition with recognizing a problem, delineating the scope and nature of a problem, and understanding how to reach a solution to the problem (cf. Davidson *et al.* 1994).

Metacognitive monitoring, especially during the final stage of solution evaluation, is critical to completing a bundle and exiting the problem nexus. Metacognition plays a critical role in the recognition of success (or failure) in solutions. The recognition of success or failure is particularly important in our model of uncertainty management, because such recognition is thought to be reflected behaviourally in the transition from one UCM bundle to another. Recognition is the event at the tipping point that precipitates transition from one bundle to another. Failure to recognize success or failure can result in a number of uncertainty management conditions. For instance, failure to recognize success could result in multiple, perhaps excessive, solution proposals (SP) and solution evaluations (SE) following problem recognition. Recognition of failure would result in articulations associated with problem recognition (PR) and then postponement of SP and SE, resulting in what we have called interrupted or non-bundled sequences.

An example of metacognition articulated in translation is exhibited in the form of the following sequence: (1) *What is this word in English?*; (2) *There are several equivalents … x, y, and z*; (3) *Parallel texts suggest that x is the correct equivalent in this context*. Note how this sequence of articulated metacognition closely resembles the uncertainty management bundle of problem recognition, solution proposal, and solution evaluation. The articulated sequence is a *metacognitive bundle* associated with the underlying problem-solving cognition sequence.

Capturing Uncertainty

Studies of metacognition in a number of activity domains suggest that articulation behaviour gathered through verbal protocols can be useful in capturing metacognitive activity (Garner 1988; Garner and Alexander 1989). If the proposal that metacognition in translation is heavily associated with problem-solving and uncertainty is correct, we should be able to elicit and then assign translator articulations from verbal reports to our problem-solving stages and other classification parameters. Although our example uses articulations as indicators, it is important to note that all UCM activity is not necessarily articulated, and can take the form of such non-articulated behaviour as information retrieval, revisions, and cursor repositioning. Eye-tracking behaviour might also mark the progress of problem-solving in uncertainty management. For instance, eye-tracking indicators, such as gaze track and the movement of the eye from one fixation point to another, might also serve to mark cognitive progression both within and between bundles. When collecting data, it is therefore critical to utilize a methodology capable of capturing both articulated and non-articulated behaviour.

To overcome the problems associated with using only verbal protocol data, Angelone's original study (2010) triangulated his uncertainty management data using a dual methodology involving voice recording of Think-Aloud Protocols (TAP) and screen recording (Camtasia Studio[2]) of non-articulated activity. The purpose of capturing both articulated and non-articulated behaviours is to create a more holistic conception of what occurs in and around a UCM bundle. The mixed data produce, of course, more complete and accurate classifications, but – even more importantly – it also supports more granular interpretations. For example, if the translator articulates 'waves break … hmm', we are aware of the fact that uncertainty has emerged and a UCM bundle may have been initiated. But, from a close reading of the articulation itself, we have no way of inferring or determining the textual level or the translation locus associated with this uncertainty. If, however, we look at any corresponding non-articulated behaviour, we can get a better sense of the translator's underlying cognitive state and infer the probable focus of metacognition. Using this same example, if the translator searches the internet for 'wave' in the SL and retrieves a definition, there is a high probability that the textual level of uncertainty is lexis and the locus of uncertainty is comprehension. If, on the other hand, the translator searches the TL equivalent of 'waves break' and seeks to retrieve information from a bilingual database, the probability is high that the textual level of uncertainty is collocation and the locus of uncertainty is transfer.

Expertise, Uncertainty and Translation Quality

We have argued that metacognitive activity is both highly associated with and drives uncertainty management. Shreve (2006) proposes that both professional and non-professional translators engage in significant metacognitive activity, yet the degree and contour of utilization will vary as a result of expertise. Angelone's earlier study indicated that this certainly holds true in uncertainty management, and that direct and indirect articulation can give clear evidence of metacognition reflecting the translator's internal cognitive states when encountering a problem nexus. Metacognitive articulation can provide data indicating the textual property or properties precipitating the uncertainty, the sequence and progression of problem-solving, and the probable locus of the translation problem. In his earlier exploratory study of the uncertainty management behaviour of a professional translator and three students of translation, Angelone (2010) observed several key expertise-related variations:

- In terms of the textual level of uncertainty management, the students focused more frequently on general language words in isolation and on terms, while the professional focused on collocations and terms. In other words, the professional tended to work with relatively larger text chunks than the students (cf. also Lörscher 2005).

- In terms of the behavioural level of uncertainty management, two interesting trends emerged. First, the professional engaged in problem recognition more frequently than the students, suggesting that professional translators may have a more finely-tuned capacity for honing in on problems. This confirms Shreve's speculation (2002) that expert translators have a greater capacity to recognize and react to cues in the source text that indicate potential translation difficulty, as well as Lörscher's observation (2005) that professional translators are more able to recognize problems in the emerging target text. Second, the students in the study engaged in solution evaluation behaviour more frequently than the professional. This pattern suggests several possibilities including, as previously indicated, an inability to recognize success or propose good solutions. The root cause of more frequent solution evaluation behaviour may be a lack of trust in their cognitive resources and a lack of confidence in problem solving as a result of significantly less translation experience.
- In terms of the metacognitive bundling of problem-solving behaviour, the professional exhibited a higher percentage of uninterrupted 'coherent' problem recognition – solution proposal – solution evaluation bundles than the students, pointing to a greater awareness of translation as a multi-step and complex task inextricably bound up in successful problem-solving. The sequential planning and focused attention underlying uninterrupted cycling emerge as primary indicators of expertise in uncertainty management. The students' manner of uncertainty management was both less coherent and apparently less effective. There were examples of bundles initiated and not completed, and cases where the elements of the bundle (recognition, proposal, evaluation) were present, but apparently weak. Cases of weak problem recognition, for instance, seem to be signalled by excessive SP or SE indicators following a PR indicator.

As we have indicated, Angelone's process-oriented study, whose results we have summarized above, did not address product-oriented questions involving the impact of differential uncertainty management behaviour on translation quality. In the remainder of this paper, we examine some of the quality questions that arise:

- What impact does metacognitive bundling (uninterrupted PR-SP-SE bundles) have on overall translation quality, as indicated by the type and frequency of errors in the target text?
- Are certain forms of uncertainty management behaviour more conducive than others in limiting translation errors?

- What is the correlation between the textual level of overall uncertainty management and the textual level of translation errors?
- Do apparent process-oriented expertise effects in uncertainty management behaviour result in product-oriented expertise effects, i.e. improved translation quality?

We formed the following three hypotheses in response to these research questions:

1. When uncertainty is encountered in translation, coherent metacognitive bundling is correlated with more successful management and better overall translation quality (fewer errors) than when uncertainty management activity is more fragmented and not bundled.
2. The higher the amount of coherent UCM management at a given textual level (lexis, collocation, etc.), the lower the frequency of errors at that level.
3. Of the three uncertainty management behavioural stages, problem recognition is most pivotal in error control. If a problem is not recognized, then uncertainty does not arise and the strategic process associated with uncertainty management cannot occur. Once a problem is recognized, then heightened attention and focus sets the stage for subsequent solution proposal and solution evaluation behaviour.

Method

Angelone's original process-oriented study (2010) had seven participants including two professionals. During the course of the investigation, three participants had to be dropped from the study, including one of the professionals, leaving one professional and three translation students. Of course, this compromised the integrity of the study and reduced the ability to generalize from its results. However, after a preliminary analysis of the data collected from the remaining four participants, it was determined that the investigation might still be valuable as an exploratory study. The research proposes some useful theoretical and methodological frameworks for studying uncertainty management and might be able to generate some theoretical speculations that would warrant further investigation with a more robust set of results.

The first of the remaining participants was a professional translator (English L1) with an M.A. in Translation from Kent State University and over ten years of professional German into English translation experience. The second participant was a German-English bilingual (raised in a bilingual household) who had completed the first year of the M.A. programme in translation at Kent State at the time of the experiment. The third and fourth participants, L1 English and L1 German respectively, were also students who had completed the first year of the M.A. programme in translation. None of the three students had professional translation experience, defined here as translation work generating at least 70 per cent of annual income over a minimum period of three months.

The participants were asked to think aloud while translating a 50-word travel blurb for the German island of Borkum from German into English. This was preceded by a practice think-aloud session for purposes of habituation. They had access to any and all online resources they needed, and had the option of thinking aloud in English, German, or both. As they translated, their verbalizations were documented using a microphone, and their onscreen activity was documented using screen recording, establishing a dual methodology for more effectively triangulating the metacognitive activity occurring during uncertainty management. All articulations and activities deemed to be indicative of metacognition were then classified in terms of textual level, behavioural focus, and translation locus, leading to the findings outlined above.

To obtain product-oriented data for this study, we had two external graders assess the four translations (which were coded for purposes of ensuring anonymity) and mark up any errors using a modified version of the American Translator Association's error encoding framework (see Appendix 1). Both graders have years of experience in using this framework in German-English practice translation courses, and one of the two graders is a certified ATA grader. Assessment was done independently with no inter-consultation. We then compared results to make sure no major discrepancies existed, and established an error profile for each participant, as outlined in Table 3:

Table 3 Participant error profile

Participant # _____

General comments:

Total # of errors made:

Textual level of errors made: ___ lexis ___ term ___ collocation ___ phrase ___ syntax ___ sentence ___ macro-level

# of errors occurring in the context of uninterrupted PR-SP-SE bundles:

# of errors occurring in non-bundled contexts:

# of errors occurring in units exhibiting problem recognition behaviour:

# of errors occurring in units exhibiting solution proposal behaviour:

# of errors occurring in units exhibiting solution evaluation behaviour:

Results and Discussion

Both graders found no errors when assessing the professional's translation, instead citing this participant's solid sense for text type and genre conventions in English. In fact, the professional was the only participant to receive such positive comments pertaining to macro-level considerations such as text type awareness. Interestingly, in terms of textual level, the professional does not demonstrate significant metacognition higher than the sentence level (see Table 4). Perhaps as a result of years of experience, the professional translator develops an inherent sense for macro-level considerations to the extent that they are not problematic and therefore do not cause a high level of uncertainty in need of extensive management behaviour? The German-English bilingual was assessed as being a competent translator, with no additional general comments provided by either grader. The same holds true for the L1 English student, with general comments focused primarily on minor terminological issues. Assessment of the L1 German student's performance indicates a tendency to translate too literally, leading to problems with idiomatic constructions and meaning. This participant engaged in metacognition relatively frequently at the lexis and term levels (see Table 4), potentially indicating a focus on word-for-word translation. It could very well be that in this participant's case, a lack of experience, coupled with the L1 into L2 translation direction, restricts the translator's confidence in transcending the word level to transfer meaning successfully.

Table 4 Textual level at which metacognitive activity was employed

PARTICIPANT	TOTAL META-COGNITION	% LEXIS	% TERM	% COLL.	% PHRASE	% SYNTAX	% SENT.	% MACRO.
Professional	97	4.12	35.05	31.96	9.28	8.25	4.12	7.22
Bilingual	43	20.93	39.54	18.60	16.28	0.00	0.00	4.65
Student L1 EN	86	34.89	13.95	15.12	19.77	3.49	3.49	3.49
Student L1 DE	105	31.43	31.43	19.05	10.48	0.00	2.86	3.81

The fifty-word experimental text proved quite sufficient in size and difficulty to generate a sizable number of metacognitive behaviour indicators (331), but did not generate a large number of errors (a total of 17: see Table 5). We believe the number of errors generated is much too small a sample to make any robust claims. Nevertheless, the patterns of error we found may be suggestive of relationships that would warrant further study.

Table 5 Error frequency and distribution according to error type

PARTICIPANT	TOTAL ERRORS	% LEXIS	% TERM	% COLL.	% PHRASE	% SYNTAX	% SENT.	% MACRO.
Professional	0	n/a	n/a	n/a	n/a	n/a	n/a	n/a
Bilingual	4	50	25	0	25	0	0	0
Student L1 EN	4	25	25	25	0	25	0	0
Student L1 DE	9	33.33	22.22	11.11	11.11	22.22	0	0

With the caveats about the sample size in mind, the fact that the translation by the professional had no errors invites a closer look at what distinguishes this participant's uncertainty management behaviour from that of the others, i.e. what did this translator do that the others did not?

Two major points of consideration surface. First, the professional engages in uninterrupted coherent PR-SP-SE metacognitive bundling more frequently than any of the three students (see Table 6). This result seems to provide some preliminary support for our hypothesis that metacognitive bundling is correlated with more successful uncertainty management and therefore better overall translation quality than non-bundled metacognitive activity, and provides a basis for further investigation.

Table 6 Errors occurring within bundled vs. non-bundled translation activity

PARTICIPANT	UNINTERRUPTED PR-SP-SE BUNDLES	TOTAL NUMBER OF ERRORS	ERRORS WITHIN BUNDLED ACTIVITY	ERRORS WITHIN NON-BUNDLED ACTIVITY
Professional	64.95%	0	n/a	n/a
Bilingual	53.49%	4	1	3
Student L1 EN	37.21%	4	0	4
Student L1 DE	54.28%	9	3	6
TOTAL	–	17	4 (24%)	13 (76%)

Second, the professional also engaged in problem recognition more frequently than the three students (see Table 7). This provides some support for our hypothesis that problem recognition is the most important form of uncertainty management behaviour based on the heightened attention, focus and tendency for subsequent sequential planning that accompany it.

Table 7 Behavioural level at which metacognitive activity was employed

PARTICIPANT	PROBLEM RECOGNITION	SOLUTION PROPOSAL	SOLUTION EVALUATION	UNCLASSIFIED
Professional	41.24%	20.62%	25.77%	12.37%
Bilingual	20.93%	13.95%	37.21%	27.91%
Student L1 EN	30.23%	15.12%	33.72%	20.93%
Student L1 DE	29.52%	19.05%	36.19%	15.24%

While the performance of the single professional translator in the group is suggestive (zero errors, metacognitive bundling, higher frequency of problem recognition behaviours), given the exploratory nature of the study we can draw no firm conclusions. The data indicate a possible correlation between translation quality and uninterrupted problem-solving bundles as well as between increased problem recognition and reduced numbers of errors. We believe a future study is warranted, with a design that includes larger, balanced groups of novices and professionals, where we could also focus on within-group quality differences associated with bundling.

For all student participants, more errors were made in situations of non-bundled activity (76 per cent) than in situations when metacognitive bundling was evident (24 per cent), supporting the notion that such bundling is critical in keeping errors at bay. This conclusion would also need to be confirmed in a further study using a longer and more difficult text, but the difference is sufficiently large to be suggestive.

It is also clear that the bilingual as well as the L1 DE student both made errors in bundled contexts, so bundling in and of itself apparently does not guarantee error-free or error-minimized translation. It would seem useful to take a closer look inside each bundle to see how variation in the contour of the three embedded uncertainty management behaviours could impact when errors are more likely to occur and when they are not. The error data (see Table 8), not unexpectedly, suggest that problem recognition (as opposed to solution proposal and solution evaluation, to be analysed in Tables 9 and 10 respectively) is the most important uncertainty management behaviour within any given PR-SP-SE bundle when it comes to limiting errors. While this result seems obvious (i.e. if a problem is not recognized it cannot be solved), it confirms the general finding in expertise studies that the development of skill in any domain is associated with a knowledge accumulation process that emphasizes the development of awareness and familiarity with the nature and structure of problems (Schenk *et al.* 1998; Glaser and Chi 1988). Investing time and attention at this initial stage of uncertainty management seems conducive to fostering successful problem solving overall through careful planning and problem delineation. Again, it was the professional who engaged in problem recognition most frequently in our study, and – most likely as a direct result – produced the best translation with the fewest number of errors. The obvious implication of the data in Table 8, of course, is that many errors produced by the students were due to a simple failure to recognize the problem.

Table 8 Errors occurring in situations of problem recognition behaviour

PARTICIPANT	TOTAL NUMBER OF ERRORS	ERRORS WHEN PR WAS EVIDENT	ERRORS WHEN PR WAS NOT EVIDENT
Professional	0	n/a	n/a
Bilingual	4	1	3
Stud. L1 EN	4	1	3
Stud. L1 DE	9	3	6
TOTAL	17	5 (29%)	12 (71%)

The solution proposal data in Table 9 suggest that solution proposal behaviour is generally also helpful in limiting errors, but not to the same extent as problem recognition behaviour. Solution proposal should be regarded as a fundamental translation competence, very much in line with Pym's (2003) minimalist approach in which generating multiple viable target text options (what we are calling solution proposals) and then narrowing them down to one viable option with confidence (what we are calling solution evaluation) are at the very core of successful translation.

Table 9 Errors occurring in situations of solution proposal behaviour

PARTICIPANT	TOTAL NUMBER OF ERRORS	ERRORS WHEN SP WAS EMPLOYED	ERRORS WHEN SP WAS NOT EMPLOYED
Professional	0	n/a	n/a
Bilingual	4	1	3
Stud. L1 EN	4	2	2
Stud. L1 DE	9	4	5
TOTAL	17	7 (41%)	10 (59%)

The solution evaluation data (see Table 10) deviate from the patterns found for problem recognition and solution proposal in that one of the participants (the L1 DE student) actually made more errors when the uncertainty management behaviour (in this case solution evaluation) was employed than when it was not. In light of the fact that this same participant also engaged in solution evaluation behaviour relatively frequently, one might be inclined to question whether or not excessive solution evaluation ultimately has a negative impact on uncertainty management and overall translation success. As suggested earlier, a desire to over-evaluate may stem from a lack of confidence and trust in instincts, or, as was proposed in Angelone's previous study, it could be that problem recognition is faulty. Too little time was spent and too little attention allocated at the problem recognition stage, leading to indecision and doubt in situations of evaluation. Just because problem recognition has occurred and solutions have been proposed does not mean that the translator has recognized the right problem, the full scope of the problem, or has the resources to generate the optimal set of solution proposals. The translator understands or suspects that something is wrong, but has not diagnosed the problem properly and has generated too few (or too few good) solutions for it. Such a circumstance could produce excessive evaluation. Thus extensive solution evaluation cannot compensate entirely for failures earlier in the problem-solving sequence.

Table 10 Errors occurring in situations of solution evaluation behaviour

PARTICIPANT	TOTAL NUMBER OF ERRORS	ERRORS WHEN SE WAS EMPLOYED	ERRORS WHEN SE WAS NOT EMPLOYED
Professional	0	n/a	n/a
Bilingual	4	2	2
Stud. L1 EN	4	0	4
Stud. L1 DE	9	6	3
TOTAL	17	8 (47%)	9 (53%)

The error data overall suggest that metacognitive bundling is associated with error avoidance. However, the case of the L1 DE student also suggests that bundles must also be efficacious, i.e. problem recognition must be effective and proposed solutions must be viable. In situations where the previous stages are clearly present and apparently effective, solution evaluation behaviour proved to be highly associated with avoiding errors, especially in the case of the L1 EN student. Despite allocating less time to solution evaluation overall, when this participant did engage in SE (as indicated by markers), the stage generally tended to follow problem recognition and solution proposal in a bundled fashion.

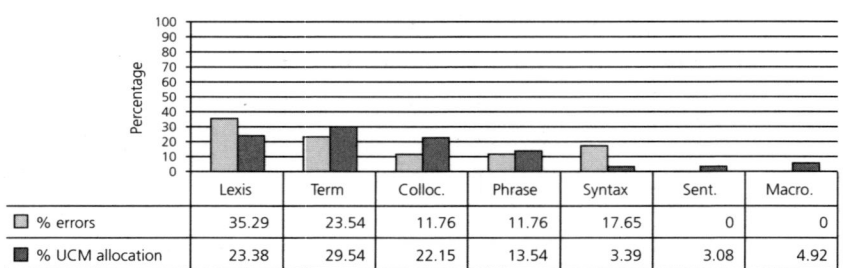

	Lexis	Term	Colloc.	Phrase	Syntax	Sent.	Macro.
☐ % errors	35.29	23.54	11.76	11.76	17.65	0	0
■ % UCM allocation	23.38	29.54	22.15	13.54	3.39	3.08	4.92

Table 11 Textual level of UCM allocation vs. textual level of errors

Table 11 displays the aggregated association of textual level of error and textual level of UCM allocation for each of the seven textual levels analysed in this study. The striped bars represent percentage of errors, while the solid bars represent percentage of uncertainty management allocation. One would expect, given our theoretical model, each solid bar to reflect a higher percentage than each corresponding striped bar, thereby indicating that uncertainty management allocation was sufficient and successful at minimizing error frequency. That is, as our second hypothesis stated, the higher the amount of coherent UCM management at a given textual level (lexis, collocation, etc.), the lower the frequency of errors at that level. We can see in the aggregated data that this is not always the case. Detailed views of the individual participant data are given below (Table 12: Textual level of UCM allocation vs. textual level of errors for Professional, Bilingual, Student L1 En and Student L1 De).

In fact, our second hypothesis is only supported for the professional translator in our study who had no errors. In the case of the bilingual student translator, uncertainty management is seemingly insufficient in limiting errors at the lexis and phrase levels. In the case of the L1 EN student, management seems to be lacking in addressing errors at the term, collocation and syntax levels. The L1 DE student's use of uncertainty management seems to come up short at the lexis and syntax levels.

It rapidly becomes evident that the mere presence of indicators of uncertainty management is not necessarily synonymous with more *effective* UCM.

Professional

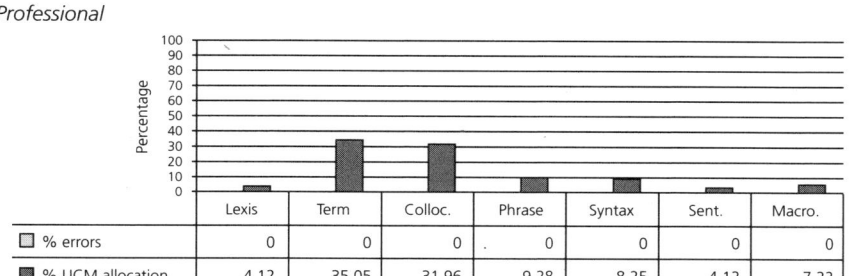

	Lexis	Term	Colloc.	Phrase	Syntax	Sent.	Macro.
☐ % errors	0	0	0	0	0	0	0
◼ % UCM allocation	4.12	35.05	31.96	9.28	8.25	4.12	7.22

Bilingual

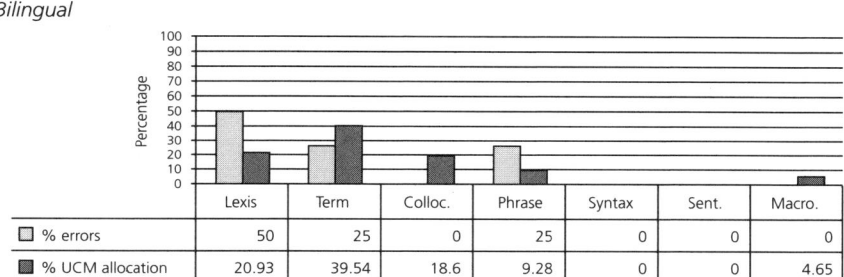

	Lexis	Term	Colloc.	Phrase	Syntax	Sent.	Macro.
☐ % errors	50	25	0	25	0	0	0
◼ % UCM allocation	20.93	39.54	18.6	9.28	0	0	4.65

Student L1 EN

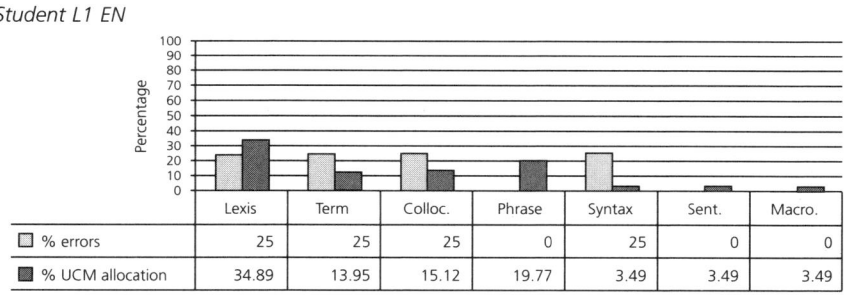

	Lexis	Term	Colloc.	Phrase	Syntax	Sent.	Macro.
☐ % errors	25	25	25	0	25	0	0
◼ % UCM allocation	34.89	13.95	15.12	19.77	3.49	3.49	3.49

Student L1 DE

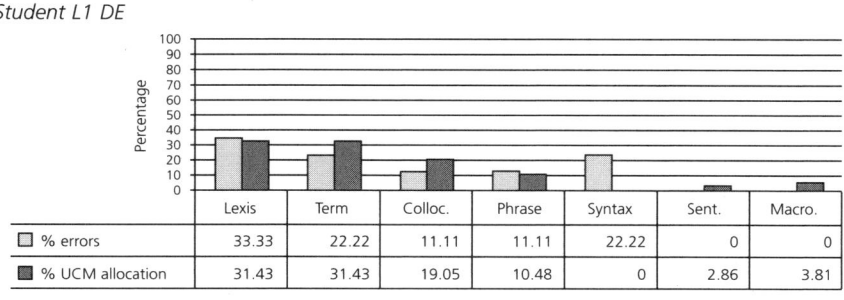

	Lexis	Term	Colloc.	Phrase	Syntax	Sent.	Macro.
☐ % errors	33.33	22.22	11.11	11.11	22.22	0	0
◼ % UCM allocation	31.43	31.43	19.05	10.48	0	2.86	3.81

For example, the data for the L1 DE student indicate that frequency of allocation of uncertainty management at the terminological level outweighs frequency of errors, leading one to assume that terminological errors should be kept in check. However, 22.22 per cent of this participant's errors were in fact terminological. This participant's relatively high percentage of solution proposal and solution evaluation contributed to a high general allocation of UCM frequency. In other words, for this participant, after the problem is recognized, subsequent solution proposal and evaluation are unsuccessful. As mentioned previously, improper or weak problem recognition can compromise the effectiveness of subsequent problem-solving stages. For novices at least, high general UCM allocation frequencies are not predictive of error frequency and, in essence, may be a faulty gauge of uncertainty management success.

Conclusions and Future Research

The small number of participants and the lower than expected number of errors make any conclusions we can draw only speculative. Nevertheless, some of the results are sufficiently suggestive that they recommend further research. We did find evidence in support of our first hypothesis, that coherent, effective metacognitive bundling is correlated with better overall translation quality (fewer errors) than when uncertainty management is not present, or when it is fragmented and interrupted. Our second hypothesis predicted that the higher the percentage of UCM management at a given textual level, the lower the frequency of errors. This hypothesis was not supported in this small sample, and, for theoretical reasons, we believe it may not generally hold true for novices, even in subsequent studies. Finally, we found support for our hypothesis that problem recognition is pivotal in error control. If a problem is not recognized, then uncertainty does not arise and the strategic metacognitive processes associated with uncertainty management cannot occur. The challenge for novices is to learn to recognize problems effectively. Once recognized, then heightened attention and focus set the stage for subsequent solution proposal and solution evaluation behaviour. However, our data show that even then, the mere fact of recognition is not sufficient. The problem must be correctly diagnosed, if subsequent solution proposal and solution evaluation are to be successful. Both the current product-oriented study and Angelone's previous process-oriented research (2010) suggest expertise effects in uncertainty management as indicated by metacognitive activity. The results from only one professional translator limit the generalizability of the results, but are interesting enough to suggest that a further study with a larger group of professionals could confirm our observations.

Clearly, the *manner* in which uncertainty management unfolds is a much more reliable indicator of potential success in translation than the simple frequency of uncertainty management behaviours. Since, as proposed by Shreve (2006), both professionals and non-professionals do in fact make use of metacognition, evaluations regarding successful application need to focus on *how* metacognition is used, rather than just on *if* it is used. Our data suggest that clear bundles of problem-solving behaviour, marked by visible indicators, and devoid of excessive solution proposal and solution evaluation, are associated with the most effective error control. Table 13 offers a comparative profile of professional and non-professional translation behaviour, combining both process- and product-oriented data from the two studies discussed in this paper. We hope it will serve as a helpful point of departure in designing future empirical research pertaining to metacognition and uncertainty management.

Table 13 A comparative profile of metacognitive application for purposes of UCM

PARAMETER	PROFESSIONAL	STUDENTS
Higher occurrence of metacognitive bundling (uninterrupted PR-SP-SE bundles)	✓	
Primary textual level(s) of uncertainty management	terms and collocations	lexis and terms
Primary behavioural level of uncertainty management	problem recognition	solution evaluation
Higher allocation of problem recognition behaviour	✓	
Higher allocation of solution evaluation behaviour		✓
Primary textual level(s) of errors	none	lexis
More errors in bundled or non-bundled contexts?	n/a	non-bundled
More errors when PR was or was not evident?	n/a	was not
More errors when SP was or was not employed?	n/a	was not
More errors when SE was or was not employed?	n/a	was not*

* With the exception of the L1 DE student, who made more errors when SE was employed than when it was not.

Earlier in this paper we argued that translation, by its very nature, is rooted in problem solving. The problem recognition – solution proposal – solution evaluation bundle theoretical construct central to this paper's conception of uncertainty management seems to be a fruitful model for examining translation processes and products from a cognitive and metacognitive perspective.

Notes

1 Macro-level is understood here as being above and beyond the sentence level, including such aspects as cohesion, coherence, genre conventions, and target reader expectations

2 For more information on the features of *Camtasia Studio* software, see: www.techsmith.com/camtasia.asp

References

Angelone, E. (2010), 'Uncertainty, uncertainty management and metacognitive problem solving in the translation task'. In G. Shreve and E. Angelone (eds), *Translation and Cognition*. Amsterdam: John Benjamins. pp. 17–40.

Asadi, P. and C. Séguinot, (2005), 'Shortcuts, strategies and general patterns in a process study of nine professionals'. *Meta*, 50 (2), 522–547.

Davidson, J., R. Deuser, and R. Sternberg, (1994), 'The role of metacognition in problem-solving'. In J. Metcalfe and A. P. Schimamura (eds), *Metacognition: Knowing about Knowing*, Cambridge, MA.: MIT Press. pp. 207–226.

Englund Dimitrova, B. (2005), *Expertise and Explicitation in the Translation Process*. Amsterdam: John Benjamins.

Fraser, J. (2000), 'What do real translators do? Developing the use of TAPs from professional translators'. In S. Tirkkonen-Condit and R. Jääskeläinen (eds), *Tapping and Mapping the Processes of Translation*. Amsterdam: John Benjamins. pp. 111–121.

Garner R. (1988), 'Verbal report data on cognitive and metacognitive strategies'. In C. Weinstein, E. Goetz, and P. Alexander (eds), *Learning and Study Strategies: Issues in Assessment, Instruction and Evaluation*. San Diego, CA: Academic Press. pp. 63–76.

Garner, R. and Alexander, P. (1989), 'Metacognition: answered and unanswered questions'. *Educational Psychologist*, 24, 143–158.

Glaser, R. and M. Chi, (1988), 'Overview'. In M. Chi, R. Glaser, and M. Farr (eds), *The Nature of Expertise*. Hillsdale, NJ: Erlbaum. pp. xv–xxvii.

Hansen, G. (2003), 'Controlling the process: Theoretical and methodological reflections on research Into translation processes'. In F. Alves (ed.), *Triangulating Translation: Perspectives in Process Oriented Research*. Amsterdam: John Benjamins. pp. 25–42.

Jakobsen, A.L. (2002), 'Translation drafting by professional translators and by translation students'. *Empirical Translation Studies: Process and Product.* Copenhagen Studies in Language 27, Copenhagen: Samfundslitteratur, pp. 191–204.

Koby, G.S. and B.J. Baer, (2005), 'From professional translation to the translator training classroom: Adapting the ATA error marking scale'. *Translation Watch Quarterly*, 1, 33–45.

Lörscher, W. (2005), 'The translation process: Methods and problems of its investigation'. *Meta* 50 (2), 597–608.

PACTE (2005), 'Investigating Translation Competence: Conceptual and Methodological Issues'. *Meta* 50 (2), 609–619.

Pym, A. (2003), 'Redefining translation competence in an electronic age. In defence of a minimalist approach'. *Meta* 48 (4), 481–497.

Schenk, K., N. Vitalari, and K. Davis, (1998), 'Differences between novice and expert systems analysts: what do we know and what do we do?' *Journal of Management Information Systems* 15 (1), 9–50.

Shreve, G.M. (2002), 'Knowing translation: Cognitive and experiential aspects of translation expertise from the perspective of expertise studies'. In A. Riccardi (ed.), *Translation Studies: Perspectives on an Emerging Discipline.* Cambridge: Cambridge University. pp. 150–171.

—— (2006), 'The deliberate practice: Translation and expertise'. *Journal of Translation Studies* 9 (1), 27–42.

—— (2009), 'Recipient-orientation and metacognition in the translation process'. In R. Dimitriu and M. Shlesinger (eds), *Translators and their readers: in homage to Eugene A. Nida.* Brussels: Les Editions du Hazard. pp. 255–270.

Sirén, S. and K. Hakkarainen, (2002), 'Expertise in translation'. *Across Languages and Cultures* 3 (1), 71–82.

Tirkkonen-Condit, S. (2000), 'Uncertainty in translation processes'. In S. Tirkkonen-Condit and R. Jääskeläinen (eds), *Tapping and Mapping the Processes of Translation.* Amsterdam: John Benjamins. pp. 123–142.

—— (2005), 'The monitor model revisited: Evidence from process research'. *Meta* 50, (2), 405–414.

Appendix 1: Modified ATA Grading Framework

CODE	REASON	LEVEL(S) OF ERROR IN OUR STUDY*
INC	Incomplete passage	not used
ILL	Illegible	not applicable
MU	Misunderstanding of the ST	not used
MT	Mistranslation into TL	phrase, term
A	Addition	not used
O	Omission	syntax
T	Terminology	lexis, term
R	Register	not used
F	Too freely translated	not used
L	Too literal; word-for-word translation	lexis, collocation
FC	False cognate	not used
IND	Indecision; gave more than one option	not used
I	Inconsistency	not used
AMB	Ambiguity	not used
G	Grammar	syntax
SY	Syntax	syntax
P	Punctuation	not applicable
SP	Spelling	not applicable
D	Accents, or other diacritical marks	not applicable
C	Case (upper/ lower)	not applicable
WF	Word form	lexis
U	Usage	collocation, phrase
ST	Style	syntax

* Each error was categorized as only one error type.

EEG, EYE and KEY: Three Simultaneous Streams of Data for Investigating the Cognitive Mechanisms of Translation

Christian Michel Lachaud

6

Chapter Outline

Introduction

The psycholinguistic study presented in this article was realized for the European Research Project 'EYE-to-IT',[1] involving collaboration between the Department of Literature, Area Studies and European Languages, University of Oslo, Norway, and the National Centre for Epilepsy, Rikshospitalet University Hospital, Oslo, Norway. Using an original technical development combining three technologies, namely electroencephalography (EEG), eye tracking (EYE) and keystroke logging (KEY), EYE-to-IT aimed to develop technical solutions for studying the cognitive mechanisms of translation and for helping translators to perform better while translating texts.

'Prompting,' or presenting online a visual message composed of a word or a sentence, offers interesting perspectives for the purpose of supporting a translator in his task. The prompting technique, already in use for online documentation and feedback systems (Cavero *et al.* 1995, Ferreira and Atkinson 2009), could be adapted for priming transcoding and translation (Finkbeiner *et al.* 2004, Duyck and Warlop 2009) – 'transcoding' being a technical term from translation theory, meaning 'translating out of context' (Lederer 2006). Because a prompting procedure should not restrict the translator's freedom, fluidity and creativity by locking a given formulation in his mind, delivering a list of possibilities from which the translator would choose the one he prefers would be inappropriate. Prompting should rather be designed as a subtle influence on the translators' mental processes, supporting them when they fail or are being challenged. This fuzzy, even subliminal influence, can only be achieved with prompts different enough from the targeted solution to avoid focusing the translator on a formulation, but related enough to support translation. Promoting targeted formal knowledge (knowledge of word form) and semantic knowledge (conceptual knowledge) in the mind of the translator can indeed be achieved with prompts having formal features (letters or sequences of letters) and/or semantic features (semantic properties) in common with the targeted translation. For instance, the Norwegian word *mannekeng* (fashion model) can be used to prompt the Norwegian transcoding of the English source word *male*, the target word *mannlig*, because both prompt and target share sublexical features (i.e. the first four letters). Similarly, a semantic prompt can be found in *bestefar* (grandpa), which is a specific representative for the category 'male'. With such inputs delivered in a timely manner, the translator would be left dealing with his own mental processes, the dynamics of which are now subtly influenced.

Although translation is carried out at the *textual* level, a systematic approach intended for future technical implementation requires that the positive effect of this prompting method on translation is evaluated step by step, starting at the word level before using in experimental settings more complex linguistic stimuli, such as phrases, sentences and texts. The study presented in this article involved the combining of EEG, EYE and KEY for investigating the effect of prompting on cognitive load (i.e. mental effort) and transcoding performance, in a population of translators facing three transcoding situations (Deceptive Cognates, True Cognates and Non-Cognates – see below for an explanation of each of these). After first exposing the transcoding challenge existing in each situation, I will discuss the advantages of each measurement technique (EEG, EYE, KEY), as well as the advantages and drawbacks in combining them. I will describe the experimental setting, before presenting the results and discussing some findings.

'Back-Engineering' the Mind of Bilinguals

The experiment presented in this article was designed to identify transcoding challenges and to start to explore the psychological nature of these challenges. It was the first in a series of four experiments which aimed at (i) identifying the transcoding challenges that a translator faces, (ii) understanding the psychological nature of these challenges, (iii) defining the type of information that could helpfully prompt the translator in order to cope with transcoding challenges, and (iv) evaluating the benefit of prompting for transcoding performance. Three logical L_2 (English) – L_1 (Norwegian) word correspondences were used in the study: Deceptive Cognates or false friends (DC), True Cognates (TC) and Non-cognates (NC) (Chamizo Domínguez and Nerlich 2002).

(i)   A DC relation exists between two words from two languages when they share the same form but not the same meaning, like 'gift', meaning 'present' in English, but 'poison' in Norwegian.

(ii) A TC relation exists between two words from two languages when they share both exactly the same form (as opposed to cognates whose form may differ slightly in a language pair) and the same meaning, like 'egg' for the English/Norwegian pair.

(iii) A NC relation exists between two words from two languages when they share the same meaning but not the same form, like 'ant' in English and '*maur*' in Norwegian.

Figure 1 shows the logical structure of L_2-L_1 correspondences at the lexical and semantic levels for DC, TC and NC, based on the architecture of Conceptual Mediation Hierarchical Models (Schwanenflugel and Rey 1986, Frenck and Pynte 1987, French and Jacquet 2004).[2]

NC corresponds to the most common transcoding situation, while TC and DC are rare. TC can be considered as a control condition in which no transcoding needs to be done, while DC and NC require the application of a transcoding procedure. In theory, transcoding an English NC Stimulus S_2

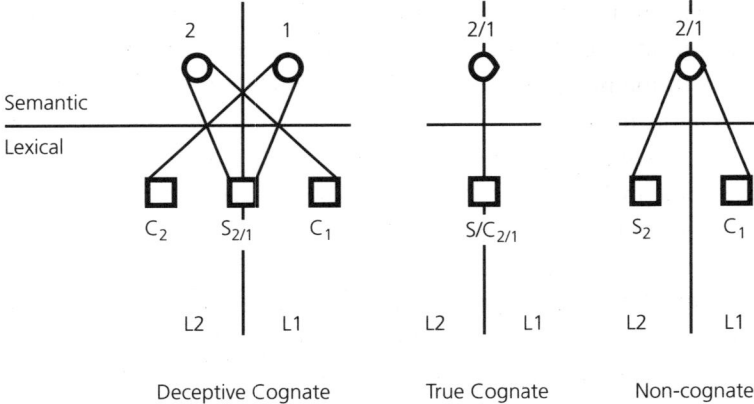

Figure 1 Logical structure of lexical and semantic L_2-L_1 relations for Deceptive Cognates, True Cognates and Non-cognates. S stands for 'Stimulus' (English word to transcode into Norwegian), C for 'Correspondence in the other language', L for Language; L_2 is the second language of the subject (English); L_1 is his mother tongue (Norwegian), into which he must transcode. The numbers 1 and 2 refer respectively to L_1 and L_2. Squares represent the mental representations of lexical information. Circles represent the mental representations of abstract information.

like 'ant' into its Norwegian correspondence C_1 '*maur*' will require four main steps: (i) recognizing the stimulus (retrieving and activating in long-term memory the mental representation of its formal aspects – symbolised by the square marked S_2 in Figure 1), (ii) accessing the meaning (activating in long-term memory the mental representation of the abstract aspects of the stimulus – symbolized by the circle marked 2/1 in Figure 1), (iii) retrieving the corresponding item in the target language (activating in long-term memory the corresponding formal representation for Norwegian, marked C_1 in Figure 1), and (iv) producing the solution (speaking, typing, writing). In the case of TCs, because both the formal and the semantic representations are identical in L_1 and L_2, no transcoding will happen. Therefore, the processing of a TC stimulus will be limited to three steps: (i) recognizing the stimulus, (ii) accessing its meaning, and (iii) producing the solution. Transcoding English DC input S_2 (like 'gift') into its Norwegian correspondence C_1 ('*gave*') will require additional processes, since S_2 is conflated with S_1 ('gift' can be an English word as well as a Norwegian word). According to parallel distributed processing models (Group 1986), whose principles are well formulated in TRACE (McClelland and Elman 1986), a psycholinguistics model of word recognition, the stimulus will not only activate meaning 2 ('present') in the

English lexicon, it will also activate meaning 1 ('poison') in the Norwegian lexicon (see also Bölte and Coenen 2002). Activation will automatically propagate in the neural network, spreading back from the semantic level of representation to the formal level of representation in the other language (Figure 1). Therefore two transcoded meanings of 'gift' will be simultaneously activated, one in Norwegian from the English meaning (C_1 '*gave*'), and one in English from the Norwegian meaning (C_2 'poison'). The consequence will be a conflict between the two lexicons during selection, both at the semantic level between meanings 1 and 2 and at the lexical level between representations C_1 and C_2. Facing a confusing situation, the translator may have four types of reactions: (i) He might automatically produce the correct Norwegian formulation ('*gave*') for the English meaning ('gift'), although probably with greater difficulty than for a NC; (ii) Confused, he might also produce an incorrect output by formulating the Norwegian meaning in English ('poison'), especially if the Norwegian language is more prominent in his mind than the English language. He may then realize his mistake and try to correct it, in which case two scenarios may occur (iii and iv). A successful correction would require him (iii) to go back from C_2 ('poison') to meaning 1 ('poison'), to $S_{2/1}$ ('gift'), and to proceed forward in the other direction, to meaning 2 ('gift'), to C_1 ('*gave*'). If successful, the time needed to produce the correct Norwegian transcoding ('*gave*') of the English stimulus ('gift') will be further increased and may have other behavioural manifestations, like typing corrections. But the translator may also be unable to correct his mistake fully, especially under time pressure, (iv) if he only reverses his transcoding, and does not transcode again. In this case, he will simply be back to the initial stimulus ('gift'), a phenomenon that was sometimes observed in our experiments.

Measuring the Mind Simultaneously with EEG, EYE and KEY

While the mind cannot be measured directly, manifestations of its activity can, such as electric potentials (EEG) and behaviour (eye movements and keystrokes). The EEG technique measures, usually on the surface of the scalp, the electric variations generated by the activity of neuron assemblies (Niedermeyer and Da Silva 2005), including that of cognitive activity, at the moment they occur in the cerebral cortex ('online' measurement). EEG can be used to track cognitive load variations as an index of processing difficulty, to locate where in the brain the activity occurs for additional knowledge about the cognitive functions involved, and/or to pinpoint the moment in time when a specific process occurs. The eye-tracking technique measures eye movements (also considered to be an 'online' measurement), a behaviour which provides indices about visual information intake. Eye movements can reveal the progression of syntactic processing and meaning building in the reader's mind, and in the cases where information intake is necessary for the translation process, or in cases where the translation processes influence information intake, eye tracking may also reveal information about the cognitive processes occurring during translation. Finally, keystroke logging, the technique of recording typing behaviour on a keyboard, can be used for studying the mental processes during translation by studying how the text was produced (also considered 'online' measurement) as well as for studying translation as a product (offline measurement), in which case keystroke logging only serves as a means to record the final text product.

Despite the fact that each technique imposes its own constraints on the experimental situation and is generally seen as exclusive of the two others, EYE-to-IT engaged researchers in the challenge of simultaneously using EEG, EYE and KEY for studying cognition during translation. By multiplying measurement techniques, a tremendous burden is placed on researchers to control their experiments well and to prepare the participants adequately. Furthermore, the risk of producing bad quality data is increased. However, combining techniques offers the invaluable advantage of yielding a thorough picture of the reality being measured.

The main technical difficulty in this study was presented by EEG and EYE. EEG requires situations which do not promote eye movements, blinks, motor activity, and any cerebral activity other than the one being studied. Therefore reading and typing while translating represent sources of artefacts that one would like to avoid, making it meaningless not only to use EYE and KEY together with EEG, but to use EEG for studying translation. However, the improvement of mathematical algorithms allows us to extract useful information from EEG with artefacts, opening its application to new research areas. Similarly, using eye tracking in a situation where the subject regularly gazes beyond the screen (typing, consulting a dictionary) is a challenge in itself, as the tracking of the eyes' position will be interrupted. Furthermore, it may be difficult, if not impossible, to distinguish, during the analysis of eye movements, between actual reading activity and the search behaviour that occurred when the translator transferred attention back to the source text.

However, eye tracking proves to be at least a very useful tool for the online detection of the difficulties that the translator is facing (longer fixation time or larger number of fixations). Subsequently, eye tracking provides inputs for analyzing the nature of the linguistic challenges and knowing when to deliver a prompt, and where on the screen. If constraints can be managed, each technique measuring a different manifestation of the mental processes underlying translation may be used in a beneficial and complementary way with other techniques. This requires clever designs and proper methods of analysis for reducing the impact of artefacts on experimental results.

In this study, we investigated (i) the amplitude variations through time in the EEG frequency bands (Time-Frequency Power Differences), which reveal cognitive load variations, (ii) the verification effort during the mental matching between L_2 and L_1, which manifests itself in the total amount of time spent gazing at both words (Total Fixation Duration), (iii) the attention demand required for processing the stimulus, the variations of which are manifested in pupil diameter through the pupillary reflex (Pupil Size Amplitude Variation, corresponding to the difference between minimum and maximum sizes), (iv) the decision difficulty, which is manifested in the amount of time required for pressing the answer key (Reaction Time), and (v) the confusion of the translator, which is manifested in the amount of response errors (Error Probability).

We expected that TC would be the easiest configuration to process (lowest cognitive load, verification effort, attention demand, difficulty and confusion), while DC would be the most difficult configuration to transcode (highest cognitive load increase, verification effort, attention demand, difficulty and confusion). Non-cognates were expected to present intermediate levels of difficulty.

Method

Independent variables

Two independent variables were manipulated in the experiment:

(i) Stimulus Type (three levels: DC, TC, NC)
(ii) Transcoding Correspondence between the L_2 and L_1 words composing a stimulus (two levels: Match – L_2 and L_1 correspond, Mismatch – L_2 and L_1 do not correspond).

The two variables were crossed according to a factorial design, generating six experimental conditions.

Dependent variables

The dependent variables, measured in the participant's brain activity and behaviour while both the English and the Norwegian words were displayed, were as follows:

(i)   Time-Frequency Power Difference (EEG) between the Match and Mismatch conditions for each stimulus type (expressed in significant Time-Frequency units – see the Data Processing section).
(ii) Total Fixation Duration (expressed in ms – EYE)
(iii) Pupil Size Amplitude Variation (expressed in arbitrary unit[3] – EYE)
(iv) Reaction Time (expressed in ms – KEY)
(v)   Error Probability (expressed in per cent – KEY)

Operational hypothesis

EEG: *Time-Frequency Power Difference* will be positive with DCs (greater cognitive load for processing the Match condition than the Mismatch condition), negative with TCs (smaller cognitive load for processing the Match condition than the Mismatch condition) and intermediate with NCs.
EYE: decreasing gradient of *Total Fixation Duration* and *Pupil Size Amplitude Variation* will be observed from DCs, to NCs, to TCs.
KEY: decreasing gradient of *Reaction Time* and *Error Probability* will be observed from DCs, to NCs, to TCs.

Experimental materials

120 English words and 240 Norwegian words were used. The English word list consisted of 40 English/Norwegian DCs like 'art' ('*art*' means 'sort, kind, or species' in Norwegian), 40 English/Norwegian TCs like 'arm' and 40 English/Norwegian NCs like 'ant'. Of the 240 Norwegian words, 120 were the Norwegian equivalents of the English words (respectively '*kunst*', '*arm*' and '*maur*'), the other 120 being unrelated. These 240 items were created by pairing each one of the 120 English words once with its Norwegian equivalent (120 items) and once with one of the 120 unrelated Norwegian (120 items). The stimulus words were all nouns. In order to avoid ambiguous situations, NC words were excluded if they could be a cognate with a slightly different

spelling (like porter/*portier*, sister/*søster*, hair/*hår*, machine/*maskin*, etc.). Spelling in English and Norwegian was strictly identical for TCs and DCs. As shown in Table 1, the average length of the English words was approximately identical across Stimulus Type conditions, as well as the Thorndike-Lorge frequency index of word occurrence in written language (Wilson 1988). Other indices known to influence processing difficulty were also computed: Age of Acquisition, Familiarity, Concreteness, and Imageability or ease with which an object could be represented with a drawing (Juhasz 2005). Although these ratings were not available for all the English words we had selected, we report in Table 1 the information available in the MRC psycholinguistic database[4] (Wilson 1988) for a random subset of items in each condition. It approximates the characteristics of the whole set, confirming that good multidimensional balance was reached between conditions, and hence that these parameters could not cause the variations observed in the results. In the absence of a

Table 1 Formal and Psychological descriptors of the English and Norwegian stimuli

		N LETTERS	LEX FRQ	AOA	FAM	CONCR	IMAG
English stimulus word	N words	40/40/40	40/40/40	10/18/35	27/32/37	27/31/37	27/32/37
	Min-Max	3–8	10–1790	222–383	424–620	311–614	384–634
		3–7	1–1430	150–406	441–644	482–635	412–630
		3–7	20–1323	166–511	401–626	323–623	397–632
	Mean/*SD*	4.33/1.01	324/383	282/52	552/52	500/92	537/67
		4.75/0.99	385/380	268/67	548/53	589/32	574/43
		5.03/1.15	347/313	304/64	542/48	519/83	543/60
Norwegian stimulus word	N words	40/40/40	40/40/40	NA			
	Min-Max	3–10	0.004–6.3				
		3–7	0.032–8.4				
		3–9	0.009–6.3				
	Mean/*SD*	5/1.5	0.87/1.5				
		4.75/1	1.23/1.8				
		5.1/1.6	0.77/1.3				

Note **N Letters**: The amount of letters composing a word, or word length. **Lex Frq**: Lexical frequency. For the English words, Thorndike-Lorge written frequency index provided by the MRC Psycholinguistics Database. For the Norwegian words, index computed by the author with the Google search engine (amount of pages written in Norwegian, located in Norway and containing the target Norwegian word at least once, expressed in millions of pages). **AoA**: Age of Acquisition. **Fam**: Familiarity. **Concr**: Concreteness. **Imag**: Imageability. AoA, Fam, Concr and Imag are **ratings** between 100 and 700, corresponding to a scale of 1 to 7. **N words**: Amount of words per category. Values in each cell are given in this order: DC, TC and NC.

psycholinguistic lexical database for the Norwegian vocabulary, the above psychological dimensions were impossible to control for the Norwegian words. However, their formal homogeneity (length and frequency) could be computed (Blair, Urland and Ma 2002) and was high between conditions (Table 1). All materials were cross-validated by a third party expert.

Experimental plan

Four lists, each containing one fourth of the 240 items, were created such that in each list, half of the items were transcoding correspondences, while the remaining half were not. Each participant was tested with two complementary lists, in order to provide data on each of the 120 English words. Additionally, a training set containing ten items was created.

Stimulation procedure

Items were selected randomly from each list and presented automatically, delivered visually at 800 by 600 screen resolution and normal pixel density (96 DPI) on a high quality 21" cathode ray tube screen (DELL P1130 Trinitron). The screen was refreshed at 100 Hz, stimulus delivery being synchronized with screen refreshment for improving timing precision of stimulus presentation. The distance between the surface of the screen and the subject's eyes was 55 cm. Words were written with the fixed-width font Courier New, in size 24 (9 mm height per letter, i.e. 0.94° visual angle). The two words composing a stimulus were separated by an empty space which varied between 9 and 18 characters depending on the length of the words. This visual layout allowed us to keep the total item length constant (24 characters, space included), as shown in Figure 2.

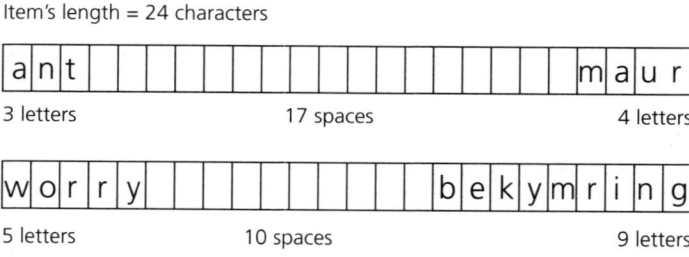

Figure 2 Items' visual layout (character boxes were not visible in the stimulus)

Furthermore, each item's length was made large enough to make it impossible to read a word while gazing at the other one, whatever the word length. Therefore participants were obliged to make a saccade (a fast movement of the eyes) to read each word, an essential constraint for analysing the data: saccadic movements produce a specific artefact in the EEG which could be used for clear time synchronization with the onset of processing of the Norwegian word.

The stimulation sequence started with the English word (WL_2 – see Figure 3) appearing randomly on the left or right half of the screen for 400 ms. Displaying WL_2 for this short duration served as a signal, attracting the gaze of the subject to ensure that the English word was always read first. After 400 ms, the Norwegian word (WL_1) was displayed on the other half of the screen, while the English word remained on the screen at its position. The two words were then displayed together until the response key was pressed or for a maximum duration of two seconds. Two additional seconds separated the end of an item's presentation from the beginning of the next (termed 'inter-stimulus interval'). Every 20 items, a resting time was offered to the participant. He was free to use it or not, for as long as he needed.

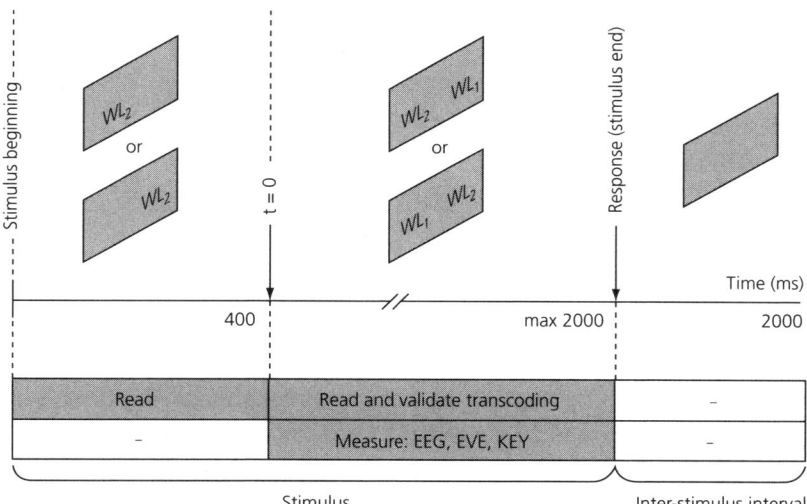

Figure 3 Summary of the experimental situation during the stimulation sequence on one item

Task

Participants performed a 'go, no-go' transcoding validation task, consisting of checking if the English and the Norwegian words (DCs, TCs, NCs) presented in the same item were transcoding correspondences, and pressing a button on a button box if the Norwegian word was the correct transcoding of the English word or doing nothing otherwise. Placed under performance pressure both for speed and accuracy, subjects had to provide a decision as fast as possible and were encouraged to avoid mistakes (see the Experimental Session section below for more details about the experimental protocol).

Recording

Three computers were used. The first computer, piloted with a script written for E-Prime (2008b),[5] presented the stimulus and measured the participant's decisions (i.e. key pressed and reaction time measured from the appearance of the Norwegian word – see Figure 3). The second computer recorded the EEG continuously at 512 Hz with the ASA software (2008a), through a 64 channels shielded cap.[6] The third computer recorded eye-movements from the appearance of the English word and until the subject had given his answer or until 2 seconds had elapsed. The eye-tracker (EyeLink 1000, SR Research Ltd., Canada, used in remote mode with a 500 Hz monocular sampling rate) was piloted directly from the first computer by additional instructions included in the E-Prime script. Computers 2 and 3 were time-synchronized with Computer 1 through communication protocols (respectively Parallel port and Etherlink), EEG and EYE data being time-stamped with triggers generated by E-Prime for the various stimulation events and for the participant's answer. The time accuracy of the equipment, programming and communication protocols were set and tested in a series of pre-tests.

Population

We were advised by the European Union Officers following EYE-to-IT to use bilinguals only at this early stage of research development. Translators are a rare and expensive population, whose use was not scientifically justified for this study. Indeed, any bilingual could transcode isolated words as well as any expert translator. In total, 52 participants were tested (52 per cent female), aged 27 on average (min 18, max 65, *SD* 9). Norwegian native speakers who were also fluent bilinguals in English were invited to undergo a two step selection procedure. A questionnaire first controlled their linguistic background and linguistic competence, checking that candidates learned English in early childhood (average age of commencement for learning English was 6.5 years, min. 0 for real bilinguals, max. 10, *SD* 3.3). Those with an adequate profile were given the online language assessment test 'Dialang' (Freie Universität Berlin *et al.* 2003), evaluating their proficiency in English. Participants with the highest reading level and a vocabulary level score above 900 out of 1,000 were selected. After signing a consent form, candidates were included in the pool of experimental subjects. None had cognitive impairment or neurological disorders. Those with corrected vision were accepted provided they wore glasses or contact lenses during the experiment. Participants were paid 500 Norwegian Kroner.

Experimental session

Experimental sessions were individual and lasted two hours. The participant was prepared (installation and plugging in of the electro-cap), instructed on how to behave with the equipment (be as still as possible, blink systematically between items, be extremely focused on the screen, use resting breaks to relax the eyes and to move if necessary), and instructed about the task to perform (read the stimulus, decide if the Norwegian word is the correct translation of the English word, and press the button of the button box if the answer was yes, do nothing otherwise. Perform the task as fast as possible and, at the same time, avoid making mistakes). Instruments were then adjusted and tested (lowest possible electric resistance for all electrodes, calibration of the eye-tracker). Before starting to train on a set of training items, the subject was asked to summarize what he had understood and remembered, and if needed, clarifications were given by the experimenter. The subject was then trained until his performance reached a minimum threshold of average speed (1200 ms) and accuracy (80 per cent). The testing part which followed was extremely brief (five minutes long) because of its high intensity. The experiment was run along with two other experiments in the same session, and took place at the ERP Laboratory of the National Centre for Epilepsy, Rikshospitalet University Hospital, Oslo, Norway, in June 2008.

Data processing

EEG: Time-Frequency analysis (Koenig, Hubl and Mueller 2002, Hoechstetter *et al.* 2004, Harmony *et al.* 2009) used the data from 44 participants only, the EEG quality from eight participants being poor. Signal processing and analysis was done with the software *BESA* (2009). Time-Frequency analysis considered EEG segments of 575 ms (-100 to 475) around the first horizontal eye movement after the appearance of the Norwegian word (beginning of the mental matching between L_2 and L_1). Longer segments could not be used (appearance of the first answers). For each *Stimulus Type* condition, the analysis compared power differences existing in the EEG between the Matching condition and its corresponding Mismatching condition, in 2 Hz frequency bands between 4 and 50 Hz, on each 25 ms time interval between -100 and $+475$ ms. Time-frequency matrices of p-values[7] were obtained, one p-value per 2 Hz by 25 ms sample (Time-Frequency sample), one matrix per channel, repeated for each one of the three *Stimulus Type* conditions. The distribution of p-values across conditions, frequency bands, time intervals, and cranial locations was analysed with multilevel modelling (Clark 1973, Hox 2002, Lachaud and Renaud 2009, Rasbash *et al.* 2009).

EYE: Eye data from all subjects were used. Raw measurements on matching items were isolated from those on mismatching items. Items with blinks or no eye detection were eliminated. The overall quality, however, was very good, because subjects were instructed to blink systematically between items and to pay great attention to the stimulus, which naturally reduced their blinking rate during item presentation. A script written by Dr. O. Spakov (EYE-to-IT, TAUCHI, University of Tampere, Finland), analysed the raw data and extracted *Total Fixation Duration* and *Pupil Size Amplitude Variation*. Outliers were filtered with Median $\pm$ 3 Median Absolute Deviation applied by subject and by item in each condition. Missing values were not replaced. Three linear multilevel models, one per dependent variable, crossed subjects and items as random variables and included *Stimulus Type* as a fixed variable.

KEY: Data from only 41 subjects were used, 11 subjects having performed the task incorrectly during part of the experiment. The procedure described above for eye movements was followed for filtering outliers and statistical analysis. Because *Error Probability* was binary, a logit binomial multilevel model was used. The model's structure is identical to the ones previously described.

For EEG, EYE and KEY, the test statistic was a large sample Chi-squared test. Results are shown as graphs in Figures 4 to 8, with 95 per cent confidence interval bars.

Results

EEG

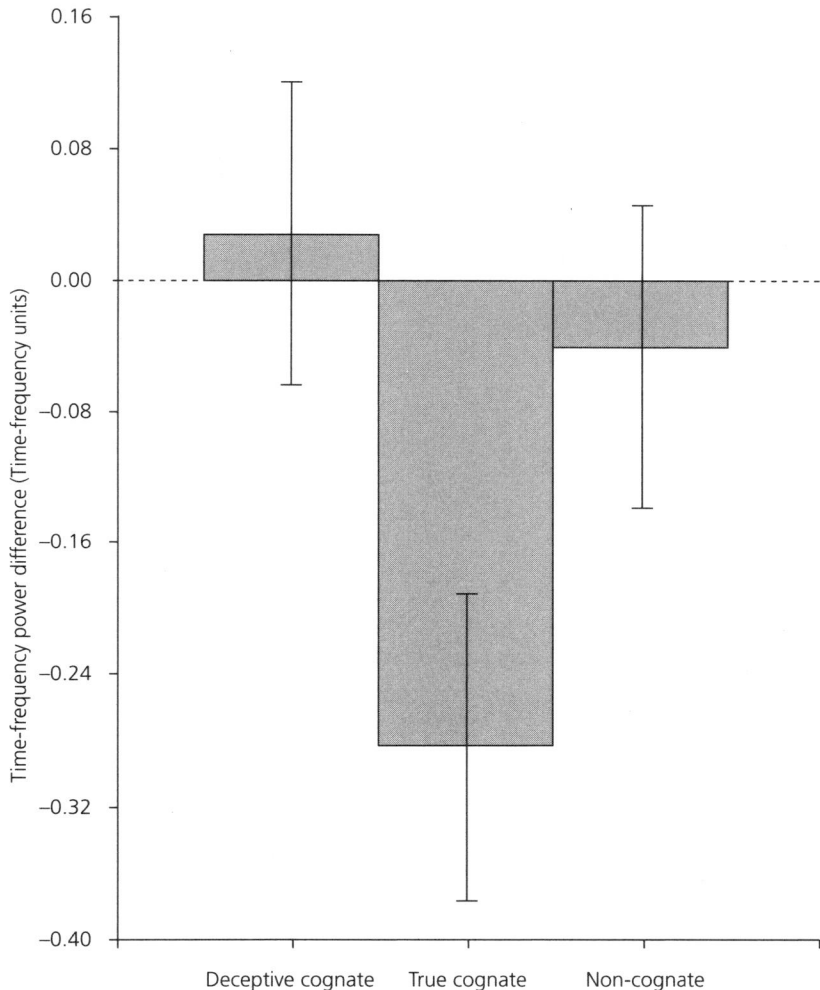

Figure 4 Time-Frequency Power Difference (in Time-Frequency units) as a function of Stimulus Type

Time-Frequency Power Difference was smaller by 0.311 Time-Frequency units with TCs than with DCs ($\chi^2_{(1, N 5 2736)}$ = 36.8, $p<$ .0001), and smaller by 0.238 Time-Frequency units than with NCs ($\chi^2_{(1, N 5 2736)}$ = 21.5, $p<$ .0001). The difference between DCs and NCs was marginal ($p<$ .16).

EYE

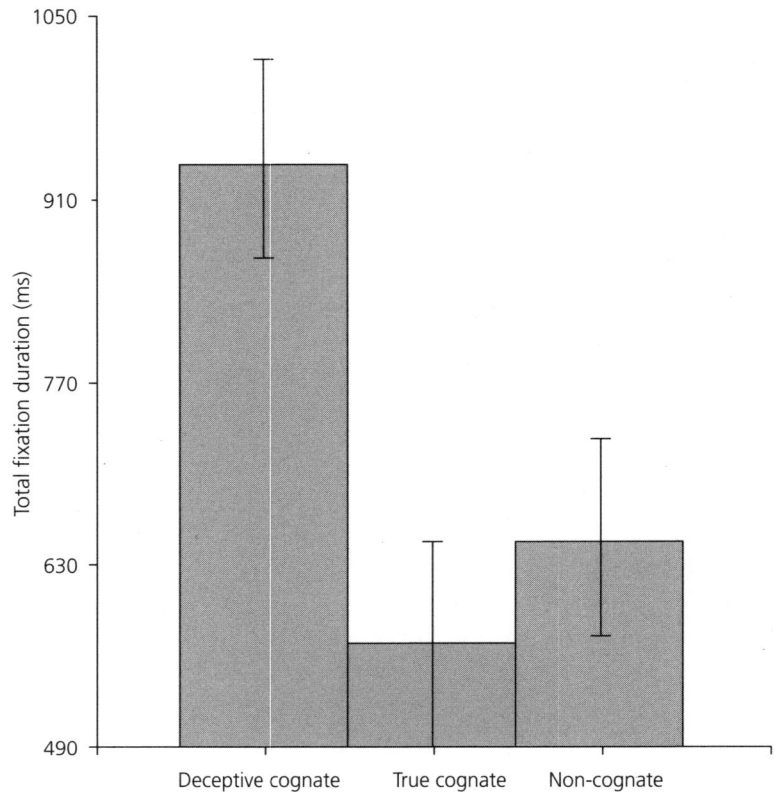

Figure 5 Total Fixation Duration (in ms) as a function of Stimulus Type

Total Fixation Duration with DCs was 368 ms longer than with TCs ($\chi^2_{(1, N 5 2827)}$ = 50.2, $p<$ .0001), and 289 ms longer than with NCs ($\chi^2_{(1, N 5 2827)}$ = 30.9, $p<$ .0001). The difference between TCs and NCs was marginal ($p<$ .13).

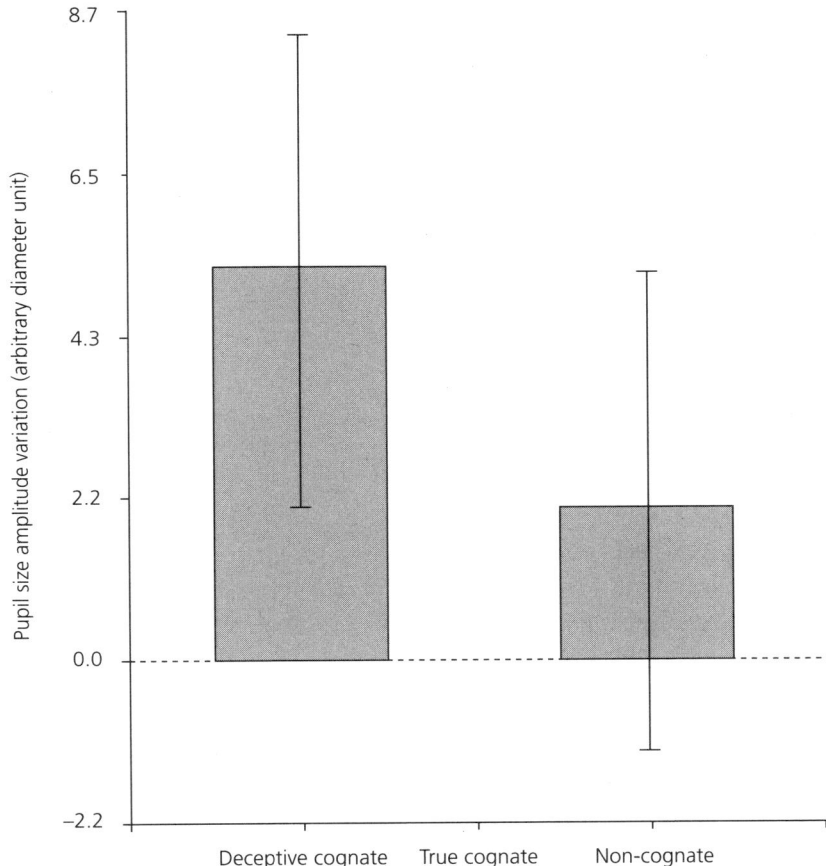

Figure 6 Pupil Size Amplitude Variation (in arbitrary diameter unit) as a function of Stimulus Type

Pupil Size Amplitude Variation with DCs was 5.3 diameter units bigger than with TCs ($\chi^2_{(1, N\,5\,2892)}$ = 10.5, $p<$ .0013) and 3.3 diameter units bigger than with NCs ($\chi^2_{(1, N\,5\,2892)}$ = 4, $p<$ .047). The difference between TCs and NCs was not significant ($p<$ .22).

KEY

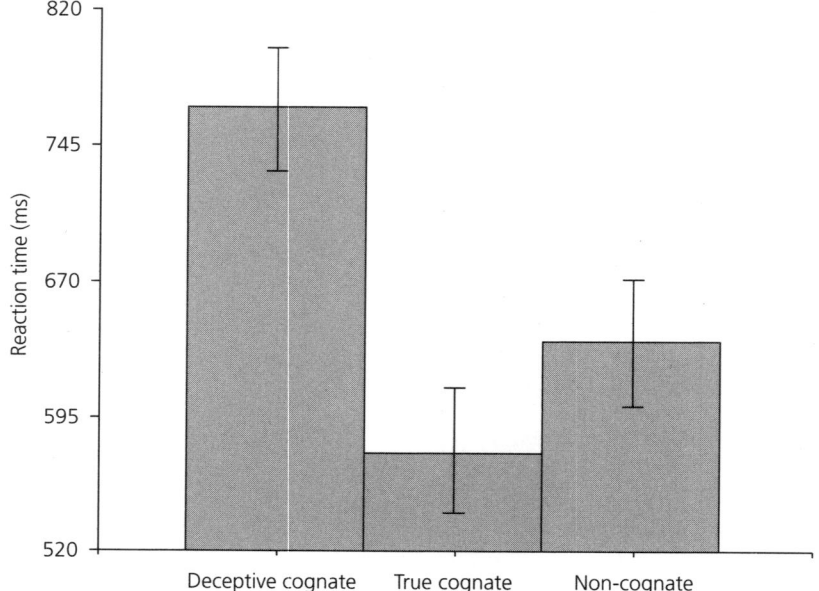

Figure 7 Reaction Time (in ms) as a function of Stimulus Type

Reaction times with DCs were 189 ms longer than with TCs ($\chi^2_{(1, N 5 2186)}$ = 99, $p<$ .0001), and 127 ms longer than with NCs ($\chi^2_{(1, N 5 2186)}$ = 44, $p<$ .0001). Additionally, reaction times were 62 ms longer with NCs than with TCs ($\chi^2_{(1, N 5 2186)}$ = 11, $p<$ .001).

Error Probability with DCs was 15 per cent greater than with TCs ($\chi^2_{(1, N 5 2460)}$ = 24, $p<$ .0001), and 14 per cent greater than with NCs ($\chi^2_{(1, N 5 2460)}$ = 20, $p<$ .0001). The difference between TCs and NCs was not significant ($p<$ .66).

Discussion

Result patterns across dependent variables give a clear, unambiguous picture of the greater difficulty participants had transcoding DCs (positive *Time-Frequency Power Difference*, longest *Total Fixation Duration*, biggest *Pupil Size Amplitude Variation*, longest *Reaction Time* and biggest *Error Probability*). The fact that TCs were easier to process is also indisputable

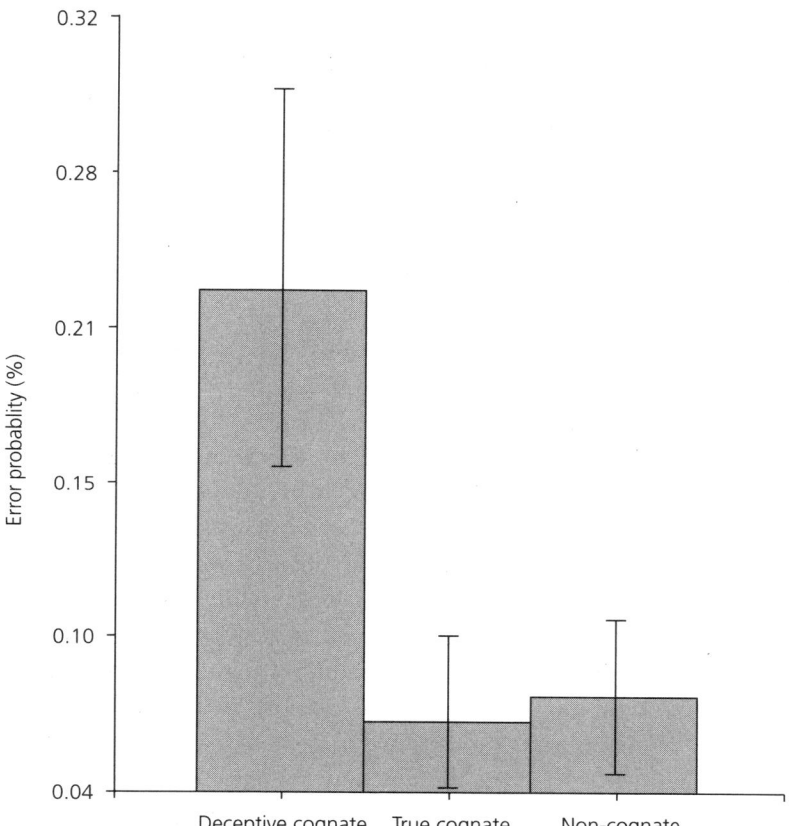

Figure 8 Error Probability (as a percentage) as a function of Stimulus Type

(biggest negative *Time-Frequency Power Difference*, shortest *Total Fixation Duration*, smallest *Pupil Size Amplitude Variation*, shortest *Reaction Time* and smallest *Error Probability*). Although an intermediate pattern was predicted for NC, analyses do not clearly confirm the hypothesis. Yes, the average of the dependent variable for NCs is always between DCs and TCs, but the difference between the three conditions is only significant for reaction times. With other dependent variables, NCs are either significantly different from TCs and not from DCs (*Time-Frequency Power Difference*), or from DCs and not from TCs (*Total Fixation Duration, Pupil Size Amplitude Variation* and *Error Probability*).

If the study had been based on one dependent variable only, the chances are high that an incorrect conclusion would have been drawn e.g.: 'NCs are as difficult to transcode as DCs', or 'NCs are as easy to process as TCs'. It is, however, likely that NCs are more difficult to process than TCs, but easier to transcode than DCs. Because each dependent variable measures a different aspect of the mind's activity, it is not surprising that varying patterns of results are obtained, hence the fundamental importance of choosing dependent variables adequately targeting the mental process that needs to be studied.

This study reveals that the processing difficulty (*Reaction Time*) is highest for DCs, lowest for TCs, and medium for NCs. The verification effort (*Total Fixation Duration*) and reading attention demand (*Pupil Size Amplitude Variation*) is highest for DCs and lowest for TCs. The verification effort is marginally bigger with NCs than with TCs, but attention demand is not statistically different. Participants were the most confused with DCs, and also confused (but less so) with TCs and NCs. The overall cognitive load is strongly reduced between the TC Mismatching and Matching conditions, and slightly reduced with NCs, indicating that less computation is required to make a decision in these matching conditions than in the corresponding mismatching conditions. The overall cognitive load is slightly increased with DCs, indicating that more computation was needed to make a decision in the matching condition than in the mismatching condition.

The Conceptual Mediation Hierarchical Model presented in Figure 1 is supported by this set of results. Because the lexical form is identical between L_2 and L_1 for TCs, verification effort, attention demand, difficulty and confusion are the lowest, and cognitive load is reduced in the matching condition compared to the mismatching condition. With NCs, the meaning of the two words is identical and serves as a link between L_2 and L_1 lexical forms. Thanks to this semantic link, the overall cognitive load is slightly reduced in the matching condition compared with the mismatching condition. Verification effort is greater with NCs than with TCs because two lexical forms are now being compared and mentally transcoded. Consequently, attention demand, confusion level and the decision-making load are also higher. DC words have the same lexical form in L_2 and L_1, but a different meaning in L_2 and L_1. DCs therefore induce the highest confusion and difficulty, as well as hesitation in the decision-making process. Thinking about possible meanings, bilinguals will eventually follow one of the four paths described in the introduction. Due to the additional computation that was not necessary in the NC condition, it is logical to find an overall cognitive load increase in the matching condition compared to the mismatching condition.

Conclusion

This study has demonstrated the possibility and the added value of simultaneously using multiple techniques to measure the cognitive load involved in transcoding TCs, NCs and DCs. The methodology has allowed us to confirm the existence of a transcoding difficulty hierarchy that translators may face at the word level: DCs are the most difficult to process, NCs represent an intermediate cognitive load, and TCs are the easiest. The results allow us to pave the way for a Translation Priming system that might help translators retrieve forms and meanings from long-term memory. For example, when processing DCs, translators might benefit from prompts related both semantically and lexically to the target. On the other hand, the processing of NCs might only require prompts at the lexical level. Finally, when processing TCs, translators might not benefit from prompting as they would not be facing any transcoding challenge. This information was essential for grounding the next steps of the study: testing the benefits of prompting on transcoding (Lachaud, Fougner Rydning and Larsson, Submitted) and translation (future research).

Notes

1 Development of Human-Computer Monitoring and Feedback Systems for the Purposes of Studying Cognition and Translation, 2006/01–2009/04, 6th Framework Program, Information Society Technologies (Contract 517590).

2 According to this type of psychological model, two languages share the same semantic system of representation in the bilingual mind, but each language is stored as a distinct system of formal representations. Both languages are therefore linked together through the common semantic system – Illes, J., Francis, W.S., Desmond, J.E., Gabrieli, J.D.E., Glover, G.H., Poldrack, R., Lee, C.J. & Wagner, A.D. (1999). Convergent Cortical Representation of Semantic Processing in Bilinguals. *Brain and Language*, 70 (3), 347–363.

3 Pupil size provided by the EyeLink 1000 is given as integer numbers in an arbitrary unit, with a noise level of 0.2 per cent of the diameter.

4 The MRC Psycholinguistic database: Cf. http://www.psych.rl.ac.uk/MRC_Psych_Db.html (Last accessed 06/01/10).

5 E-Prime is software specifically developed for psychological research. It allows the presentation

of visual, auditory, or audio-visual stimuli to human subjects, and records their behavior in automated experimental sessions.

6   WaveGuard™ cap (ANT) with a 64 channels 10-20 international layout, using 64 sintered Ag/AgCl electrodes, Hirose HD connectors.

7   Statistical index giving the probability that the null hypothesis is true. The scientific standard threshold is p< .05. It means that the probability to observe a given pattern in the data due to chance is below 5 per cent.

References

(2008a). Advanced Signal Analysis. Enschede, Netherlands: Advanced Neuro Technology Software BV (ANT).

(2008b). E-Prime. Pittsburgh, PA, USA: Psychology Software Tools, Inc.

(2009). Brain Electrical Source Analysis. Gräfelfing, Germany: MEGIS Software GmbH.

Blair, I. V., G.R. Urland, and J. E. Ma, (2002), 'Using Internet search engines to estimate word frequency'. *Behavior Research Methods, Instruments & Computers*, 2 (34), 286–290.

Bölte, J. and E. Coenen, (2002), 'Is phonological information mapped onto semantic information in a one-to-one manner?' *Brain and Language*, 81 (1–3), 384–397.

Cavero, L., P. Concejero, J. Gili, K.O. Yuichiro Anzai, and M. Hirohiko, (1995), 'Help and prompting in broad band multimedia services'. *Advances in Human Factors/Ergonomics. Amsterdam*: Elsevier. pp. 225–230.

Chamizo Domínguez, P.J. and B. Nerlich, (2002), 'False friends: their origin and semantics in some selected languages'. *Journal of Pragmatics*, 34 (12), 1833–1849.

Clark, H.H. (1973), 'The language-as-fixed-effect fallacy: a critique of language statistics in psychological research'. *Journal of Verbal Learning and Verbal Behavior*, 12, 335–359.

Duyck, W. and N. Warlop, (2009), 'Translation Priming Between the Native Language and a Second Language: New Evidence From Dutch-French Bilinguals'. *Experimental Psychology*, 56 (3), 173–179.

Ferreira, A. and J. Atkinson, (2009), 'Designing a feedback component of an intelligent tutoring system for foreign language'. *Knowledge-Based Systems*, 22 (7), 496–501.

Finkbeiner, M., K. Forster, J. Nicol, and K. Nakamura, (2004), 'The role of polysemy in masked semantic and translation priming'. *Journal of memory and language*, 51 (1), 1–22.

Freie Universität Berlin, G., Jyväskylän yliopisto, F., Lancaster University, U., CITO groep, N., Karl-Franzens-Universität Graz, A., Vrije Universiteit Brussel, B., Handelshøjskolen i Århus, D., Århus Kommunes Sprogcenter, D., Generalitat de Catalunya, E., Aristotelio PanepistimioThessalonikis, G., ITÉ Dublin, I., Háskóli Íslands, I., INVaISI, I., Universitetet i Bergen, N., Universidade de Aveiro, P., Universidade de Coimbra, P., Göteborgs Universitet, S. & Lunds Universitet, S. (2003). DIALANG. European project for the development of diagnostic language tests in 14 European languages.

French, R.M. and M. Jacquet, (2004), 'Understanding bilingual memory: models and data'. *Trends in Cognitive Sciences*, 8 (2), 87–93.

Frenck, C. and J. Pynte, (1987), 'Semantic representation and surface forms: A look at across-language priming in bilinguals'. *Journal of Psycholinguistic Research*, 16 (4), 383–396.

Group, C.P.R. (1986), *Parallel distributed processing: explorations in the microstructure of cognition.* Cambridge, MA, USA: MIT Press.

Harmony, T., A. Alba, J.L. Marroquín, and B. González-Frankenberger, (2009), 'Time-frequency-topographic analysis of induced power and synchrony of EEG signals during a Go/No-Go task'. *International Journal of Psychophysiology*, 71 (1), 9–16.

Hoechstetter, K., H., Bornfleth, D., Weckesser, N., Ille, P. Berg, and M. Scherg, (2004), 'BESA Source Coherence: A New Method to Study Cortical Oscillatory Coupling'. *Brain Topography*, 16 (4), 233–238.

Hox, J. (2002), *Multilevel analysis: techniques and applications.* London: Lawrence Erlbaum Associates.

Illes, J., W.S. Francis, J.E., Desmond, J.D.E., Gabrieli, G.H., Glover, R., Poldrack, C.J. Lee, and A.D. Wagner, (1999), 'Convergent Cortical Representation of Semantic Processing in Bilinguals'. *Brain and Language*, 70 (3), 347–363.

Juhasz, B.J. (2005), 'Age-of-Acquisition Effects in Word and Picture Identification'. *Psychological Bulletin*, 131 (5), 684–712.

Koenig, T., D. Hubl, and T.J. Mueller, (2002), 'Decomposing the EEG in time, space and frequency: a formal model, existing methods, and new proposals'. *International Congress Series*, 1232, 317–321.

Lachaud, C.M., A. Fougner Rydning, and P.G. Larsson, (Submitted). 'Towards online automatic systems for improving human text translation: Transcoding performance and cognitive load variations after prompting'. *International Journal of Human-Computer Studies.*

Lachaud, C.M. and O. Renaud, (2009), 'A tutorial for analyzing human reaction times: How to filter data, to manage missing values, and to chose a statistical model?'. *Applied Psycholinguistics*, accepted.

Lederer, M. (2006). 'Défense et illustration de la théorie interprétative de la traduction'. In F. Israël & M. Lederer (eds), *La Théorie Interprétative de la Traduction: Genèse et Développement.* Paris: Miraud.

McClelland, J.L. and J.L. Elman, (1986), 'The TRACE model of speech perception'. *Cognitive Psychology*, 18 (1), 1–86.

Niedermeyer, E. and F. L. Da Silva, (2005). *Electroencephalography Basic Principles, Clinical Applications, and Related Fields.* Philadelphia, PA, USA: Lippincott Williams & Wilkins.

Rasbash, J., C. Charlton, W.J. Browne, M. Healy, and B. Cameron, (2009), *MLwiN.* Bristol, UK: Centre for Multilevel Modelling, University of Bristol.

Schwanenflugel, P.J. and M. Rey, (1986), 'Interlingual semantic facilitation: Evidence for a common representational system in the bilingual lexicon'. *Journal of Memory and Language*, 25 (5), 605–618.

Wilson, M.D. (1988), 'The MRC psycholinguistic database: Machine readable dictionary, version 2'. *Behavioural Research Methods, Instruments and Computers*, 20, 6–11.

Translation Directionality and the Revised Hierarchical Model: An Eye-Tracking Study[1]

Vincent Chieh-Ying Chang

Chapter Outline

Introduction

Background

There has been a limited number of pioneering eye-tracking studies on the way cognitive loading varies with different translation tasks; therefore, much still needs to be learned regarding (1) whether 'eye tracking' can be adequately applied to the study of the effect of directionality on cognitive loading at a *textual* level; and (2) whether the predictions suggested by the Revised Hierarchical Model (Kroll and Stewart 1994) regarding 'translation asymmetry' (see Translation Directionality below) are valid at a *textual* level. 'Translation asymmetry' refers to asymmetrical levels of cognitive loading caused by different translation directions; it is a function of translation directionality, and refers to a phenomenon where translating from language A into language B is more cognitively demanding than the reverse direction. In particular, 'translation asymmetry' has only been investigated in the case of highly competent professional interpreters/translators or non-translator/

interpreter bilinguals (De Groot *et al.* 1994; Altarriba and Mathis 1997; Jiang 1999; Rinne *et al.* 2000; Tokowicz and Kroll 2007). The limited evidence suggests it is likely to be a much more significant phenomenon among novice translators, and highlights this under-researched population as potential research subjects. In fact, Rinne *et al.* (2000: 88) specifically recommended that further studies using 'less proficient students of translation studies as subjects' would be useful.

Research significance and motivation

In the translation and interpreting market place, bilateral translation and interpreting is commonplace (Malkiel 2004) and translation into the second language is gaining ground (Wilss 1996: 8). It has also been revealed that most professional translators work into their second language (Weatherby 1998: 21). If it can be established that translating into the second language is generally more cognitively demanding than working into the first language, then it is arguable that translator training should take this into account in its curricula, so that future students will be better equipped to face future market requirements.

Translation directionality

It has been argued by Kroll and Stewart (1994) that more cognitive effort is required when a person performs a single-word translation task from her/his first language into her/his second language (A→B), whereas relatively less is required in the opposite direction (B→A). This claim is based on their findings from experimental research in which bilingual undergraduate students were instructed to perform two kinds of task: (1) verbally naming an item presented in a list of pictorial representations of concrete objects, and (2) translating a word presented in a word list. Sixteen bilingual subjects with the language pair of Dutch (A) and English (B) participated in the first task, and twenty four bilingual subjects with the same language combination participated in the second. The cognitive loading generated when participants provided the required word in response to the picture or word cue was measured by reaction times. The list in which the pictures to be named or the words to be translated were located could comprise objects either in a similar conceptual category (e.g. scarf, shoes, stockings) or in random categories (e.g. horse, skates, cherry), and the subjects could be required to name the pictorial object either in their first or second language, as well as to carry out single-word A→B or B→A translation.

The experimenters' hypothesis was that, when a general category was stimulated by a list of related objects or words, many lexical representations would be simultaneously activated. As a result, when required to name a particular item or translate a single word in the list, other words would compete in the subject's mind, creating 'category interference' and slowing the mental process.

Interestingly, their results confirmed that category interference did indeed occur (i.e. longer reaction times were observed) when the bilingual subjects worked A→B, but no such interference was found when they worked B→A. Kroll and Stewart (1994) argued that this 'translation asymmetry' demonstrated the existence of conceptual as well as lexical associations in the minds of bilingual individuals. They devised a Revised Hierarchical Model (Kroll and Stewart 1994) (Figure 1) to explain *a posteriori* this theoretical interpretation of their findings. Further, the Revised Hierarchical Model explicitly suggests a strong correlation between reaction time and cognitive loading; in other words, cognitive loading is measurable by reaction time – the longer the reaction time is, the higher the cognitive loading. This claim has been supported by the findings of other studies (e.g. Heredia 1996; Brysbaert and Dijkstra 2006).

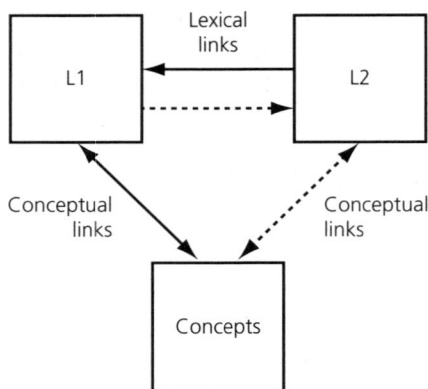

Figure 1 Revised Hierarchical Model
Source: Adapted from Kroll & Stewart (1994: 158)
Arrows represent the directions of associations or links. Bold arrows represent comparatively stronger links and dotted-line arrows represent weaker links.

However, up to now, investigations into the effect of directionality on translation have suffered from a number of weaknesses. First, little work has been done with novice translators (e.g. Pavlović and Jensen 2009). Studying the population of novice translators is of great significance, because other potential novice-related factors may impact on the effect of directionality. For instance, de Groot (1994) shows that word concreteness has an effect on how quickly an individual completes A→B and B→A translations, and the result contradicts the predictions suggested by the Revised Hierarchical Model. A number of factors, such as years of training and experience, have been shown to have an impact, and therefore to what extent translation asymmetry can be confirmed or disconfirmed by the population warrants further investigation.

In addition, the experimental tasks have involved only associations between single words, as opposed to authentic translation tasks with texts. In fact, the Revised Hierarchical Model assumes that meaning resides in single words; however, whether or not the predictions regarding 'translation asymmetry' suggested by the model are valid at a *textual* level has yet to be explored. A further criticism is that the distinction the model makes between lexical and conceptual links has been inferred from purely behavioural evidence (reaction times) and lacks direct physiological confirmation. Last but not least, the Revised Hierarchical Model can only make predictions on single-word translations of, for instance, different language combinations and varying levels of word lengths and frequencies, but not on texts. This point has been confirmed by Kroll (2009). The model's predictive capacity is therefore limited. Our motivation for this study was to explore whether or not the predictions regarding translation asymmetry, suggested by the Revised Hierarchical Model, are valid at a textual level.

Eye-tracking studies on translation and interpreting

To date, only a limited number of studies applying eye tracking to Translation and Interpreting (T&I) research have been published (Tommola and Niemi 1986; Hyönä *et al.* 1995; O'Brien 2006; Sharmin *et al.* 2008; Dragsted and Hansen 2008; Sjørup 2008; Jakobsen and Jensen 2008; Caffrey 2008; Carl *et al.* 2008; Jensen 2008; Alves *et al.* (Online) and Pavlović and Jensen 2009). The EU-sponsored EYE-to-IT project (Online) also investigated the cognitive processes involved in translation; publications from the project are forthcoming. The review below aims to show that (1) little work has been conducted on the effect of directionality on cognitive loading; and (2) more topics on translation and interpreting could be investigated, using eye tracking as a method.

Tommola and Niemi (1986) were the first to present a preliminary investigation of cognitive loading of online simultaneous interpreting, using data on pupil diameter. A larger pupil diameter indicates a heavier amount of cognitive loading (Rayner 1998). One female subject was recruited to carry out simultaneous interpreting of five Finnish texts into English. Due to the syntactic differences between Finnish and English, restructuring of the output English sentences was required. In the study, they reported peaks of pupil diameter where restructuring was necessary in the English output.

Hyönä et al. (1995) were the second to apply the method of eye tracking to translation and interpreting studies. They tested whether or not pupil diameter change could be used to investigate the cognitive processing load for simultaneous interpreting (SI) and other language tasks. In their first experiment, nine Finnish-English translation and interpretation students were recruited to carry out three tasks: SI, shadowing (listening to and repeating a text without translating it) and passive listening. Their results demonstrated that pupillometric measures strongly correlated with the difficulty of the task. The pupil dilated significantly more during SI than during shadowing, and more during shadowing than during passive listening. In their second experiment, eighteen Finnish-English translators were recruited to conduct three tasks: (1) single-word passive listening, but with the added instruction to say YES when they recognized the aurally presented word; (2) single-word shadowing; and (3) single-word translation. Both Finnish and English vocabulary was presented and the words were classified as difficult or easy. A multifactorial analysis showed that there was a significant correlation between pupil size and the type of task, the input language and the difficulty of the words (for a review on how pupil size correlates with a task's difficulty level, see Janisse 1977; Beatty 1982).

A third study that tested the usefulness of eye tracking for translation studies was conducted by O'Brien (2006). In her study, four professional translators were recruited to translate a text using a translation memory (TM) tool. Their pupil dilation data were recorded and used as a measure of the cognitive loads required to process different types of TM matches: No Match, Fuzzy Match, MT Match and Exact Match. Her results showed that a No Match required the most cognitive effort and Exact Match the least. Gaze replay, where participants retrospectively watch a video of their own eye movements during the experimental task, was also used in combination with retrospective interviews that prompted the subjects to recall what they did during the translation task. The study was an initial test of the usefulness of eye tracking for investigating cognitive load in translation, specifically when translators use translation technology.

Sharmin *et al.* (2008) aimed to explore the effect of time pressure and text complexity on fixation patterns of translators. They reported a significant effect of text complexity and no significant effect of time pressure on the translators' fixations on their computer screen.

Dragsted and Hansen (2008) employed keystroke logging and eye tracking as research methods, and based on data from eight participants, they suggested the concept of eye-key span, i.e. the temporal duration between 'a given ST fixation and the production of its TT equivalent' (ibid.: 27). Further, their results suggested that a translation segment involves reading and comprehending a segment of the ST, as well as writing and producing its equivalent in the TT. This means that typing is intrinsic to the task of translation.

In a pilot study, Sjørup (2008) explored the optimal way to design an eye-tracking experiment, using three professional translators, to determine potentially different patterns of eye-movement behaviour when processing metaphors during translation. The study suggested that processing metaphors, in comparison with literal expressions, required more fixation time, and that processing metaphors was cognitively more demanding.

Jackobsen and Jensen (2008) recruited a group of six professional translators and a group of six translation students to carry out four tasks: (1) reading for comprehension only; (2) reading in preparation for translating; (3) reading while verbally translating into their native language, i.e. Danish (also referred to as B→A sight translating or interpreting); and (4) reading while producing a translation by typing. Data analysis included task time, fixation count, fixation duration and fixation transitions between the ST and TT. The results suggested that, compared with the first two tasks, the third and the fourth tasks required a significantly longer time, more fixations and longer fixation durations, regardless of participant grouping. The results also suggested that translation students needed a significantly longer time, more fixations, longer fixation durations and more transitions between the ST and TT for all translation-related tasks.

Using fixation-based and pupillometric data, Caffrey (2008) recruited twenty participants to explore how TV anime were processed in four different subtitling conditions: (1) one-line subtitling; (2) two-line subtitling; (3) one-line subtitling with pop-up glosses that were used to convey cultural information intrinsic to Japanese anime; and (4) two-line subtitling with pop-up glosses. Results revealed that both the number of lines used for subtitling and the use of pop-up glosses had a significant effect on cognitive processing. The study suggested that processing two-line subtitling generated more cognitive loading, compared with one-line subtitling, and that two-line subtitling with glosses created the most cognitive loading. It was also suggested that the presence of glosses contributed to a re-distribution of attention between the subtitling and the glosses, and that whenever glosses were presented, more subtitles were omitted.

To investigate the phenomenon of translation, Carl *et al.* (2008) proposed a new bimodal cognitive research design of 'user-activity data' (UAD) that incorporates keystroke logging and eye-movement data. Three participants were requested to translate a number of texts from English into Danish, and their preliminary results based on keystrokes and fixations suggested the usefulness of the research design.

Alves *et al.* (Online) recruited two expert translators who were requested to translate from German into English, and such methods as keystroke logging and eye tracking were utilized. They aimed to investigate *units of translation* and *grammatical metaphor*. 'Grammatical metaphor' refers to 'semantic units mapped on to different grammatical units' (ibid.: 1). The study suggests that eye tracking is a viable method for investigating the field of translation and interpreting.

Pavlović and Jensen (2009) carried out the latest eye-tracking based study of directionality in translation to date. This experiment sought to measure the cognitive loading related to translation directionality with the language combination of Danish (A) and English (B). The eye-tracking data analysed included fixation time, average fixation duration, task time and pupil size and were collected from a group of eight translation students and another group of eight professional translators. Text stimuli were used and controlled for genre, syllable count and sentence length. Their results suggested that (1) processing TT generated more cognitive loading, and this was consistent with the findings of Sharmin *et al.* (2008); (2) regardless of participant grouping, A→B translation was significantly more cognitively demanding than B→A translation, based on the data of task time and pupil size; and (3) regardless of translation direction, translation students experienced significantly more cognitive loading, compared to professional translators. Two hypotheses the study set out to test were non-conclusive, i.e. (1) processing ST during A→B translation would be more cognitively demanding than during B→A translation; and (2) producing TT would be more cognitively demanding during A→B translation than during B→A translation.

However, the study by Pavlović and Jensen (2009) could potentially have been strengthened. First, the text stimuli were made comparable by controlling for factors, such as genre, readability, grade level, syllable count and sentence length. However, for text stimuli to be comparable in a study closely related to translation directionality, a translatability test has to be conducted in order to avoid potential confounding factors at a *textual* level (see Text Selection below). Secondly, the study did not report behavioural data, by which we mean the accuracy of the product data produced by all the participants.

To sum up, the previous research has to a certain extent suggested eye tracking as a viable method for studying translation or interpreting. However, the number of eye-tracking studies specifically investigating the phenomenon of translation or interpreting is still very limited. Therefore, whether or not eye tracking has a broader applicability to the field of Translation Studies investigating other research topics warrants further testing. In addition, very few studies have investigated the effect of directionality on cognitive loading at a textual level, and this is a gap this paper aims to bridge.

Methodology

As mentioned in the Introduction, the study presented here was interested in investigating cognitive loading in translation directionality to see if the predictions of the Revised Hierarchical Model are applicable at the textual level.

Experimental design

To test if there is any significant difference between cognitive loading for A→B and B→A translation using eye tracking, one English text and one Mandarin text were selected for participants to translate. Task sequence was randomized across participants.

Participants

Given practical and geographical constraints, the number of qualified participants available for the study was limited. Sixteen healthy female subjects with a language combination of Mandarin Chinese as language A and English as language B participated. All had completed a one-year postgraduate translation and/or interpretation program at one of the UK universities. The data from one subject were excluded from analyses because she did not follow the investigator's instructions.[2] Therefore data from fifteen participants were analysed.

Text selection

Text selection was a critical aspect of the study design. Several elements were considered, in terms of criteria for text selection. First, the study aimed to achieve as much ecological validity as possible. To maximize ecological validity of the study, written texts, as opposed to single words, were used as stimuli to simulate real-life situations where translators are requested to conduct textual translations. Nevertheless, no claim of having achieved perfect ecological validity can be made in relation to this study because of the fact that the texts were selected and controlled to some extent, and because the study was conducted in a laboratory setting that could have a potentially adverse effect on the level of ecological validity.

In addition, since the study was interested only in investigating cognitive loading for different translation directions, simple and non-technical texts were selected in order to eliminate any potential confounding variables such as lack of domain knowledge. The simple, non-technical texts were tested to ensure that they were comparable in terms of grade level, word count, comprehensibility, readability and translatability (see details below). It is worth pointing out that the use of the translatability test was an improvement on the study by Pavlović and Jensen (2009), because the test further ensured text comparability.

The English text from one children's story book (Milne 1980) was selected, and the Mandarin text was chosen from a Mandarin textbook used in Taiwan (Lai 2006).

Grade Level

Grade level refers to educational stages in a system of grades. The selected English texts scored 4.5 on the Flesch-Kincaid Grade Level Test (this can be calculated using Microsoft Word 2002 and later versions). This means that the English text was usable and understandable by pupils in the second semester of grade four in an elementary school in the US educational system. As the

Flesch-Kincaid Grade Level Test could not score Mandarin texts and no test was available to score Mandarin texts, a Mandarin textbook used in the second semester of grade 4 in Taiwan[3] was obtained (grade level = 4.5). The short text was extracted from the textbook to ensure that it was comparable with the English text in terms of grade level. A low grade level minimized the text-related difficulty factor in the study.

Word Count

Both texts consisted of fifty words in total. The concept of an orthographic word as understood in the English language is different from the idea of a word in an ideogram-based language such as Mandarin, where 'words' are often composed of two 'characters', forming a compound unit that is equal to a word unit in English. For example, the Chinese character 電 means 'electricity' and 腦 means 'brain'. Juxtaposing the two characters would yield a compound word 電腦 (meaning 'computer'). Therefore to control word counts for the text, two Mandarin language and translation teachers with Mandarin as their language A and English as their language B agreed on the total word counts of all four texts after modifications. First, they used Microsoft Word 2000 to compute the word counts of the English text. To ensure that the English text was composed of fifty words exactly, a number of English words were deleted or changed without affecting the grammar and meanings of the texts. Second, the two teachers individually calculated the word counts of the selected Mandarin text. After careful deliberation and modifications without affecting the grammar and meaning, they reached a consensus that the Mandarin text consisted of fifty 'words'. By doing so, the potential effect of differing word counts was minimized.

Comprehensibility

Ten bilinguals with Mandarin as their language A and English as their language B were instructed to read and rate the English and the Mandarin texts in terms of comprehensibility, using a scoring system of 1 = very easy, 2 = easy, 3 = medium, 4 = difficult, 5 = very difficult. They were asked to rate the texts, based on how easy it was for them to understand the texts. The two texts were on average rated at 1.6 or 1.7 respectively. This indicates that the two texts were fairly easy to comprehend and minimized, insofar as possible, any effect that varying levels of text comprehensibility might have had on the results.

Readability

The same ten bilinguals with Mandarin as their first language and English as their second were asked to read and rate the two texts for readability, using the same scoring system of 1 = very easy, 2 = easy, 3 = medium, 4 = difficult, 5 = very difficult. They were instructed to rate the texts based on how easy it was for them to read the texts. We differentiate here between comprehensibility and readability. For example, a high school literary piece may be easy to read and yet difficult to comprehend. Both texts were, on average, rated as 1.6 and 1.5 respectively. This shows that the two texts were considered to be fairly easy to read by the raters and the potentially confounding variable of readability was, therefore, hopefully minimized.

Translatability

In the study, translatability was defined as how difficult or easy it was for a qualified novice translator to translate a text. The comprehensibility and readability tests could be administered to bilinguals. However, the translatability test could only be carried out by qualified professional translators, which were difficult to come by. Cohen (1960: 37) argues that at least two judges are needed to 'determine the degree, significance, and sampling stability of their agreement'. Therefore two evaluators were recruited to complete the translatability test. While more raters would have been desirable, practical constraints dictated that only two would be used.

It has often been assumed that the fact that a text is easily readable and comprehensible and used at an elementary level means that it is easy to translate (McGillis 1998). However, this is not necessarily the case. In order to reduce the effect of another potentially confounding variable, a translatability test was administered. Two professional translation teachers, with Mandarin as their first language and English as their second, were asked to read and rate both texts in terms of translatability level, based on the scoring system of 1 = very easy, 2 = easy, 3 = medium, 4 = difficult, 5 = very difficult. Both the professional translation teachers gave a score of 1 to both texts, and suggested that the texts were very easy to translate.

Stimuli presentation

An ASL (Applied Sciences Laboratory) Model 504 non-head-mounted monocular eye-tracker[4] was used in the study. Two professional translators' opinions were sought regarding how the windows should be displayed in order to simulate the way they would normally translate, and both reported that they usually had their source text on their left-hand side to read, while working on the computer screen on the right-hand side for text production. The window environment in the participants' monitor was arranged so that there were two split windows side-by-side, with the text (presented or to be produced) at the top of the window. Regardless of the translation direction, the source text was always presented in the split window on the left-hand side, whereas the window on the right was used for target text production. The text alignment was set as 'align to the left'. The font of both source and target texts was set as size 14 (so that words or characters were large enough to be easily visible), bold, and black in colour. The background colours of the two split windows were switched to gray. This prevented light-sensitive pupils from sudden constriction (Winn *et al.* 1994) when the participants embarked on the tasks after eye calibration. Another reason for this was to ensure consistency with the calibration step, as the calibration map was also gray. After calibration was completed, the participants were instructed to minimize the map and switch to the split-window environment. Figure 2 shows how the split windows and stimuli were displayed during the experiments. Further, all

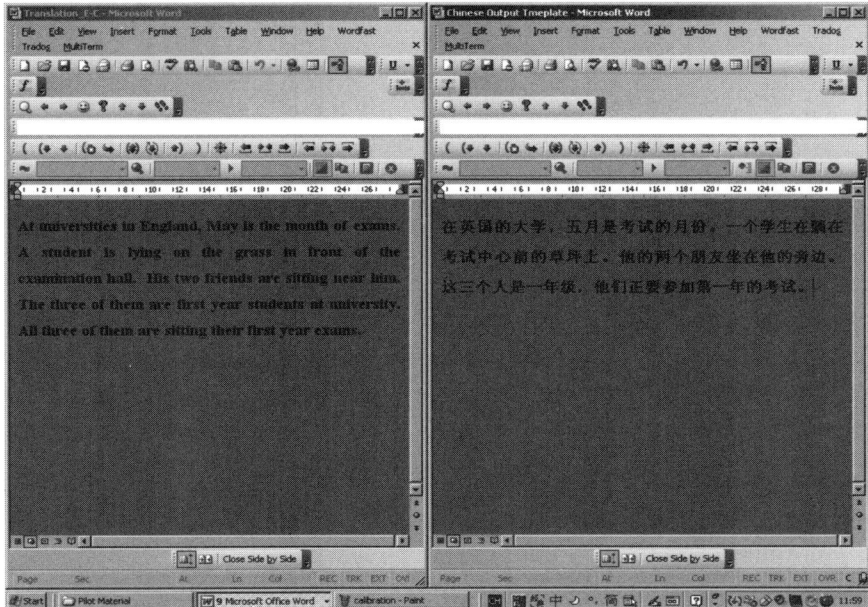

Figure 2 Split Window for Stimuli Presentation and Text Production

the participants were native speakers of Mandarin Chinese, but came from different parts of the Mandarin-speaking world.[5] The format of Mandarin used for source text display and target language production was adjusted accordingly, in order to avoid extra cognitive loading for having to produce the other form of Mandarin they were not familiar with.

Dependent Variables

Pupil Diameter

Pupil diameter is defined as 'the measure through the centre of the adjustable opening in the iris of the eye, terminated at both ends by its circumference' (Cogain, Online); it has been used as a measure of cognitive loading (Rayner 1998; Rayner *et al.* 2006). In the study, with the lighting level of the laboratory room kept constant as well as the background colour of the computer screen, the dependent variable of pupil size was measured. The eye tracker recorded data on pupil diameter variations over time during the translation task. The unit of measurement was millimeters.

Fixation Count

In a generic reading experiment, a fixation is normally defined as a gaze at a particular point for 200 to 300 milliseconds (ms) (Rayner 1998). Majaranta (Online: 6) outlines a number of people who define a fixation as a gaze at a particular point between 200 to 600 ms, on the assumption that the more cognitively demanding a task is, the higher the number of fixations is required. Translating is arguably more cognitively demanding than merely reading in one's mother tongue, because it involves reading comprehension, language conversion and text production. Given a relatively higher complexity level of translating, the study threshold for the definition of a fixation at 500 ms, a level higher than the 200 to 300 ms often associated with a fixation during monolingual reading in the mother tongue (Rayner *et al.* 2006).

Task Time

Time spent on completing each translation task by each participant was recorded in the study. Such data is referred to as 'task time', and its unit is in minutes (min). Task time has been demonstrated to be a useful indicator of cognitive loading of a task (Pavlović and Jensen 2009).

Fixation Frequency

Fixation frequency refers to the frequency at which fixations appear on a particular area, and has been demonstrated to be a useful measure of cognitive loading (Orden *et al.* 2001). The algorithm involved in computing fixation frequency is the temporal definition of a fixation in a study (500 ms in this study) divided by the number of fixations that take place in an area in question (Cogain, 2008).

It has to be acknowledged that there has been a controversy regarding how fixation frequency is computed. For example, Radach and Kennedy (2004: 6) explicitly defined fixation frequency as 'mean absolute number of fixations per word, for the current pass'. However, the algorithm for the computing of fixation frequency already built into the software program (EYENAL) used in the present study adopted COGAIN's definition (COGAIN, Online). Using EYENAL, values regarding fixation frequency were automatically yielded for data analysis, and the researcher had no control over how to compute fixation frequency for the study. Even so, at the very least, COGAIN's computation can still to a certain extent create useful values for statistical analyses. When the numerator within a fraction stays constant, whilst the denominator varies, the values generated are still useful for comparison. In the study, 500 ms was the constant numerator within the fraction, whereas the denominator changed whenever the total fixation count for different conditions of different participants varied. The EYENAL in-built computation method created different values for different conditions for different subjects, and the computation remained constant across all conditions and subjects. This computation therefore at the very least generated a certain level of value and usefulness for further analyses and did not negatively affect the statistical analyses in the study. However, it is worth noting that future researchers should give consideration to these varying definitions of fixation frequency.

Blink Frequency

Blink frequency refers to how frequently the eye blinks during a task, and this measurement has been shown to correlate strongly with cognitive loading (Rayner 1998). When an individual blinks, the values of pupil size samples during blinking will be zero. Upon completion of the task, the total count of zeros divided by the total number of samples obtained will yield blink frequency.

Results

In this section, first, behavioural results (end products) are described. Second, paired samples *t*-tests were conducted on the data and results are reported.

Behaviour during the experiment

It is crucial to ascertain that the participants actually followed the instructions during the experiment. Departure from the investigator's instructions could produce inaccurate outputs, which would have invalidated the physiological data. Therefore adherence to instructions for translating had to be verified. To that end, two Mandarin language/translation teachers with English as their second language graded the translation and typing outputs, based on a standard scoring scheme (100 = full marks or 100% accuracy; 60 = pass or 60% accuracy). This scoring standard was selected because in the Mandarin-speaking domain, 60 is generally a score threshold for a pass. Given that the experiments involved native Mandarin speakers and raters, this pass mark was deemed appropriate. Table 1 shows the scoring results for translating from Mandarin into English and translating from English into Mandarin Chinese:

Table 1 Descriptive Statistics on Scoring of the Outputs (Mandarin & English)

	VALID NUMBER OF SUBJECTS	LOWEST SCORE	HIGHEST SCORE	MEAN	STD. DEVIATION
Translation Mandarin→ English	15	87	95	91.40	2.772
Translation English→ Mandarin	15	90	99	94.93	2.434

The behavioural results indicated that the subjects did conduct the tasks as instructed by the investigator; their translation products scored a very high accuracy level. This validated the physiological data, which were then deemed usable for further statistical analyses. Translations into English scored lower than into Chinese. One possible interpretation for this is that translating into the second language generates more cognitive loading than into the first language. However, it has to be acknowledged that a translation could be of lower quality for reasons that are independent of cognitive loading.

Further, based on the high scores, it can be argued that the texts were extremely easy to understand and translate, and this confirms the effectiveness of the tests administered (see Text Selection above) to remove difficulty as a variable and to ensure the texts were comparable with the primary aim of investigating the effect of directionality, not difficulty.

Pupil size (measured in millimetres)

The average pupil size when translating from Mandarin Chinese (language A) into English (language B) ($M = 5.09$, $SD = 0.17$) was found to be significantly larger than that of translating from English (B) into Mandarin Chinese (A) ($M = 4.87$, $SD = 0.15$, $t(14) = 2.33$, $p = 0.036$, $r = 0.53$).

Overall fixation count across texts on the screen

The fixation count when translating from Mandarin Chinese into English ($M = 123.47$, $SD = 12.33$) was significantly larger than that during translation from English into Mandarin Chinese ($M = 79.80$, $SD = 12.65$, $t(14) = 5.24$, $p < 0.001$, $r = 0.81$).

Task time (measured in minutes)

Translating from Mandarin Chinese into English ($M = 2.79$, $SD = 0.18$) was significantly longer than that for translating from English into Mandarin Chinese ($M = 1.85$, $SD = 0.35$, $t(14) = 0.85$, $p < 0.001$, $r = 0.79$).

Fixation frequency across texts on the screen (measured in decimal numbers)

Fixation frequency while translating from Mandarin Chinese into English ($M = 0.62$, $SD = 0.03$) was significantly higher than that during translating from English into Mandarin Chinese ($M = 0.54$, $SD = 0.04$, $t(14) = 2.39$, $p = 0.031$, $r = 0.54$).

Blink frequency (measured in decimal numbers)

No significance (p = 0.419) was yielded. This indicates that, as the participants were allowed to look down during the translation task and this may have contaminated the blink data, blink frequency was not a very reliable source of information. It has to be acknowledged that because the non-head-mounted model of the eye-tracker was used in the study to ensure a relatively higher level of ecological validity, the issue of statistical non-significance was anticipated.

Conclusions, Discussion and Recommended Future Work

To conclude, the results presented above consistently suggest that A→B translation was more cognitively demanding than B→A translation. This also indicates that the predictions suggested by the Revised Hierarchical Model were valid at a textual level.

The findings generated from the research have a number of limitations. Given the language pair, the results must not be assumed to be universal. Additionally, since the study was carried out in a laboratory setting, no claim has been made regarding perfect simulation of real-life translation scenarios. Moreover, the study was solely interested in the effect of directionality on cognitive loading, so various factors were controlled to ensure comparability of the texts, and this rendered the texts very simple. The results are therefore not generalizable to texts with greater levels of difficulty or to texts from other genres. Nonetheless, there is potential for investigating directionality and cognitive load in texts with higher levels of complexity, from other genres and with different language pairs.

Further, given the non-head-mounted model of the monocular eye-tracker used in the study, blink frequency, a potentially important indicator of cognitive loading, was not accurately recorded. Further work which employs a model in which blink frequency can be measured is thus desirable. In addition, given that the applicability of eye tracking to the field of translation and interpreting has been demonstrated, the use of eye tracking can be extended to investigate other research topics within the realm of translation and interpreting. For example: (1) How do people visually process subtitles? (2) What is the general length of a 'meaning unit' in a source text for a translator to have to process before s/he starts to produce the target text? (3) During the very act of interpreting, what do interpreters look at in a conference venue to help obtain non-text-related information to facilitate interpreting? (4) Where is it best to place a translated text in a video game, so as to attract the highest level of visual attention? This paper has laid a foundation that encourages future researchers to use eye tracking to study topics associated with translation and interpreting.

It will be remembered that the predictions of the Revised Hierarchical Model have been demonstrated to be valid by this research program for textual translation which requires dealing with both concrete and abstract concepts. It has to be acknowledged, though, that the texts used in the research presented in this paper were simple, non-technical short texts, because factors such as text difficulty and text type may have an effect on translation asymmetry.

In addition, a longitudinal study recording the different cognitive loading between A→B and B→A translation or interpreting could be interesting, as it could potentially test if training over time has an effect on cognitive loading. Such results can also help to inform translator/interpreter pedagogy. If it can be established that more training reduces cognitive loading, schools should take into account the importance of incorporating more A→B training into curricular designs.

Lastly, pupillometry and other ocular measures are only some of the physiological indicators for cognitive loading. Other physiological measures are heart rate, skin conductance, blood pressure, and neuroendocrine secretion. To elucidate, the higher the stress, the more an individual perspires, and the higher the skin electricity conductance. Secretion of cortisol (stress hormone) also increases proportionately to the level of stress involved. How to apply these methods adequately to the field of T&I Studies to converge different types of data in order to further strengthen the results and findings is a question that has remained hugely under-researched. There is great scope for collaboration with other fields in order to study such phenomena.

Notes

1 I would like to acknowledge the assistance of Mr. Stephen Oliver of S. Oliver Associates who provided an eye-tracker for this research.

2 The task involved in the study was for the participants to translate a short text to the best of their

ability as quickly as possible without any revision. However, one of them conducted revision, and hence these data were excluded.

3 The educational system in Taiwan is modelled on the US educational system. Therefore it is argued that the grade levels of the two countries are comparable.

4 The non-head-mounted model was selected in the study in order to maintain as much ecological validity as possible. With this model, the participants were free to look at the computer monitor or look down at the keyboard when necessary.

5 Taiwan and Hong Kong use traditional Mandarin Chinese whereas Mainland China and Singapore use Simplified Mandarin.

References

Alves, F., A. Pagano, S. Hansen-Schirra, S. Neumann and E. Steiner [Online], 'Units of translation and grammatical shifts: product and process perspectives'. www.cbs.dk/content/download/103126/.../Alves%20et%20a1.pdf. Accessed 12 December 2009.

Altarriba, J. and K.M. Mathis (1997), 'Conceptual and lexical development in second language acquisition'. *Journal of Memory and Language,* 36, 550–568.

Beatty, J. (1982), 'Task-evoked pupillary responses, processing load, and the structure of processing resources'. *Psychological Bulletin,* 91, 276–292.

Brysbaert, M. and T. Dijkstra (2006), 'Changing views on word recognition in bilinguals'. In J. Morais and G. D'ydewalle (eds), *Bilingualism and Second Language Acquisition.* Brussels: KVAB.

Caffrey, C. (2008), 'Using pupillometric, fixation-based and subjective measures to measure the processing effort experienced when viewing subtitled TV anime with pop-up gloss'. In S. Göpferich, A.L. Jakobsen and I.M. Mees (eds), *Looking at Eyes: Eye-Tracking Studies of Reading and Translation Processing.* Copenhagen Studies in Language 36. Copenhagen: Samfundslitteratur. pp. 125–144.

Carl, M., A.L. Jakobsen and K.T.H. Jensen (2008), 'Studying Human Translation Behavior with User-Activity Data'. In *Proceedings of NLPCS workshop at ICEIS.* Barcelona. pp. 114–123.

COGAIN (Online), Retrieved at http://www.cogain.org/glossary/. Accessed 14 January 2008.

Cohen, J. (1960), 'A coefficient of agreement for nominal scales'. *Educational and Psychological Measurement,* 20, 37–46.

De Groot, A.M.B., L. Dannenburg and J.G. van Hell (1994), 'Forward and backward word translation by bilinguals'. *Journal of Memory and Language,* 33, 600–629.

Dragsted, B. and I.G. Hansen (2008), 'Comprehension and production in translation: a pilot study on segmentation and the coordiation of reading and writing processes'. In S. Göpferich, A.L. Jakobsen and I.M. Mees (eds), *Looking at Eyes: Eye-Tracking Studies of Reading and Translation Processing.* Copenhagen Studies in Language 36. Copenhagen: Samfundslitteratur. pp. 9–30.

Eye-to-IT (Online), *Retrieved at http://cogs.nbu.bg/eye-to-it/.* Accessed 14 Feb. 2009.

Heredia, R.R. (1996), 'Bilingual memory: A re-revised version of the hierarchical model of bilingual memory'. *The Newsletter of the Center For Research in Language,* 10, pp. 3–6.

Hyönä, J., J. Tommola and A. Alaja (1995), 'Pupil dilation as a measure of processing load in simultaneous interpretation and other language tasks'. *The Quarterly Journal of Experimental Psychology,* 48A, 598–612.

Jackobsen, A.L. and K.T.H. Jensen (2008), 'Eye movement behaviour across four different types of reading task'. In S. Göpferich, A.L. Jakobsen and I.M. Mees (eds), *Looking at Eyes: Eye-Tracking Studies of Reading and Translation Processing.* Copenhagen Studies in Language 36. Copenhagen: Samfundslitteratur. pp. 103–124.

Janisse, M.P. (1977), *Pupillometry: The Psychology of the Pupillary Response.* Washington: Hemisphere Publishing.

Jiang, N. (1999), 'Testing processing explanations for the asymmetry in masked cross-language priming'. *Bilingualism: Language and Cognition,* 2, 59–75.

Kroll, J.F. (2009), '*Re: VERY URGENT: A quick question please*'. Personal email to C.-Y. Chang (chc131@mail.harvard.edu).

Kroll, J.F. and E. Stewart (1994), 'Category interference in translation and picture naming: Evidence for asymmetric connections between bilingual memory representations'. *Journal of Memory and Language,* 33, 149–174.

Lai, C.S. (2006), *Chinese Mandarin: Second Semester of the Fourth Year.* Taipei, Taiwan, Kang Hsuan Publishing.

Majaranta, P. (Online), 'Implementation of New Interaction Techniques: Eye Tracking' (online lecture slides). Retrieved at http://www.cs.uta.fi/init/slides/INIT-2008-EyeTracking-01.pdf, Visual Interaction Research Group, Tampere Unit for Computer-Human Interaction, Accessed 13 August 2008.

Malkiel, B. (2004), 'Directionality and translational difficulty'. *Perspectives: Studies in Translatology,* 12, 208–221.

McGillis, R. (1998), 'Children's Literature Comes of Age: Toward a New Aesthetic (review)'. *The Lion and the Unicorn,* 22, 1, 111–117.

Milne, J. (1980), *The Long Tunnel.* London, Heinemann Educational Books, Ltd.

O'Brien, S. (2006), 'Eye-tracking and translation memory matches'. *Perspectives: Studies in Translatology,* 14, 185–205.

Orden, K.F.V., W. Limbert, S. Makeig and T.-P. Jung (2001), 'Eye activity correlates of workload during a visuospatial memory task'. *Human factors: The Journal of the Human Factors and Ergonomics Society,* 43, 111–121.

Pavlović, N. and K.T.H. Jensen (2009), 'Eye tracking translation directionality'. In A. Pym and A. Perekrestenko (eds), *Translation Research Projects 2.* Tarragona, Intercultural Studies Group.

Radach, R. and A. Kennedy (2004), 'Theoretical perspectives on eye movements in reading: Past controversies, current issues, and an agenda for future research'. *European Journal of Cognitive Psychology,* 16, 3–26.

Rayner, K. (1998), 'Eye movements and information processing: 20 years of research'. *Psychological Bulletin,* 124, 372–422.

Rayner, K., C.K.H., T.J. Slattery and J. Ashby (2006), 'Eye movements as reflections of comprehension processes in reading'. *Scientific Studies of Reading*, 10, 241–255.

Rinne, J.O., J. Tommola, M. Laine, B.J. Krause, D. Schmidt, V. Kaasinen, M. Teras, H. Sipila and M. Sunnari (2000), 'The translating brain: cerebral activation patterns during simultaneous interpreting'. *Neurosci Lett*, 294, 85–8.

Sharmin, S., O. Špakov, K.-J. Räihä and A.L. Jakobsen (2008), '*Effects of time pressure and text complexity on translators' fixations*'. In K.-J. Räihä and A. Duchowski (eds), *Proceedings of the Eye Tracking Research & Application Symposium, ETRA 2008*. Savannah, Georgia: USA, ACM. pp. 123–126.

Sjørup, A.C. (2008), 'Metaphor comprehension in translation: methodological issues in a pilot study'. In S. Göpferich, A.L. Jakobsen and I.M. Mees (eds), *Looking at Eyes: Eye-Tracking Studies of Reading and Translation Processing*. Copenhagen Studies in Language 36. Copenhagen: Samfundslitteratur. pp. 53–78.

Tokowicz, N. and J.F. Kroll (2007), 'Number of meanings and concreteness: Consequences of ambiguity within and across languages'. *Language and Cognitive Processes*, 22, 727–779.

Tommola, J. and P. Niemi (1986), 'Mental load in simultaneous interpreting: An on-line pilot study'. In L. Evensen (ed.), *Nordic research in text linguistics and discourse analysis*. Trondheim: Tapir. pp. 171–184.

Weatherby, J. (1998), 'Teaching Translation into L2. A TT- Oriented Approach'. In K. Malmkjaer (ed.), *Translation and Language Teaching – Language Teaching and Translation*. Manchester: St. Jerome. pp. 21–38.

Wilss, W. (1996), *Knowledge and skills in translator behavior*. Amsterdam & Philadelphia: John Benjamins.

Winn, B., D. Whitaker, D.B. Elliott and N.J. Phillips (1994), 'Factors affecting light-adapted pupil size in normal human subjects'. *Investigative Ophthalmology & Visual Science*, 35, 1132–1137.

Towards an Investigation of Reading Modalities in/for Translation: an Exploratory Study Using Eye-tracking Data

Fabio Alves, Adriana Pagano and Igor da Silva

Chapter Outline

Introduction

Reading as a cognitive activity related to translation has scarcely been investigated. First attempts to do so relied mostly on reading time measurements (Shreve *et al.* 1993) or on findings from related disciplines (Danks and Griffin 1997). Other attempts used key logging (Jakobsen 2002) or combined verbal reports and direct observation with either key logging (Alves 2005) or screen logging (PACTE 2005). These studies made use of a limited number of methodological tools to track reading processes experimentally. More recently, with the use of eye tracking in translation process research (O'Brien 2006; Sharmin *et al.* 2008; Jakobsen and Jensen 2008), tracking eye movements has allowed researchers to investigate reading in/for translation relying on quantitative data that can be interpreted in connection with other types of experimental data.

This paper reports on results of an exploratory study following a similar design to the one used by Jakobsen and Jensen (2008), but introducing an additional condition in an attempt partially to test their methodology and examine eye-tracking data in different reading performances associated with different tasks and stimulus patterns. The study involved reading for three specific purposes: (i) answering reading comprehension questions, (ii) producing an oral summary of a text, and (iii) translating a text orally while reading it (sight translation). The study design consisted of two experimental conditions: in Condition 1, subjects were requested to read three short newspaper reports on the same piece of news but published in different news websites and therefore having different rhetorical structures; in Condition 2, subjects were requested to read three short popular science texts constructed along similar rhetorical structures but dealing with three different topics. The study relied on two main assumptions. The first one was that subjects would spend more time and show a higher number of and longer fixations as they dealt with increasing complexity of the tasks requested, answering reading comprehension questions being the least effortful and sight translation being the most demanding task in terms of cognitive effort, due to the concurrent reading of a text and the verbalization of its translation. The second assumption was that using two different experimental conditions would allow us to investigate whether the findings would point to the same tendencies in the variables under scrutiny irrespective of changes in topic and in rhetorical structure.

Background

Shreve *et al.* (1993) were among the first authors to attempt to investigate the role of reading in/for translation in the course of the translation process. The authors investigated differences in reading-for-translation, reading-for-paraphrasing, and reading-for-comprehension in an attempt to verify if translators behave differently when performing the three tasks. Shreve *et al.* (1993) assumed that most professional translators do not read the source text before translating and usually only skim or read selected passages before starting to translate. For them, this indicates a reading strategy and, thus, 'it might be possible to begin translating sentences and build up comprehension as one goes' (Shreve *et al.* 1993: 21). Their results showed that reading time increased slightly in anticipation of problems related to translation. According to Shreve *et al.* this finding points to the importance of investigating the reading process of translators to find out whether reading ability increases as professional translators improve their skills.

Danks and Griffin (1997) discussed reading for translation in comparison with general (monolingual) reading processes. According to them, novice translators tend to translate word-by-word whereas more expert translators seem to favor meaning-to-meaning translation at a higher level of processing. These findings show an interaction between the level of translation skill and that of processing. On the basis of these findings, the authors argue that reading depends on the reader's level of skill and processing capacity. They relate their conclusions to those presented by Shreve *et al.* (1993), establishing a relationship between the level of processing of the source text and the level of expertise of translators. For Danks and Griffin (1997), processing source texts at a higher level of understanding may depend on translators being more skilled as comprehenders.

Jakobsen (2002), PACTE (2005) and Alves (2005) also dealt with reading in/for translation as they attempted to investigate orientation as a first phase in the translation process, a phase which is mostly concerned with reading and understanding the source text. Jakobsen (2002) investigated the translation process of novice and professional translators and tried to identify the main traits of the three phases of the translation process, namely orientation, drafting, and revision. Jakobsen (2002) was able to show that the orientation phase, which one assumes to be predominantly about reading the source text, requires the least amount of time from subjects. Alves (2005) and PACTE (2005) also showed that orientation can be nearly non-existent for quite a number of subjects and that, when it does occur, it is always the shortest phase in the translation process. Because the empirical data obtained in all these studies did not provide direct traceable evidence of reading processing, results end up being generic and holding little evidence about the specificity of reading for translation.

Differences in reading-for-translation and reading-for-repetition have also been investigated from a standard psycholinguistic standpoint. Macizo and Bajo (2006) found that reading-for-translation consumes more working memory resources than reading-for-repetition. Macizo and Bajo (2006) argued that this finding is consistent with theories of translation that posit that partial reformulation processes are required while the translator reads the source text in order to translate it.

More recently, eye tracking was introduced into translation process research in an attempt to gather empirical data that can be interpreted towards an assessment of the role played by reading in translation. Studies have, so far, investigated the impact of reading on the translator's performance with relevant results focusing on the relationship between reading and translation memory matches (O'Brien 2006), reading, time pressure and text complexity (Sharmin *et al.* 2008), the integration of eye-tracking data with key-logging data and retrospective protocols (Carl *et al.* 2008), in what is called User Activity Data (UAD), and reading for different purposes (Jakobsen and Jensen 2008).

Eye-tracker manufacturers provide the following account of this technology:

> Eye tracking works by reflecting invisible infrared light onto an eye, recording the reflection pattern with a sensor system, and then calculating the exact point of gaze using a geometrical model. Once the point of gaze is determined, it can be visualized and shown on a computer monitor. The point of gaze can also be used to control and interface with different machines. This technique is referred to as eye control.[1]

Among the several data that can be gathered by this technology, eye-tracking software provides qualitative and quantitative data related to fixation length and fixation count. A fixation is a segment of the signal corresponding to the exact point of gaze which is of constant or slowly changing mean due to drift. If there is an abrupt change in the mean, this is considered a saccade. In eye-tracking studies, a reading activity is one involving successive fixations and saccades that can be mapped on to the text (although not necessarily on to all individual words). The underlying assumption in such studies is that long and high numbers of fixations and backward movements (e.g. saccades representing revision of text strings) are signals of effort in processing.

In a recent study using eye-tracking technology, Jakobsen and Jensen (2008) had 12 subjects, six Danish translation students and six Danish professional translators, perform four different tasks involving four different purposes, namely reading for comprehension, reading for a prospective translation task, reading while performing an oral translation and reading while performing a written translation. The authors aimed to compare professional and student performance as well as to assess, among others, variables such as task time, number of fixations, and fixation length with a view to exploring the impact of the independent variable, reading/translating modality. The authors concluded that 'reading purpose had a clear effect on eye movements and gaze time' (Jakobsen and Jensen 2008: 120). The specificities of task demands 'caused participants to undertake considerable processing additional to what was the case following an instruction to read a text for comprehension'. In Jakobsen and Jensen, task complexity was related to longer time and a higher number of fixations as observed among the subjects of their study.

This article builds on Jakobsen and Jensen (2008) and, by means of an analogous experimental design, aims at comparing our results with the results of their study. Replication of experiments is seldom carried out in the area of translation process research. As shown in Alves (2003), difficulties which hinder replication are, among others, specificities of the language pairs involved in the experimental designs, as well as discrepancies in translators' profiles (including language proficiency and professional experience), familiarity with text domain and directionality. These difficulties notwithstanding, replication of experiments is thought to offer the possibility of strengthening the generalization power for translation process research, and is therefore, desirable. Bearing these considerations in mind and drawing on previous studies, we also seek to address issues such as the extent to which higher levels of reading comprehension may depend on higher levels of expertise, i.e. whether subject profile plays a role in the results. Finally, on the basis of our data and results, we discuss methodological implications that the use of eye tracking may have for translation process research.

Materials and Methods

As stated in the introduction, the study reported here targeted the performance of subjects in three tasks involving reading for three specific purposes: (i) answering reading comprehension questions (Task A), (ii) producing an oral summary of a text (Task B) and (iii) translating a text orally while reading it (sight translation) (Task C). The study design consisted of two experimental conditions: in Condition 1, subjects were requested to read three short newspaper reports on the same piece of news but published on different news websites and therefore having different rhetorical structures; in Condition 2, subjects were requested to read three short popular science texts constructed along similar rhetorical structures (Ask the Expert column in a popular science magazine) but dealing with three different topics. All tasks involved reading texts written in English, the subjects' L2, and providing answers, summaries or oral translations in Brazilian Portuguese, their L1.

The texts selected for experimental Condition 1 had an average number of 193 words and were identical to those used by Jakobsen and Jensen's (2008) study. They are about the end of Tony Blair's term as British Prime Minister. Since the news was reported differently by each of the three websites, differences in rhetorical structure could be observed among the three texts (see Appendix). In Condition 2, three short texts with an average of 105 words were selected from the column Ask the Expert in the magazine *Scientific American* (see Appendix). They are about three different topics – scars and tattoos, HIV contamination, and comets –, but all three rely on the same rhetorical structure. This was assessed drawing on Rhetorical Structure Theory (Taboada and Mann 2006) and basically comprised an answer to a question formulated (*solutionhood*) in the highest hierarchical level, consisting of a projected answer (*projection*) provided to a question involving *unconditional circumstances*.[2]

Details on the texts and tasks in our experimental design are summarized in Table 1.

Table 1 Texts and associated tasks in the two experimental conditions

CONDITION	TEXT TITLE	TEXT SIZE	TASK
	Historic day as Blair surrenders power and Brown finally moves into No 10	197 words 1,102 char. 8 sentences	**Task A1:** Answering reading comprehension questions
Condition 1	Finally Blair exits the stage	187 words 1,115 char. 8 sentences	**Task B1:** Producing an oral summary of text
	Blair exits British politics as new era begins with Tory defection	194 words 1,106 char. 7 sentences	**Task C1:** Sight translation
	If the cells of our skin are replaced regularly, why do scars and tattoos persist indefinitely?	99 words 526 char. 7 sentences	**Task A2:** Answering reading comprehension questions
Condition 2	If a used needle can transmit HIV, why can't a mosquito?	109 words 485 char. 6 sentences	**Task B2:** Producing an oral summary of text
	If comets melt, why do they seem to last for long periods of time?	107 words 502 char. 6 sentences	**Task C2:** Sight translation

The texts were displayed in 16-point, double-spaced Times New Roman font, and were inserted as an image in a new project created with the software package Tobii Studio 1.5. The subjects' eye movements were recorded by a Tobii T60 eye-tracker. Subjects wore no head apparatus nor did they use chin rests, and they sat at a distance of 60–70 cms from a 17" LCD screen at a resolution of 16 bits and 1280 × 1024 pixels. A built-in camera and an external microphone were available to record subjects' oral outputs, as a means to ensure ecological validity of the experiments.[3]

Twelve subjects, six Brazilian translation students and six Brazilian professional translators, were recruited to participate. All subjects received initial training to become familiar with the experimental environment and the eye-tracking equipment. The study initially involved a sample of 17 subjects, belonging to two clear-cut groups: professional translators (8 subjects, with reported experience in written translations), and translation students (9 novice subjects, attending either undergraduate or graduate translation-oriented courses). The experimental conditions required subjects to avoid unnecessary movements of their heads away from the screen and to keep the distance range previously established. Two subjects – a student and a professional translator – could not comply with this condition. Their average fixation length fell below the mean values recommended by Jakobsen and Jensen (2008), namely 175ms. Therefore their data proved to be partially unreliable and were discarded. Among the remaining ones, twelve subjects were randomly selected to compose two groups of six subjects each, labeled S1, S2, S3, S4, S5, and S6 in the case of students and P1, P2, P3, P4, P5, and P6 in the case of professionals.

As mentioned earlier, Jakobsen and Jensen (2008) controlled their experiment for task impact by implementing the same task order for all subjects but changing the text used in each task. That is to say, subjects performed all tasks in the same sequence. In our study, we decided to control for task impact by changing the task order but maintaining the text used for each specific task. In other words, our subjects performed the three tasks in a different sequence, but the text used for each specific task was the same for all subjects. However, as a means of neutralizing skewing effects, subjects performed their tasks in a random fashion; the task order is provided in Tables 2 and 6 displayed in the section on findings and analysis. The tasks were carried out in a row with each subject performing all tasks in succession. For the tasks involving either reading for answering comprehension questions or reading for summarizing the text, subjects were allowed to read the texts as many times as necessary before declaring themselves to be ready for the task. For the sight translation task, subjects were requested not to read the text before the actual translation, and only read it as they performed their tasks.

Our independent variable was task modality (reading for comprehension, reading for summarizing and reading for sight translation) under two experimental conditions: Condition 1 (texts on the same topic) and Condition 2 (texts having the same rhetorical structure). Dependent variables were (1) reading time (task time in seconds), (2) absolute number of fixations, and (3) average fixation length (in milliseconds). Building on data filtered through the default Tobii fixation filter (35 fixation radius)[4] and rounded to exclude decimals, results were compared across the two conditions. Results for Condition 1 were also compared to Jakobsen and Jensen's (2008) analyses. Assuming increased difficulty from reading for comprehension to reading for sight translation, paired samples t tests were run to establish the significance of mean results for fixation count and length.

Findings and Analysis

In this section, findings are presented separately for each one of the conditions regarding total task time, number and length of fixations (i.e. fixation count and fixation length, respectively). The findings will then be compared and discussed in the next section.

Condition 1

Total task time

Table 2 shows task time (in seconds) and task order for each subject, as well as means per group. As mentioned in the methodology section, subjects were selected in a random fashion out of a relatively larger sample, which explains why there is no occurrence of Task C1 as the second task performed among students.

Table 2 Individual and mean task time (in seconds) in Condition 1 according to group

GROUP	SUBJECT	TASK A1*	TASK B1*	TASK C1*	TASK ORDER
	S1	100	85	313	A1,B1,C1
	S2	79	160	234	C1,A1,B1
	S3	190	171	320	B1,A1,C1
Students	S4	178	288	327	A1,B1,C1
	S5	142	126	259	C1,B1,A1
	S6	124	112	445	B1,A1,C1
	Means	136	157	316	
	P1	75	90	177	A1,B1,C1
	P2	32	44	181	C1,B1,A1
	P3	186	142	410	B1,A1,C1
Professionals	P4	83	75	290	C1,A1,B1
	P5	130	101	272	B1,C1,A1
	P6	66	86	253	A1,C1,B1
	Means	95	90	264	

* A1=reading for comprehension; B1=reading for summarizing; C1=sight translating.

Considering the small sample and our hypothesis that there is a progression in total task time from Task A1 to Task C1, it is necessary to analyse means more closely. For the students, means from Tasks A1 to B1 decrease for 4 subjects, the differences being not greater than 15 per cent. In the other two cases (S2 and S4), means increase, the differences being greater than 60 per cent. For the professionals, means from Tasks A1 to B1 increase for half of the sample. In either direction, variations do not exceed 38 per cent (P2).

Table 3 Recomputed mean* task time (in seconds) for professionals and students in Condition 1 in comparison to Jakobsen and Jensen's findings

TASK	PROFESSIONALS		TRANSLATION STUDENTS	
	J & J (2008)	CONDITION 1 DATA	J & J (2008)	CONDITION 1 DATA
A: Reading for Comprehension	40	95	61	139
B: Reading for Summarizing	57	90	103	124
C: Reading for Sight Translation	154	225	204	334

* means are rounded for comparability reasons.

Taking into account that the variations for S2 and S4 are very high in relation to those subjects who showed decreasing values from Task B1 to Task A1, Table 3 shows means excluding S2's and S4's data and is thus assumed to be more representative of the tendencies in the sample.

As shown in Tables 2 (with all subjects) and 3 (excluding S2 and S4), students spent more time on average performing all the tasks and this is consistent with Jakobsen and Jensen's (2008) findings. Both professionals and students in our study spent more time performing the tasks than the subjects in Jakobsen and Jensen (2008). Task A1 stands out in particular, as the students in our experiment spent at least twice as much time as those in Jakobsen and Jensen's experiment. Moreover, contrary to our expectations, both professionals and students spent more time on Task A1 (reading for comprehension) than on Task B1 (reading for summarizing), the latter having been conceived as a task that would require both reading for the sake of understanding the text (reading comprehension) and deciding which pieces of information would be the most relevant for a summary.

There may be several possible explanations for the differences observed between the results of Jakobsen and Jensen (2008) and those of the present study. A possible reason may relate to the differences in subject profile. Although groups in the two studies consisted of six professional translators and six translation students, their levels of proficiency and expertise were not previously assessed in either of the studies. Drawing on Muñoz's (2009) claim that subject profiling is important for comparability across samples, one could assume that differences in subject profiles may account for the differences between the results of Jakobsen and Jensen (2008) and the results for the Tasks A1 and B1 in the present study. As for the sight translation task, subject profile can be related to the familiarity with the task: most of the Brazilian subjects reported spontaneously that sight translation was an unfamiliar task, whereas there is no reference to the subject's level of familiarity with this task in Jakobsen and Jensen (2008). On the basis of the data available, it is not possible to say whether the Danish subjects were more or less familiar with this task than their Brazilian counterparts.

In the case of Task A1 demanding more effort and time than (or as much as) Task B1, there is no explanation in terms of task sequencing. As shown in Table 3, S2 and S4 are the only subjects in the students' group who spent more time on Task B1, but that was not the first task for either of them. P1, P2 and P6 are the subjects in the professional group who spent more time on Task B1, and again that was not the first task for any of them. This may imply that, unlike the subjects in Jakobsen and Jensen (2008), for our subjects Task A1 was apparently more demanding than Task B1.

Another possible explanation for such differences could be related to the possibility that in Jakobsen and Jensen (2008) the task ended when participants signalled that they had finished reading. It is not clear, however, whether the subjects were instructed or allowed to re-read the texts. If subjects in Jakobsen and Jensen were allowed to read the texts only once, that would explain why the subjects in our experiment spent considerably more time on their tasks since they were allowed to read the texts for tasks A1 and B1 as many times as they wished.

Fixation Count

Table 4 shows the total number of fixations in Condition 1.

Table 4 Mean* total number of fixations found for professionals and students in Condition 1 in comparison to Jakobsen and Jensen's findings

TASK	PROFESSIONALS		TRANSLATION STUDENTS	
	J & J (2008)	CONDITION 1 DATA	J & J (2008)	CONDITION 1 DATA
A: Reading for Comprehension	132	184	170	177
B: Reading for Summarizing	373	194	643	181
C: Reading for Sight Translation	520+	160	520+	152

* means are rounded for comparability reasons.
+ J & J (2008) provide the means for both students and professional translators altogether (in our case, that would be 156).

Unlike Jakobsen and Jensen's (2008) findings, the results in Table 4 point to no apparently clear-cut differences across groups and across tasks, professionals having a slightly higher number of fixation counts for all the tasks and Task C1 (sight translating) being the one with the lowest fixation count for both groups. The overall increase from Task A1 (181) to Task B1 (188) is not significant ($t=1.450$; $df=11$; $p=0.175$), but the decrease from Task B1 (188) to Task C1 (156) is indeed significant ($t=4.793$; $df=11$; $p<0.001$).

Finally, the differences between the findings of the present study and the findings in Jakobsen and Jensen (2008) are likely to be related to eye-tracking data filter configurations. As argued in Alves *et al.* (2009), filter configuration determines parameters to include or exclude fixation data in the analysis, as a means of disregarding unreliable data, or data that may refer to random gazes or drifts. The authors' analysis of the same set of data shows that results within subjects are completely different as a consequence of changes in filter configurations. Bearing in mind that eye tracking is an emergent technology in the field of translation studies and that studies like Jakobsen and Jensen (2008) are pioneering ones in the field, insights gathered from comparing results, such as Jakobsen and Jensen's and ours, highlight the importance of publications including details of filter configuration when reporting experiment set-up and analysis so as to allow studies to be replicated and thus generate comparable data.

Fixation Length

Table 5 shows the fixation length for each task in Condition 1.

Table 5 Mean length of fixations (*in milliseconds*) found for professionals and students in Condition 1 and overall data in Condition 1 in comparison to Jakobsen and Jensen's findings

TASK	CONDITION 1 DATA PER GROUP		OVERALL DATA	
	PROFESSIONALS	STUDENTS	J & J (2008)*	CONDITION 1 DATA
A: Reading for Comprehension	300	360	205	330
B: Reading for Summarizing	306	344	205	325
C: Reading for Sight Translation	391	402	235	396

* Jakobsen and Jensen (2008) do not provide means per group.

Similar to Jakobsen and Jensen (2008), the results of the present study do not show much difference between reading for comprehension (Task A1) and reading for summarizing (Task B1), the overall decrease from 330 to 325 being statistically non-significant ($t=0.631$; $df=11$; $p=0.541$). Nevertheless, although the differences across groups for the sight translation task is not considerable, the overall increase from 325 in Task B1 to 396 in Task C1 is significant ($t=-5.200$; $df=11$; $p<0.001$).

Condition 2

Total task time

Table 6 shows task time (in seconds) for each subject, as well as mean time per group. Again, as stated earlier, the absence of Task C2 as the second task in the student group is the result of the random selection of the subjects.

Table 6 Individual and mean task time (in seconds) in Condition 2 according to group

GROUP	SUBJECT	TEXT A2*	TEXT B2*	TEXT C2*	TASK ORDER
	S1	32	69	128	A2,B2,C2
	S2	50	84	111	C2,A2,B2
	S3	43	45	130	B2,A2,C2
Students	S4	47	88	141	A2,B2,C2
	S5	57	80	107	C2,B2,A2
	S6	55	52	150	B2,A2,C2
	Means	47	70	128	
	P1	23	25	70	C2,B2,A2
	P2	64	111	160	B2,A2,C2
	P3	44	48	112	C2,A2,B2
Professionals	P4	51	89	101	B2,C2,A2
	P5	27	36	93	A2,C2,B2
	P6	32	69	128	A2,B2,C2
	Means	40	84	111	

* A2=reading for comprehension; B2=reading for summarizing; C2=sight translation.

Regardless of task sequence, Table 6 shows that Task C2 demanded more time than Task B2, while Task A2 was the task that demanded the least time from most subjects. S6 is the only subject who does not follow this tendency of increasing time spent on the execution of Tasks A2, B2 and C2. This result cannot be associated with task sequencing, since Task B2 was performed first and consumed the shortest amount of time within the tasks performed by S6. Table 6 also shows that P2 has values considerably higher than the other professional subjects.

Table 7 presents the findings of Conditions 1 and 2 regarding task time.

Table 7 Mean* task time in Conditions 1 and 2 (in seconds) according to group of subjects

TASK	PROFESSIONALS		TRANSLATION STUDENTS	
	CONDITION 1	CONDITION 2	CONDITION 1+	CONDITION 2
A: Reading for Comprehension	95	40	136; 139	47
B: Reading for Summarizing	90	63	157; 124	70
C: Reading for Sight Translation	264	110	316; 334	128

* means are rounded for comparability reasons.

+ left values include all subjects; right values exclude S2 and S4.

As shown in Table 7, the professional subjects spent less time than students performing their tasks. Unlike in Condition 1, in Condition 2 there is a clear increase in time for tasks A2, B2 and C2.

Fixation Count

Table 8 shows the total number of fixations for Condition 2.

Table 8 Mean* total number of fixations in Conditions 1 and 2 according to group of subjects

TASK	PROFESSIONALS		TRANSLATION STUDENTS	
	CONDITION 1	CONDITION 2	CONDITION 1	CONDITION 2
A: Reading for Comprehension	184	120	177	134
B: Reading for Summarizing	194	137	181	167
C: Reading for Sight Translation	160	148	152	138

* means are rounded for comparability reasons.

Once again, fixation count proved not to be a measure of the assumed progressive difficulty level of the tasks. Task B2 demanded a higher average fixation count than Task A2 from both groups, but Task C2 required fewer counts than Task B2 among the students. The overall increase from Task A2 (127) to Task B2 (152) is not significant ($t=-0.084$; $df=11$; $p=0.934$), but the overall decrease from Task B2 (152) to Task C2 (143) is in fact significant ($t=4.229$; $df=11$; $p<0.001$). It is relevant to observe that the fixation count is not much lower than the fixation count for Condition 1 although the text size is considerably shorter and subjects spent less time completing Condition 2. One possible explanation for this would be that since texts in Condition 2 are shorter than those in Condition 1, after having coped with longer texts in Condition 1, subjects felt they could actually read more attentively, which would involve fixating on a higher number of words. As mentioned earlier the differences between the results of the present experiment and the findings in Jakobsen and Jensen (2008) are likely to be related to filter configurations, highlighting once again the importance of filter configuration for assessing and comparing data.

Fixation length

Table 9 shows the fixation length for each task in Condition 2.

Table 9 Length of fixations (*in milliseconds*) found for each group of subjects in Condition 2 in comparison to Condition 1

TASK	PROFESSIONALS		TRANSLATION STUDENTS	
	CONDITION 1	CONDITION 2	CONDITION 1	CONDITION 2
A: Reading for Comprehension	300	306	360	333
B: Reading for Summarizing	306	301	344	358
C: Reading for Sight Translation	391	413	402	410

Table 9 shows that the average fixation lengths for Condition 2 are quite similar to those for Condition 1. Again, the results do not show much difference from Task A2 to Task B2, the overall increase from 319 to 329 being non-significant (t=0.631; df=11; p=0.541). Nevertheless, although the difference across groups for Task C2 is not great, the overall increase from 329 in Task B2 to 412 in Task C2 is significant (t=−3.652; df=11; p=0.005).

Discussion

The results of the present study can be analysed from two different yet complementary perspectives. The first perspective compares the results of Condition 1 with the results shown in the study carried out by Jakobsen and Jensen (2008). The second perspective contrasts the results of Conditions 1 and 2. Tables 10 and 11 below consolidate the two perspectives. Both tables exclude data from S2 and S4 for the task time variable, for the reasons previously stated.

Table 10 shows that there are similarities and differences when comparing the findings of Jakobsen and Jensen with the results of Condition 1 in our study. As already mentioned, the decrease in task time from Task A to Task B may be related to the perceived complexity of these tasks as well as subject profiles, and differences in fixation counts are probably due to differences in methodological procedures. More specifically, Condition 1, although similar in terms of design, tasks and subjects, showed differences potentially ascribable to filter settings, and perhaps the use of different software packages, namely ClearView for Jakobsen and Jensen (2008) and Tobii Studio for the present study.

Table 10 Comparison of progression (from Task A to Task C) in Jakobsen and Jensen's and Condition 1 results for task time, fixation count and average fixation length

VARIABLE	TASK A		TASK B		TASK C	
	J & J (2008)	CONDITION 1	J & J (2008)	CONDITION 1	J & J (2008)	CONDITION 1
Task Time	–	–	↑	↓	↑	↑
Fixation Count	–	–	↑	↑	↑	↓
Average Fixation Length	–	–	=	≡	↑	↑

Legend: – (no possible comparison); ↑↓ (increase or decrease in relation to the previous task); =/≡ (equal or similar results).

Alves *et al.* (2009) discuss the need to standardize parameters for filter settings when eye tracking is used so that studies can be compared and replicated. The findings of this article reinforce their conclusions, since results diverge in terms of fixation count.

On the other hand, a different picture emerges when results of Conditions 1 and 2 are compared. Even though there are still differences for task time, Table 11 shows that the comparison yields similar results in the case of fixation count and length.

Table 11 Comparison of progression (from Task A to Task C) in Conditions 1 and 2 results for task time, fixation count and average fixation length

VARIABLE	TASK A		TASK B		TASK C	
	CONDITION 1	CONDITION 2	CONDITION 1	CONDITION 2	CONDITION 1	CONDITION 2
Task Time	–	–	↓	↑	↑	↑
Fixation Count	–	–	↑	↑	↓	↓
Average Fixation Length	–	–	≡	≡	↑	↑

Legend: – (no possible comparison); ↑↓ (increase or decrease in relation to the previous task); =/≡ (equal or similar results).

The different results for fixation counts observed in Tables 10 and 11 highlight relevant issues for research in reading processes and eye-tracking research in translation. First, task time itself seems to be a variable that is not capable of explaining difficulty progression in reading, especially for modalities demanding a subsequent output (i.e. answering comprehension questions and summarizing a task). Our results for task time in Condition 1 diverge from Jakobsen and Jensen's (2008) findings and from our own findings in Condition 2. This suggests a spurious relationship demanding the analysis of several other intervening variables, such as subject profile and perception of the task/text complexity. In the case of comparisons of modalities demanding subsequent and consequent outputs, as is the case of sight translation, however, task time does seem to be a relevant variable. In other words, subjects responded similarly in terms of task time (as well as average fixation length) when we compare either Tasks B and C or Tasks A and C.

On the other hand, the similarities in our results related to eye-tracking data in both conditions, as opposed to the results found in comparison to Jakobsen's and Jensen's experiment, reinforces Alves *et al.*'s (2009) claim that filter configuration is probably an intervening variable for comparability across experimental studies using eye tracking. Further studies are necessary to determine the most accurate filter configurations to be used in translation process research and to explain why our subjects, even though spending more time, had around one third of the fixation counts of those observed in the subjects in Jakobsen and Jensen's (2008) study.

Final Remarks

The results point out the importance of accurate methodological procedures to allow the comparison of studies. As shown, one possible explanation for the different results of Jakobsen and Jensen's (2008) research and those of the present study could be related to the parameters used in each study. One could also argue that the differences might be due to proficiency levels and familiarity with task demands among the Danish and Brazilian experimental groups. This points to the importance of assessing subject profiles beforehand. Task order also seems to be a fundamental factor in the performance of subjects. To account for the possible effect of these variables in Jakobsen and Jensen's research (2008), in the present study a second experimental condition was introduced with the same subjects and same tasks. The analysis of Conditions 1 and 2 reveals similar tendencies and shows comparable results. This suggests that subjects performed similarly in both conditions and that replication was therefore possible. The use of eye tracking in translation process research is still in its infancy. We hope our results and the methodological considerations arising from them contribute to paving the way for future studies.

Notes

1 Cf.: www.tobii.com/corporate/eye_tracking/what_is_eye_tracking.aspx. Accessed on: 15 Dec. 2009.
2 For a basic introduction to Rhetorical Structure Theory, see: www.sfu.ca/rst/.
3 The accuracy or adequacy of subjects' output is not an issue of concern in this paper.
4 According to the Tobii Handbook, a fixation radius is the smallest distance in pixels that can separate fixations.

References

Alves, F. (ed.) (2003), *Triangulation Translation. Perspectives in Process Oriented Research.* Amsterdam: John Benjamins.

Alves, F. (2005), 'Ritmo cognitivo, meta-reflexão e experiência: parâmetros de análise processual no desempenho de tradutores novatos e experientes'. In A. Pagano, C.C. Magalhães and F. Alves (eds) *Competência em Tradução: cognição e discurso.* Belo Horizonte: Editora da UFMG. pp. 109–153.

Alves, F., A. Pagano and I. Silva (2009), 'A new window on translators' cognitive activity: methodological issues in the combined use of eye tracking, key logging and retrospective protocols'. In I.M. Mees, F. Alves and S. Göpferich (eds) *Methodology, Technology and Innovation in Translation Process Research. A Tribute to Arnt Lykke Jakobsen.* Copenhagen Studies in Language 38 Copenhagen: Samfundslitteratur. pp. 267–291.

Carl, M., A.L. Jakobsen and K.T.H. Jensen (2008), 'Studying human translator behavior with user-activity data'. *Natural Language Processing and Cognitive Science (NLPCS 2008) at the International Conference of Enterprise Information Systems (ICEIS).* Barcelona, Spain. pp. 114–123.

Danks, J.H. and J. Griffin (1997), 'Reading and translation: A psycholinguistic perspective'. In J.H. Danks, G.M. Griffin, S.B. Fountain and M.K. McBeath (eds) *Cognitive processes in translation and interpreting.* Thousand Oaks: Sage. pp. 161–195.

Jakobsen, A.L. (2002), 'Translation drafting by professional translators and by translation students'. In G. Hansen (ed.) *Empirical Translation Studies.* Copenhagen Studies in Language 27. Copenhagen: Samfundslitteratur. pp. 191–204.

Jakobsen, A.L. and K.T.H. Jensen (2008), 'Eye movement behaviour across four different types of reading task'. In S. Göpferich, A.L. Jakobsen and I.M. Mees (eds) *Looking at Eyes: Eye-Tracking Studies of Reading and Translation Processing.* Copenhagen Studies in Language 36. Copenhagen: Samfundslitteratur. pp. 103–124.

Macizo, P. and M.T. Bajo (2006), 'Reading for repetition and reading for translation: do they involve the same processes?' *Cognition* 99: 1–34.

Muñoz, R. (2009), 'The way they were: subject profiling in translation process research'. In I.M. Mees, F. Alves and S. Göpferich (eds) *Methodology, Technology and Innovation in Translation Process Research. A Tribute to Arnt Lykke Jakobsen.* Copenhagen Studies in Language 38. Copenhagen: Samfundslitteratur. pp. 87–108.

O'Brien, S. (2006), 'Eye-tracking and translation memory matches'. *Perspectives: Studies in Translatology* 14: 185–203.

PACTE. (2005), 'Investigating translation competence: conceptual and methodological issues'. *Meta* 50(2): 609–619.

Sharmin, S., O. Špakov, K. Räihä and A.L. Jakobsen (2008), 'Effects of time pressure and text complexity on translators' fixations'. *Proceedings of the Eye Tracking Research and Applications Symposium (ETRA08).* Savannah, Georgia. pp. 123–126.

Shreve, G.M., C. Schäffner and J.H. Danks (1993), 'Is there a special kind of "reading" for translation: an empirical investigation of reading in the translation process'. *Target* 5(1): 21–41.

Taboada, M. and W. Mann (2006), 'Rhetorical Structure Theory: looking back and moving ahead'. *Discourse Studies* 8(3): 423–459.

Appendix

SOURCE TEXTS IN EXPERIMENTAL CONDITION 1

Task A1

Historic day as Blair surrenders power and Brown finally moves into No 10.

Tony Blair surrendered on his own terms today as Gordon Brown ushered in a new radical era of change. Ending a decade of relentless controversy, wars and even a police inquiry, Labour's longest-serving Prime Minister was set to stroll out of No 10 with his head held high. It is also the day Mr Blair is expected to announce that he is turning his back on British politics for good to take up a job as special envoy to the Middle East. He is poised to resign as an MP on the same day he steps down as Prime Minister – triggering a by-election in his constituency of Sedgefield, which could be held as early as July 19.

His decision to stand down after 24 years in Parliament will allow him to "throw himself" into the role as the international community's key peace-maker in the Middle East, his close allies said. Today at Downing Street, crowds of well-wishers, and protesters were gathering in Whitehall to watch, cheer or jeer his final progress from Downing Street to the Commons for his final Prime Minister's Questions.

Adapted from www.dailymail.co.uk

Task B1

Finally, Blair exits the stage

Tony Blair will say farewell to Downing Street and domestic politics today, bringing to an end a remarkable decade in power which began with extraordinarily high hopes but ended with opinion divided over his legacy to the country. After his last appearance at the dispatch box at Prime Minister's questions Mr Blair will return to Downing Street to make an emotional farewell to his staff, some of whom have been with him since he became Leader of the Opposition in the heady days of 1994 and the birth of New Labour.

Mr Blair, Labour's most successful leader after an unprecedented three election victories, making him – alongside Margaret Thatcher – one of the dominant political figures since the war, will drive up The Mall to Buckingham Palace with his wife Cherie to tender his resignation to the Queen. In contrast to his arrival as Prime Minister in May 1997 when Downing Street was lined with handpicked Labour Party members cheering, and waving Union flags, Mr Blair will make a low-key exit. Today it will be photographers, not supporters, recording his reluctant departure.

Adapted from www.telegraph.co.uk

Task C1

Blair exits British politics as new era begins with a Tory defection

A new political order in Britain will take shape this afternoon when Tony Blair flies to his Sedgefield constituency to resign from parliament with immediate effect, and Gordon Brown enters No 10 to prepare a shakeup of government which will see at least six ministers quit the cabinet. Mr Brown's allies said the new ministerial line-up would be deliberately inclusive, and not settle scores with Mr Blair's supporters. Mr Blair had planned to keep the decision to quit as an MP secret until after his 318th and final prime minister's questions at noon today. But news leaked that his local party was being called to an extraordinary meeting to be addressed tonight by Mr Blair.

Two of his aides in No 10 are expected to join him in his new life as a Middle East envoy. If, as expected, the role is confirmed today, Mr Blair will resign as an MP, triggering a by-election which may take place as early as July. His departure from parliament means his earnings from the lecture circuit will be kept from the register of members' interests.

Adapted from http://politics.guardian.co.uk

SOURCE TEXTS IN EXPERIMENTAL CONDITION 2

Task A2

If the cells of our skin are replaced regularly, why do scars and tattoos persist indefinitely?

The public information office of the Dermatology Associates of Atlanta provides this brief reply:

"The answer is really quite simple. The cells in the superficial or upper layers of skin, known as epidermis, are constantly replacing themselves. This process of renewal is basically exfoliation (shedding) of the epidermis. But the deeper layers of skin, called the dermis, do not go through this cellular turnover and so do not replace themselves. Thus, foreign bodies, such as tattoo dyes, implanted in the dermis will remain."

Adapted from www.scientificamerican.com/article.
cfm?id=if-the-cells-of-our-skin

Task B2

If a used needle can transmit HIV, why can't a mosquito?

Laurence Corash, chief medical officer of Cerus Corporation, provides the following explanation:

The AIDS virus (HIV) on used needles is infectious when injected into a human where the virus can bind to T cells and start to replicate. The human T cell is a very specific host cell for HIV. When a mosquito feeds on a person with HIV in his or her blood, the HIV enters the insect's gut, which does not contain human T cells. The virus thus has no host cell in which to replicate and it is broken down by the mosquito's digestive system.

Adapted from www.scientificamerican.com/article.
cfm?id=if-a-used-needle-can-tran

TASK C2
If comets melt, why do they seem to last for long periods of time?

Greg Lyzenga, associate professor of physics at Harvey Mudd College, has the answer.

Comets do not melt in the strict sense of becoming liquid. However, since they are composed partly of ice and other volatile compounds, they vaporize (turn directly to gas) when warmed in the vacuum of space by passing near the sun. It is this escaping gas that forms the comet's luminous tail. "Near" in this context means closer than several astronomical units (AU) from the sun; one AU is about 93 million miles, the average radius of the earth's orbit.

Adapted from www.scientificamerican.com/article.
cfm?id=if-comets-melt-why-do-the

Cognitive Effort in Metaphor Translation: An Eye-tracking Study

9

Annette C. Sjørup

Chapter Outline

Introduction

This paper explores the way in which translators process the meaning of non-literal expressions by investigating the gaze times associated with these expressions. Specifically, we wish to investigate whether professional translators invest more cognitive effort in the translation of metaphorical expressions than in non-metaphorical expressions. Eye tracking was used to collect data, a methodology that enables us to observe – albeit indirectly – the cognitive processes of the participants. An increase in gaze time was taken to indicate an increase in cognitive effort, as is the norm in research employing eye tracking (Rayner and Sereno 1994: 58, Jakobsen and Jensen 2008: 114). It was hypothesized that the participants would display longer gaze times for metaphorical expressions compared with those for non-metaphorical expressions. The basis for this hypothesis is that when translating metaphorical expressions, several translation strategies are available to translators, and accordingly they have to evaluate the suitability of the metaphorical expression in the target language. A consideration unique to the task of translating metaphors is whether or not to keep the metaphorical image or to paraphrase into a literal expression.

Studying the translation of metaphors is particularly interesting because of the high number of translation options available to the translator. The optimal translation strategy is highly dependent on the nature of the metaphorical expression as well as the context and target reader, and the professional translator therefore has to make strategic translation decisions continuously throughout the translation task.

As stated by Lakoff and Johnson in their preface to *Metaphors We Live By* (1980), metaphors are not isolated phenomena in literary fiction but an integral part of every type of language usage. Metaphors are found in abundance in nearly all types of text and language styles. Most research on metaphors has been in the field of cognitive linguistics and has focused on various aspects of metaphor comprehension (Lakoff and Johnson 1999, Gibbs and Steen 1997). Following Jakobsen and Jensen (2008), who studied differences between reading for comprehension and reading for translation, we have here assumed that although there has been convincing research in recent years documenting that metaphor comprehension need not be more time-consuming than the comprehension of literal expressions, this does not necessarily mean that the two processes are identical (as argued by Gerrig 1989: 237). Understanding the processing of metaphors, which is one small niche in the study of translation, may contribute towards a fuller understanding of the overall cognitive processes in translation. Studies of metaphor processing in translation are now beginning to appear (see, for example, Andersen 2004 and Tirkkonen-Condit 2002).

It was decided to recreate a genuine translation situation to the fullest extent possible, but in an experimental setting. For this reason, authentic text was used in the experiments. Deignan (2005: 117) points out that the majority of other research on metaphor processing has used constructed texts, which 'may be forcing participants to tackle problems that are not faced in normal discourse'. It seems reasonable to assume that authentic text will produce a more realistic simulation of the natural processing of texts, as metaphor comprehension is highly sensitive to context (Dobrzyńska 1995: 596). Another reason for opting for authentic texts from news magazines as the basis for the experiments was the opportunity they offered to find novel and innovative metaphors. Novel metaphors have not lost any of their imagery properties whereas conventional metaphors may have. This view is also shared by Croft and Cruse (2004). They argue that newly created metaphors are the only instances of metaphorical expressions which have retained all their original properties whereas 'conventionalized metaphors have irrecoverably lost at least some of their original properties' (2004: 204). Although the use of authentic text makes it more difficult to control for variables such as word position, sentence length and comparability of experimental texts, these disadvantages were thought to be outweighed by the advantages, notably that it was in this way possible to obtain a higher level of ecological validity.

The experiment was triangulated using eye-tracking data, keystroke log data, and retrospective interviews. This paper reports the findings from the eye-tracking data only, as the other two data sources await analysis.

Theoretical Framework

Metaphor theory

Establishing a consistent and workable definition of the constituents of a metaphor is a crucial challenge, perhaps even more important in a project using eye-tracking technology, as it is necessary to be able to identify clearly the word or words to be included in the 'Areas Of Interest' (AOIs). As pointed out by Cienki and Müller, definitions may vary according to the aim of the research project (2008: 496). The identification process may be further complicated by the requirement to take context into account, as put forward by Black (1981: 29): 'the recognition and interpretation of a metaphor may require attention to the **particular circumstances** of its utterance' (emphasis in original). In other words, it is necessary to take the context into consideration when determining whether a segment is metaphorical or not (see also Andersen 2004).

Andersen (2004: 35) cites a definition by Steen (1994), which was used as a point of departure in this study for the identification of a metaphorical expression: 'linguistic metaphors are those expressions that *can* be analysed on formal grounds as involving two semantic domains'. Lakoff and Johnson (1980: 5) have also defined the essence of metaphor as 'understanding and experiencing one kind of thing in terms of another'. In keeping with these views, this project took into account the semantic domains of the two experimental texts in their entirety in order to identify the metaphorical expressions and their boundaries.

Convincing arguments have been put forward for the lack of ambiguity in metaphors. Glucksberg (2001: 28) states in his work on understanding figurative language that, if embedded in a context, metaphors are not ambiguous and will not be interpreted literally. In an eye-tracking study, Inhoff *et al.* (1984) investigated the cognitive effort invested in metaphor comprehension. They found that metaphor *comprehension* does not constitute an increase in cognitive effort as compared with literal expressions. In contrast with this, a recent (2007) Event-Related Potential (ERP) study, measuring participants' electrophysiological responses to stimuli containing literal expressions, conventional and novel metaphors as well as anomalous expressions, found that both conventional and novel metaphors required a higher processing effort and that novel metaphors in particular required 'a sustained effort' (Lai *et al.* 2007).

However, the above research projects focus on metaphor comprehension and their findings may not necessarily apply directly to metaphor *translation*. This paper hopes to be able to contribute to the ongoing debate.

Mandelblit's 'cognitive translation hypothesis' from 1996 (reported in Tirkkonen-Condit 2002: 101) states that metaphors require more time to translate if the metaphorical expressions use a cognitive domain that is different from the available expressions in the target language. However, this hypothesis and the support it receives from Tirkkonen-Condit's (2002) research is not directly transferable to this study as the cognitive translation hypothesis would appear to be concerned with the translation of idiomatic expressions rather than metaphorical expressions, although no such distinction is expressed. Idioms differ from metaphors in that they are fixed collocations in which the individual components do not make any sense. The idiom is, in other words, comprehended as one lexical unit (Jakobsen *et al.* 2007: 218). Unlike metaphors, idioms are always frozen in the images they represent both in the source and target languages. However, both forms of speech are figurative expressions and share many features, and the distinction between idioms and frozen or dead metaphors is debatable (see e.g. Gibbs 1993), which is why these findings were regarded as likely to hold true for metaphorical expressions as well.

In their study of the translation and interpretation of idioms, Jakobsen *et al.* (2007: 233) found that 'the presence of idiomatic expressions slowed down production.' It was also shown that language-specific idioms, i.e. non-cognate idioms, involved the most time-consuming translation process (2007: 226).

As mentioned previously, there are several strategies available to the translator when translating a metaphor. The definition of these vary according to the research project and researcher in question, but they essentially all cover the same basic elements. Dobrzynska (1995: 595) suggests that translators have the following metaphor translation strategies at their disposal:

- use of an exact equivalent of the original metaphor (M–M),
- choice of another metaphorical phrase with the same meaning (M1–M2) or
- paraphrase (M–P)

Examples of the three translation strategies taken from the translations produced in this study can be seen in Table 1:

Table 1 Examples of participants' translation strategies for metaphors

ORIGINAL TEXT	USE OF AN EXACT EQUIVALENT OF THE ORIGINAL METAPHOR (M–M)	CHOICE OF ANOTHER METAPHORICAL PHRASE WITH THE SAME MEANING (M1–M2)	PARAPHRASE (M–P)
The path from the altar is strewn with failed corporate marriages	Vejen fra alteret er bestrøet med selskabsskilsmisser (*the way from the altar is strewn with company divorces*)		Der er utallige eksempler på fejlslagne fusioner (*there are numerous examples of failed mergers*)
Financial and economic convulsions		Finansielle og økonomiske turbulens (*financial and economic turbulence*)	

For this study, it was assumed that the choice of translation strategy would have an effect on the cognitive effort involved in metaphor translation, and hence an effect on the gaze times. Cristofoli *et al.* (1998:178) argue that a novel metaphor (labelled an 'original' metaphor in their classification system) should preferably be translated with a novel metaphor and a conventional metaphor with a conventional metaphor. This study hypothesizes that the use of a direct metaphorical equivalent (M–M), or, as a second preference, another metaphorical phrase (M1–M2), would in fact not only be the preferred translation strategies, but that these two strategies would also require less cognitive effort than the paraphrasing strategy (M–P). This latter strategy not only requires an evaluation of the appropriateness of the source metaphor in the target language and culture, as is also the case for the other two translation strategies, but also requires an additional shift from the metaphorical to the literal. This additional shift is assumed to constitute an increase in cognitive effort.

Eye-tracking indicators and experimental hypotheses

Research shows that there is a strong link between cognitive effort and the location of the eye's fixation (Rayner 1998). In reading, the eye remains fixated on a particular word for as long as the word is being processed (Just and Carpenter 1980: 330), and Just and Carpenter's eye-mind assumption posits that 'there is no appreciable lag between what is being fixated and what is being processed' (1980: 331). Therefore, it was assumed that gaze data are indicative of underlying (though not directly observable) cognitive processes that take place during a particular task, in this case a translation task.

Following the rationale of the eye-mind assumption, the present study investigated total gaze time (not including saccades), which is here defined as the combined duration, in milliseconds, of all the fixations on a given area of the screen during a given task. An increase in total gaze time was taken to be indicative of more cognitive effort. The measure of total gaze time is a general overall measure, which may at a later stage of the study be supplemented with the measures of first-pass gaze time and number of fixations, as well as other gaze measures, which may all contribute to a fuller picture of the gaze behaviour of the participant. For practical reasons, however, the total gaze time was chosen for the study at its current stage as the most comprehensive measure.

The mean total gaze time for all participants and for all linguistic metaphors was divided by the total number of characters in the metaphor not including spaces. This value was then compared with the total gaze time for the entire text divided by the total number of characters in the entire text (excluding gaze time and characters in metaphors). These calculations enabled us to compare gaze times for the metaphorical expressions with gaze times for the experimental text in its entirety. Using a gaze time per character measurement should not be taken to mean that any assumption was made about cognitive processing taking place at character level. The gaze time per character measurement was merely employed as a measure to enable comparisons of gaze times for segments of varying lengths.

Methodology

Equipment and analysis tools

The participants were seated in front of a Tobii 1750 eye tracker at a distance of no more than 55 cms from the monitor. Calibration was done in both Translog/GWM (Gaze-to-Word Mapping) and ClearView, the latter running in the background while the participants worked in Translog. Translog, as well as enabling the participant to view both the source and target texts simultaneously, also logs keystrokes and keystroke pauses (Jakobsen and Schou 1999). As previously mentioned, the keystroke logging will be analysed at a later stage. ClearView is a software package which records raw gaze data as well as enabling the experimenter to register manually associations between fixations and textual units (Jensen 2008: 158).

Translog presents the source text in the upper half of the application window while the target text appears in the lower half of the application window. ClearView was used for collecting the eye-tracking data. The areas

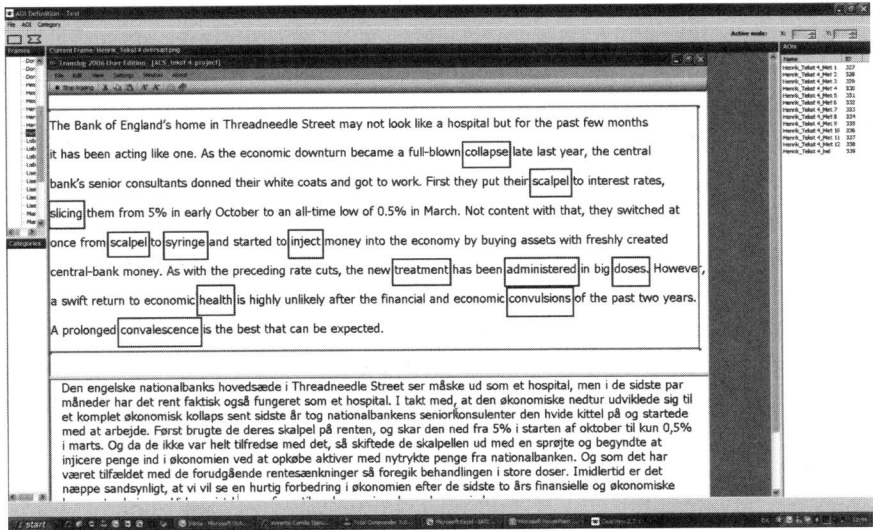

Figure 1 Screenshot of ClearView with defined AOIs

occupied on the screen by the metaphors were defined as AOIs for the eye-tracking analysis. The font of the experimental texts was Tahoma, size 18, with double spacing. The borders of the AOIs extended halfway into the space to the words on both sides of the individual AOI and also halfway to the lines above and below the line of the AOI. This was done to compensate for any inaccuracies in the eye-tracking equipment. The screenshot in Figure 1 illustrates how the AOI frames the individual word to be analysed.

Participants

The participants for this study were all Danish translators with at least 12 months of professional translation experience. The background of the participants varied in terms of the fields they normally work in, ranging from translation of literature to translation of medical texts. Data from ten participants were analysed for this paper. All participants except one were female.

Experimental texts

As stated above, to improve the ecological validity of the study, the project used authentic text shown in its entirety rather than presenting individual sentences one at a time. The two experimental texts, which can be found in Appendices A and B, each consisted of approximately 150 words in English (the participants' L2). The individual sentences were extracted from an English news magazine article and edited into an abridged version of the original article. No further modifications were made to the sentences.

According to the Flesch reading ease index scores, the difficulty level of the two experimental texts was comparable. Text 1 had a score of 74.6 and Text 2 a score of 69.3. The index score range is from 0–100; the higher the score, the easier the text (www.editcentral.com). Although the Flesch reading ease index was developed for readers with English as a first language, the professional background of the participants was deemed sufficiently similar to make it possible to apply the scores to the reading of texts for translation by L2 readers.

As both texts were abridged versions of longer texts, they were subjectively evaluated by a third party to ensure that they read as coherent text units. This evaluation was done by asking the evaluator to read the text and comment upon any abnormalities in it, and evaluate whether or not the text made sense and could be read fluently. The individual sentences were not altered, but several intermediate sentences were eliminated to keep the text length to a maximum of 150 words. Attention was given to ensuring that the contexts of the metaphors were clear from the outset. The two texts were on different subjects (company mergers and the British economy respectively).

The experimental texts contained 23 linguistic metaphors in total, constituting 23 AOIs, with ten linguistic metaphors in Text 1 and 13 linguistic metaphors in Text 2. The mean length of the AOIs was 12 characters (without spaces) in Text 1 and 9 in Text 2. For the purposes of this project, the boundaries of each individual metaphor were identified using the criterion that the constituents of the metaphorical expressions must differ from the text in terms of semantic domain.

To illustrate what is meant by a different semantic domain, an example from one of the experimental texts may be helpful: 'But the suitors must first gain the approval of regulators, who are sure to supervise the courtship with care because of the size of the dowry'. The subject of the text was the current high number of mergers between companies, and the overriding metaphorical semantic domain for the merger is marriage, and the parties and processes involved in a marriage. 'Suitors' is used as a metaphor for the two companies involved in a specific merger, and as 'suitors' differs in terms of semantic domain from the text's general semantic domain of business and mergers, 'suitors' is identified as the linguistic metaphor in its entirety, and consequently constitutes the AOI to be analysed. The other two linguistic metaphors in this example are 'courtship' and 'dowry', which were analysed separately.

The majority of the metaphors were single words, but a few metaphors consisted of multiple words, which is why the gaze time per character measurement was chosen as the preferred baseline measure for this study, in which ecological validity received higher priority than exact text comparability in terms of variables. Not all AOIs were fixated by all participants, which could be due to inaccuracy in the eye-tracking equipment and software or, more likely, it could be due to the fact that not all words are necessarily fixated when we read. However, as this study relied on averages across words and participants, the effects of non-fixations were assumed to be negligible in the final result.

Task

The participants were asked to translate two texts from English into Danish (L2 into L1). The presentation order of the two texts was counterbalanced among participants. The participants were told that they were free to review the translated text and to go back in the text to make revisions. They were informed that the target audience for the translation was readers of a Danish financial news magazine, i.e. an audience similar to the readership of the source text. The participants were also informed that they would be asked questions on comprehension and translation of the text afterwards in order to motivate them to work carefully with the texts. After translation of both texts was completed, the participants were asked questions on potential comprehension difficulties, the content, and also on any difficulties the participant may have had in the translation task. The questions were open-ended and were given in Danish to encourage answers given freely and spontaneously.

No time constraints were imposed for either of the two texts. No translation aids of any kind were available as the main aim was to keep the participant's gaze on the source and target texts to gain the highest possible data quality with the minimum number of gazes away from the monitor.

Results

In this paper, only the eye-tracking data from the translation task have been analysed. The preliminary findings from the translation task are tentative to the extent that a number of variables have yet to be controlled for. These variables include word frequency, length, and repetition of both words and metaphors. One other variable which could have an effect on the results is position of the metaphor (AOI) in the sentence. Both sentence-initial and sentence-final positions (and indeed line-initial and line-final positions) are considered undesirable AOI positions as studies have shown that they may be skipped more frequently or receive longer fixations (Frenck-Mestre 2005: 178). However, when using authentic text, it is not always possible to control for these variables, although they were taken into account to the greatest extent possible by modifying the font size and line breaks to minimize the number of AOIs placed at line-initial and line-final positions.

The metaphors in the first of the two experimental texts involved the

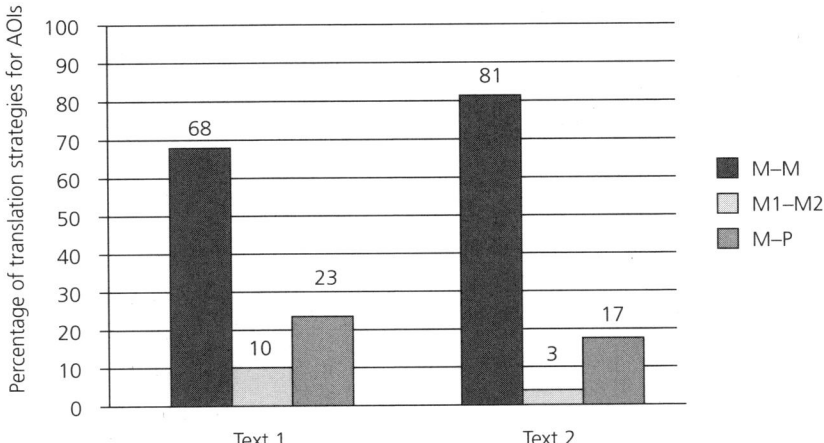

Figure 2 Mean distribution of translation strategies in percentages

semantic domain of marriage as a metaphor for business mergers. The second text, on the crisis in the British economy, used the semantic domain of patient and health as a metaphor for the national economy.

The data suggest that there is a link between the translation strategy chosen by the participants and the gaze time data (see Figure 2). Text 1 on business mergers contained a higher percentage of the translation strategies M1–M2 (a new image with the same meaning) and M–P (paraphrasing) than Text 2 on the British national economy as a patient. The mean distribution of the translation strategies is illustrated in percentages in Figure 2.

It is interesting to note that there seems to be a slight correlation between the distribution of translation strategies in the two texts and the mean gaze times. This claim is based on the higher number of M1–M2 and M–P strategies in Text 1 and the higher gaze time for the metaphorical AOIs relative to the rest of the text as illustrated in Figure 3. Text 2 shows a negligible difference in gaze times, which is assumed to be related to the high percentage of the M–M translation strategy.

Figure 3 shows the differences in gaze time between the two experimental texts. As noted earlier, the gaze time is calculated per character, not because it is assumed that there is any cognitive processing at character level but only to provide a measure of comparability between the metaphorical expressions and the entire text in which the metaphor occurs. Gaze time values from AOIs

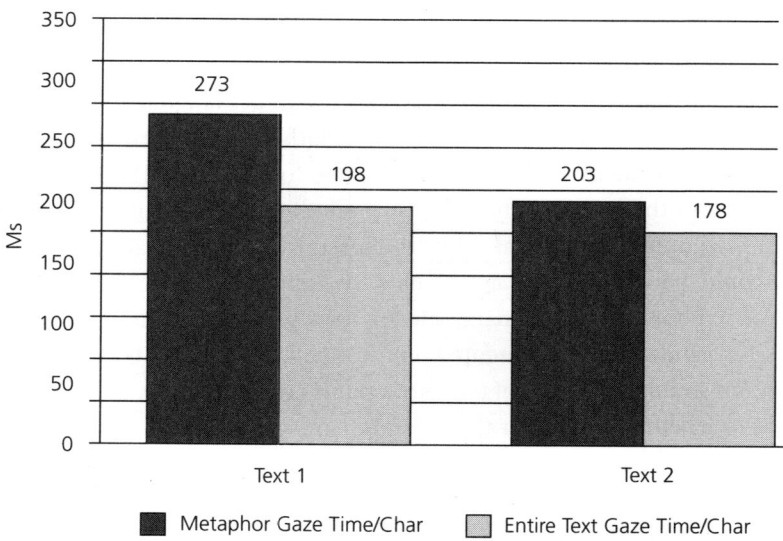

Figure 3 Mean within-subject gaze time per character

located at sentence-initial or sentence-final positions or at line breaks were included in the calculations and were treated in the same way as AOIs in other positions. Zero values were the only gaze time values that were excluded from the calculation; there were only 12 zero values out of a total of 230 AOI gaze values (10 participants × 23 AOIs/linguistic metaphors).

There is marked individual variation with gaze times per character ranging from less than 100 milliseconds to more than 300 milliseconds. For this reason, a mean value may therefore be misleading. But what turned out to be interesting is the variability across the two texts, which we are unable to explain by examining potential lexical problems. The first text, which consisted of linguistic metaphors from the semantic domain of marriage, yielded longer gaze time per character values for the metaphorical expressions compared with the text in its entirety, whereas the second text, which consisted of metaphors originating from the semantic domain of patient and health, showed only a negligible difference in gaze time. A tentative explanation could be that Danish news articles on business mergers may use more conventional linguistic metaphors based on the semantic domain of marriage, and as a preliminary review of the responses to the retrospective interviews revealed, some of the participants did not feel that the source text metaphor was equally prevalent in the target language. This resulted in a higher percentage of the M–P translation strategy in Text 1. In Text 2, the majority of participants chose the translation strategy of M–M, i.e. they made a more or less direct transfer of the metaphor into the target language, maintaining formal and semantic properties. However, another of the participants chose the translation strategy M–P, i.e. paraphrasing, for 10 out of 13 metaphorical expressions in the text. In other words, the individual variability is not only seen in gaze time values but also in the chosen translation strategies.

As could be expected in a text of only approximately 150 words with 10–13 metaphors, the participants did spot the presence of the metaphorical expressions and several commented on them and reflected on the appropriate translation strategy. Five out of ten participants commented on their deliberations as to whether to transfer the metaphorical image or not.

Discussion

In this type of research, it is difficult to decide whether to opt for a carefully controlled experiment or an experiment with high ecological validity without being able to control for a large number of variables, resulting in findings which may perhaps more easily be questioned. However, the overriding aim of this project was to gain insights into the cognitive processes of a professional translator when he or she is working with a text containing metaphors. This ambition could not be fulfilled using carefully constructed text with constructed metaphors, perhaps even presented in individual sentences. Of course, the experiment reported in this paper does not entirely simulate a natural translation task, as the experimenter was sitting in the same room and the participants were requested not to move their heads too much or to use any translation aids. However, it is still the best option until eye-tracking equipment has become a standard feature in every monitor in every office.

Another consequence of using authentic text is that, in the case of the experimental texts reported on in this study, all the metaphors in each text belong to the same semantic domain, i.e. there is cohesion between the metaphors, which could result in some form of metaphor priming effect. In other words, this could mean that subsequent linguistic metaphors from a semantic domain already encountered in preceding metaphors would be processed faster, resulting in shorter gaze times. This claim has not been investigated in this study but will be analysed at a later stage.

Another issue to consider is the lack of information about the translation production process. For this we need to analyse the key-logging data, which is the next step in the project. The problem with the eye-tracking data is that the fixations relate to both the comprehension and production processes and it is impossible to identify with any level of certainty the percentage of the gaze time which should be ascribed to either process. The key-logging data will be able to provide insight into the production process alone.

A third and equally relevant issue relates to the measure of means. The current data reveal marked individual differences in both the translation strategies chosen and gaze times. There seems to be no obvious link between the translators' everyday field of expertise and the translation strategy preferred in the experimental texts. However, it should be noted that in Text 1, two participants preferred the strategy M–P whereas the remaining participants overwhelmingly applied the translation strategy of M–M. Interestingly, one of these two participants primarily translates literature and may therefore be more familiar with the translation of metaphors, and the second participant teaches classes on working with texts and translation strategies. It is very likely that these two participants would be more aware of the benefits and disadvantages of each individual translation strategy than the rest of the participants, who may have simply chosen the strategy of M–M as the default strategy without further consideration.

Obviously, these individual differences may result in misleading findings when a mean is used as a measure, and for this reason it is necessary to study a higher number of participants – perhaps twice as many. However, as it is the aim of this study to be able to generalize about the cognitive processes taking place in a metaphor translation task, a measure of the mean value rather than individual analysis seems preferable. It may of course be that these marked individual variations are in fact a part of the pattern of the cognitive process of metaphor translation and perhaps also of translation in general.

Conclusion

There seems to be some indication that the cognitive effort invested in the translation of a metaphor is in fact related both to the frequency and applicability of the metaphorical image in the target language. This tentative claim is based on the apparent correlation between an increase in the percentages of M1–M2 and M–P translation options and an increase in metaphor gaze time in Text 1 relative to Text 2. It is perhaps not surprising that paraphrasing

(M–P) seems to require a higher cognitive effort than direct transfer of the image (M–M). Paraphrasing not only requires a shift from one semantic domain to another – as in the case of M1–M2 – but also a shift from the metaphorical to the literal. This tentative claim requires further study with investigation of gaze times distributed across translation strategies.

Total gaze time was used as the baseline measure as it is the most comprehensive measure in eye-tracking methodology, but fixation duration, number of fixations, and regressions may also contribute important information to the type of research reported in the project and will be included in future analyses.

Triangulation of the research data can be achieved by using both qualitative and quantitative approaches and comparing the results of the two methodologies. Qualitatively, we intend to undertake an in-depth analysis of the responses to the interviews and obtain third-party evaluations of the quality of the translations. Quantitatively, not only the data from the eye tracking but also that of the key-logging applications will be analysed. Cued retrospection by the participants in which they are presented with the eye-tracking recordings is likely to provide even more insightful responses than the ones gained so far, as the participants very quickly forget all but the major deliberations made during the translation. As this is a very time-consuming process, it will probably only be feasible with a few of the participants.

The evaluation of the translations themselves by a third party will provide an interesting insight into which of the chosen translation options is deemed most appropriate for the target text. It is possible that the participants' preferred strategy of direct transfer of the metaphorical image (M–M) is in fact also assessed as the most suitable solution, but it is also possible that paraphrasing (M–P) is regarded as the optimal strategy when the source text metaphor is not found to be suitable in the target language. Evaluation of a translation will always be subjective, at least to some degree, but one of the main criteria of a good translation is that it should not read as a translation. It therefore follows that a metaphor which does not seem to be a natural part of the target language and culture will stand out and should be paraphrased instead.

The difference in the semantic domains of the two experimental texts and the related differences in the preferred translation strategies certainly seem to indicate that any generalizations about the cognitive processes in metaphor translation must take into account both the context and the frequency of the semantic domain used metaphorically in the target language. Results such as these would not have emerged in a standard type of experiment with isolated constructed sentences out of context. This paper has sought to argue the value of naturalistic experiments with high ecological validity, as well as to take a step in the direction of a deeper understanding of a translator's cognitive processes in the translation of metaphors. But, more importantly, this research may also contribute to a better understanding of a translator's more general cognitive processes.

References

Andersen, M.S. (2004), *Metaforkompetence – en empirisk undersøgelse af semi-professionelle oversætteres metaforviden* [Metaphor competence – an empirical study of semi-professional translators' metaphor knowledge]. Copenhagen: Copenhagen Working Papers in LSP.

Black, M. (1981), *Models and Metaphors – Studies in Language and Philosophy.* 7th edn. New York: Cornell University Press.

Cienki, A. and C. Müller (2008), 'Metaphor, gesture, and thought'. In R.W. Gibbs (ed.), *The Cambridge Handbook of Metaphor and Thought.* New York: Cambridge University Press. pp. 483–501.

Cristofoli, M., G. Dyrberg and L. Stage (1998), 'Metaphor, Meaning and Translation'. *Hermes – Journal of Linguistics* 20. Aarhus: Det Erhvervssproglige Fakultet, Handelshøjskolen i Århus. 165–179.

Croft, W. and D.A. Cruse (2004), *Cognitive Linguistics.* Cambridge: Cambridge University Press.

Deignan, A. (2005), *Metaphor and Corpus Linguistics. Vol. 6: Converging Evidence in Language and Communication Research.* Amsterdam: John Benjamins.

Dobrzynska, T. (1995), 'Translating metaphor: problems of meaning'. *Journal of Pragmatics* 24 (6), 597–603.

Frenck-Mestre, C. (2005), 'Eye-movement recording as a tool for studying syntactic processing in a second language: a review of methodologies and experimental findings'. *Second Language Research* 21 (2), 175–198.

Gerrig, R.J. (1989), 'Empirical constraints on computational theories of metaphor: Comments on Indurkhya'. *Cognitive Science: A Multidisciplinary Journal 13 (2),* 235–241.

Gibbs, R. W. Jr. (1993), 'Why idioms are not dead metaphors'. In C. Cacciari and P. Tabossi (eds), *Idioms: Processing, Structure, and Interpretation.* Hillsdale: Lawrence Erlbaum Associates. pp. 57–78.

Gibbs, R.W. Jr. and G.J. Steen (1999), *Metaphor in Cognitive Linguistics – Selected papers from the fifth international cognitive linguistics conference, Amsterdam, July 1997.* Amsterdam: John Benjamins.

Glucksberg, S. (2001), 'Understanding figurative language – from metaphors to idioms'. *Oxford Psychology Series* 36. New York: Oxford University Press.

Inhoff, A.W., S.D. Lima and P.J. Carroll (1984), 'Contextual effects on metaphor comprehension in reading'. *Memory and Cognition* 12 (6), 558–567.

Jakobsen, A.L. and L. Schou (1999), 'Translog documentation'. In G. Hansen (ed.), *Probing the Process in Translation. Methods and results*. Copenhagen: Samfundslitteratur. pp. 151–186.

Jakobsen, A.L., K.T.H. Jensen and I.M. Mees (2007), 'Comparing modalities: Idioms as a case in point'. In F. Pöchhacker, A L. Jakobsen and I. M. Mees (eds), *Interpreting Studies and Beyond. A Tribute to Miriam Shlesinger*. Copenhagen: Samfundslitteratur Press. pp. 217–249.

Jakobsen, A.L. and K.T.H. Jensen (2008), 'Eye movement behaviour across four different types of reading task'. In S. Göpferich, A.L. Jakobsen and I.M. Mees (eds), *Looking at Eyes. Eye-Tracking Studies of Reading and Translation Processing*. Copenhagen: Samfundslitteratur. pp. 103–124.

Jensen, C. (2008), 'Assessing eye-tracking accuracy in translation studies'. In S. Göpferich, A.L. Jakobsen and I.M. Mees (eds), *Looking at Eyes. Eye-Tracking Studies of Reading and Translation Processing*. Copenhagen: Samfundslitteratur. pp. 157–174.

Just, M.A. and P.A. Carpenter (1980), 'A theory of reading: from eye fixations to comprehension'. *Psychological Review* 87, 329–354.

Lai, V. T., T. Curran and L. Menn (2007), 'The comprehension of conventional and novel metaphors: an ERP Study'. Poster presented at the 13th Annual Conference on Architectures and Mechanisms for Language Processing, Turku, Finland 24–27 August 2007.

Lakoff, G. and M. Johnson (1980), *Metaphors We Live By*. Chicago: University of Chicago Press.

—— (1999), *Philosophy in the Flesh*. New York: Basic Books.

Rayner, K. and S. Sereno (1994), 'Eye movements in reading'. In M.A. Gernsbacher (ed.), *Handbook of Psycholinguistics*. San Diego: Academic Press Inc. pp. 57–81.

Rayner, K. (1998), 'Eye movements in reading and information processing: 20 years of research'. *Psychological Bulletin* 124 (3), 372–422.

Steen, G.J. (1994), *Understanding Metaphor in Literature: An Empirical Approach*. New York: Longman.

Tirkkonen-Condit, S. (2002), 'Metaphoric expressions in translation processes'. *Across Languages and Cultures* 3 (1), 101–116.

www.editcentral.com [accessed 16 June 2009 from http://www.editcentral.com].

Appendix 1

Text 1

Every time you look around, it seems like companies are trying to hook up. The proposed marriage of Air France-KLM and Delta Air Lines is the latest to make the rounds. But the suitors must first gain the approval of regulators, who are sure to supervise the courtship with care because of the size of the dowry. The path from the altar is strewn with failed corporate marriages. Still, the matchmaking continues apace. British Airways and Spanish carrier Iberia have been wooing one another for the better part of a year. In March, pharmaceutical giants Merck and Plough-Schering announced their intention to wed. Fiat has ambitious plans to merge with Chrysler and the European operations of General Motors to spin off into a new car company. And the on-again, off-again plans of Porsche and Volkswagen to tie the knot have been dominating the business pages for months.

Appendix 2

Text 2

The Bank of England's home in Threadneedle Street may not look like a hospital but for the past few months it has been acting like one. As the economic downturn became a full-blown collapse late last year, the central bank's senior consultants donned their white coats and got to work. First they put their scalpel to interest rates, slicing them from 5% in early October to an all-time low of 0.5% in March. Not content with that, they switched at once from scalpel to syringe and started to inject money into the economy by buying assets with freshly created central-bank money. As with the preceding rate cuts, the new treatment has been administered in big doses. However, a swift return to economic health is highly unlikely after the financial and economic convulsions of the past two years. A prolonged convalescence is the best that can be expected.

Distribution of Attention Between Source Text and Target Text During Translation[1]

Kristian T.H. Jensen

Introduction

Cognitive translation processes have traditionally been studied using methods such as think-aloud protocols, retrospection and, more recently, key logging. Eye tracking, which is a relatively new method of tapping into the indirectly observable processes that take place during translation, provides the experimenter with information that was previously inaccessible. We are now, with reasonable accuracy, able to detect which word a translator is gazing at, at what time. By combining key logging and eye tracking we can obtain more detailed translation process data than if we were to apply only one technology. Key logging has proved to be a very useful means of investigating *production* processes in translation (e.g. Hansen 1999, Dragsted 2004, Jakobsen 2005).

However, in order to obtain stronger evidence of comprehension processes, key logging needs to be supplemented with eye tracking. This is a very useful tool for examining both comprehension and production processes in translation (e.g. Dragsted and Hansen 2008, Jakobsen and Jensen 2008, O'Brien 2009), though it is obviously ineffectual when the translator looks away from the monitor. In the experiment described below, it was anticipated that by combining eye tracking and key logging we would overcome this limitation in eye tracking.

In our study, key logging and eye tracking have been employed to investigate source text (ST) and target text (TT) attention during translation from L2 English into L1 Danish. More specifically, the aim is to explore the distribution of attention and the shifts in attention between ST and TT throughout a translation task. Attention that is relevant to the translation task manifests itself when gaze activity in the ST and TT areas of the monitor is registered or when typing takes place. The shifts in attention tell us (1) how many attentional segments a translator processes in a given task, and they give us information about (2) the duration of these attentional segments. The evidence underlying an attentional segment is the activity recorded between two shifts. The activity is either ST reading, TT reading/production, or overlapping activity. (How this was coded is explained below in the section on data collection, coding and analysis.) For instance, an ST attentional segment may start when ST reading begins and ends when ST reading ends and another type of activity begins. A secondary aim of the experiment is to find out if translation is carried out in a serial manner or in a parallel manner (e.g. Seleskovitch 1976, Grainger 1993, De Groot 1997, Ruiz *et al.* 2007). Put differently, does TT production take place only when the meaning of an ST segment has been interpreted, or do TT production and ST interpretation occur simultaneously? The translations of a compound expression by one student and one professional translator are analysed later to exemplify how shifts in attention can help explain differences in level of expertise.

Background

Attention during translation

Translation involves three main cognitive processes: ST comprehension, TT production, and switching between two linguistic codes (e.g. Gile 1995, Ruiz *et al.* 2007). ST comprehension involves constructing a mental representation of the source language (SL) message; TT production involves formulating a target language (TL) representation of the mental representation of the SL message; switching codes, or coordination (Dragsted and Hansen 2008), relates to the task of coordinating SL comprehension and TL production as efficiently as possible.

In psychological research, attention is considered to be the select allocation of cognitive processing resources (Anderson 2000: 47). Thus we choose where to direct our attention and we choose to ignore other things. For instance, motivated by a desire to produce a qualitatively acceptable translation within a reasonable time frame, translators would have to decide where to allocate their attentional resources, since the efforts of ST comprehension, TT production and switching codes all compete for attention. Sharmin *et al.* (2008) observed that the TT very systematically received significantly longer fixations than the ST. Based on their study, it could be speculated that translators allocate more attention to the TT than to the ST.

In the analyses of the attentional segments identified in the process data from translated texts below, we will try to determine if there is a relationship between distribution of attention, the number of segments and the duration of attentional segments across three independent variables: level of expertise (Group), level of text complexity (TextType), and the type of segment (SegmentType, either ST, TT or parallel attention (PA), cf. below) to which attention is being paid.

The attentional segments discussed throughout this paper are not to be confused with the type of segments that have been identified as reflecting cognitive segmentation in translation (e.g. Jakobsen 1998, Dragsted 2004, O'Brien 2006), where the boundaries of segments are generally defined by pauses in typing, although recent research using eye tracking calls for a redefinition (Dragsted and Hansen 2008: 23). In the study reported here, the boundaries of attentional segments are defined by the attentional shifts (e.g. from an ST segment to a TT segment and back) that precede and succeed every attentional segment. What type of attentional segment we are dealing with is therefore defined by what is attended to between two attentional shifts (i.e. the ST, TT or both). For instance, we are dealing with an ST segment if uninterrupted visual attention to the ST area of the monitor takes place.

Three views of the translation process

As Ruiz *et al.* point out, there is some disagreement between researchers as to how comprehension and production are coordinated in the translation process (2007: 490). The vertical translation view proposes that translation output is the product of a serial translation process. The ST must be fully comprehended before any TT production can take place, i.e. TT production occurs only when comprehension of the ST message has been completed (De Groot 1997: 30). In contrast, the horizontal translation view (i.e. the parallel view) maintains that ST comprehension and TT production occur in parallel, in the sense that linguistic features of the source language (SL) are instantly replaced in the TT (ibid.). Finally, a third hybrid view proposes that the translation process involves both vertical and horizontal elements (Ruiz *et al.* 2007: 490).

Seleskovitch (1976: 97) observes that interpreters process segments in parallel (particularly in simultaneous interpreting), though she makes no similar claims for translators. However in a study on translation processing, Ruiz *et al.* (2007: 491) found that when reading for translation, experienced translators activate lexical entries in the TT and process ST meaning simultaneously. There is also evidence to suggest that bilinguals activate their two languages in parallel during language comprehension when processing visual input (e.g. Grainger 1993).

Indicators of attention

(a) Visual attention

Several researchers have studied the relationship between attention and eye movements. Just and Carpenter formulated the 'eye-mind hypothesis', which assumes that: 'there is no appreciable lag between what is being fixated and what is being processed' (1980: 331). In his comprehensive review of eye-tracking research, Rayner (1998: 374) observes that psychological research has identified a strong connection between the location of the eye's fixation and cognitive effort (e.g. Posner 1980, Anderson 2000). Anderson points out that 'we are attending to that part of the visual field which we are fixating' (2000: 81). In line with these observations and with previous translation research employing eye-tracking technology (e.g. Pavlović and Jensen 2009), we assume that observable gaze data and key-logging data are indicative of cognitive processes.

Computation of gaze duration has generally taken account only of fixation durations, and not saccade[2] durations (Rayner 1998: 378). However, research has shown that cognitive processing continues during saccades and that these, therefore, should be included in the computation of gaze duration (ibid.). Thus, following Rayner's recommendations, our measurement of visual attention is based on both fixations and saccades.

(b) Keyboard activity

Typing is a production-oriented task. Therefore we assume that keyboard activity relates to the TT rather than to the ST.

Research questions

To examine the characteristics of attention in translation, some research questions have been formulated:

- How is attention distributed during a translation task?
- How frequently do professional translators and translation students perform attentional shifts during a translation task?
- What is the duration of ST and TT attentional segments in translation?
- To what extent do text complexity and level of expertise affect attention distribution, segment duration and the amount of attentional shifting that takes place?
- To what extent is translation processed serially or in parallel?

Research design and method

Participants

Translation process data from two groups of participants were analysed in this study. The first group consisted of 12 professional translators, who had at least two years of experience as full-time translators translating between English (L2) and Danish (L1). The second group consisted of 12 MA students of translation specializing in translation between English (L2) and Danish (L1). None of the participants were bilingual. Data from an additional four participants (three professionals and one student) were discarded due to poor eye-tracking data quality (see section on Data collection, coding and analysis below). Participants received a gift certificate for their participation.

Task

The participants were each tasked with translating one warm-up text and three experimental texts. Only two of these (Text A and Text B) were analysed for the present paper. The first text presented to each participant was the warm-up text. This was followed by the three experimental texts. The sequence in which these were given was semi-randomized so that a third of the total number of participants translated 'Text A' as their first text, a third 'Text B' and a third 'Text C'. The participants were asked to produce translations that would satisfy their usual quality criteria. No offline translation aids were made available as this would result in less analysable eye-tracking data as the participants look away from the monitor. Similarly, no online translation aids were made available since the data would partially reflect gaze activity that does not involve ST or TT reading. This would considerably complicate the analysis of the eye-tracking data.

Texts

The two experimental texts (A, B), from which data were analysed in this paper, were articles on current topics that appeared in British newspapers in 2008. Text A is from *The Independent* and is about a hospital nurse who had been poisoning elderly patients; Text B is from the *The Times* and is about the crisis in Darfur and China's Africa policy (see Appendix A). The experimental texts are rather short (Text A: 837 characters, Text B: 856 characters). Texts longer than this would require that the participants scroll the ST window when reading. Since the eye-tracking analysis software relies on a static image of the ST being displayed at the same location throughout the translation session, longer texts were deemed impractical for this type of experiment.

Both articles were manipulated with two aims in mind. First, they had to be comparable both in terms of the total character length and the length of their headlines to create a uniform basis for comparison. Second, since the aim was to investigate differences in the distribution of attention and differences in the number and duration of attentional segments, the levels of complexity of Texts A and Text B were made to vary.

The levels of complexity of the experimental texts were established using three quantitative indicators (Jensen 2009): readability indices, calculations of word frequency, and calculations of the number of occurrences of non-literal expressions, i.e. idioms, metaphors, and metonyms. All indices[3] applied to test the levels of readability showed an increase in the level of complexity from A to B. The U.S. grade level indices revealed that 7.8 years of schooling were needed to comprehend successfully Text A, while 17.3 years of schooling were needed to comprehend successfully Text B. With regard to our second parameter, word frequency, Text A was found to contain the fewest number of low-frequency words[4] (10.7 per cent), while Text B contained 28.1 per cent low-frequency words. Our third criterion, the number of non-literal expressions, also showed an increase in the level of complexity, Text A containing one non-literal expression as against 15 non-literal expressions in Text B.

The level of difficulty of a text may prove problematic to gauge, and the experience of a text's level of difficulty may be very individual. A complex text is not necessarily difficult to translate – this depends very much on the routines, skills and specialization of the translator (Jensen 2009: 62–63). However, since a complex text is often experienced as a difficult text, these relatively crude measures can nevertheless be employed. Since Text B was more complex than Text A by all the objective criteria, we have assumed that Text B is more difficult to translate.

Data collection, coding and analysis

Two streams of translation process data were collected. Eye-tracking data were gathered with Tobii's 1750 eye tracker and Tobii's data collection/analysis software Clearview (www.tobii.se). Key-logging data were obtained using the eye tracker/Clearview and the Translog software (Jakobsen and Schou 1999). In this paper, only eye-tracking and key-logging data from Tobii's 1750 eye tracker/Clearview have been analysed.

During data collection, Translog was used to display the text. The monitor was divided into two main areas: the upper part displayed the experimental texts (i.e. ST window) and the participants typed their translations in the lower part (i.e. TT window).

The 1750 eye tracker runs at 50 Hz, which means that it records gaze activity every 20 milliseconds. Such a resolution was considered high enough for the purposes of this study. The spatial resolution of the 1750 eye tracker is accurate to 0.5 of a degree, which corresponds to up to 1 cm of inaccuracy. Other types of eye trackers (such as the Eye Link www.sr-research.com) work at higher temporal and spatial resolutions. However, often they require that the position of the participant's head is fixed or that the equipment is head-mounted, which is undesirable in a naturalistic experiment such as this.

Microsoft Excel was used to analyse the raw data log files exported from the Tobii 1750 analysis software Clearview. In the log files, eye data and key data are aligned in individual (vertical) columns. For each (horizontal) sample row, the position of the eye (ST area of the monitor, TT area of the monitor, or outside the ST/TT areas of the monitor) was compared to potential key data found in adjacent rows in the key data column. If ST eye data were found but no typing took place, we coded this as an ST attentional segment. If TT eye data were registered but no typing took place, we coded this as a TT attentional segment. If no eye data were recorded but typing took place, we coded this as a TT attentional segment. If ST eye data and key data coincided in time, we coded such a segment as an instance of parallel attention (PA). Finally, if no eye data and no key data were observed, this was registered as 'no data'. In summary, the data may indicate three different types of attention throughout a translation task: ST attention, TT attention, and parallel attention. In addition there may be 'no data'.

The quality of the eye-tracking data is sensitive to a number of external factors, including eye colour, participants who use optical aids, poor lighting, participants' distance from the monitor, etc. (O'Brien 2009). To minimize the extent of some of these potentially error-inducing factors, various measures were taken: curtains were drawn to reduce the amount of natural light; the eye tracker was placed on a separate table with which the participants had no direct contact in order to minimize the risk of tremors; the participants sat in a fixed chair, so that they would not move about and potentially increase the distance to the monitor (they were seated between 55 cm and 65 cm from the eye tracker).

Despite these precautions, we still risked obtaining unreliable data, which could skew the results, and consequently a quality assessment was conducted. Based on Rayner and Sereno's (1994: 58) observation that the mean fixation duration in reading is 200 to 250 ms, a minimum fixation duration threshold of 175 ms was set. If participants' mean fixation durations were lower than this, their data were discarded. This turned out to be the case with three professionals and one student.

Results and Discussion

Statistical methods

Two separate statistical analyses were performed. First, we tested to what extent the *number of segments* was affected by our three independent variables Group (Professionals/Students), TextType (Text A/Text B), and SegmentType (ST segments/TT segments/PA segments). Subsequently, we tested to what extent *attentional segment duration* was affected by Group, TextType, and SegmentType. Three-way analyses of variance (ANOVAs) were carried out.

Distribution of attention

The mean task time for the professional translators was 353.3 seconds for Text A, and 404.1 seconds for Text B. For both texts, students spent more time

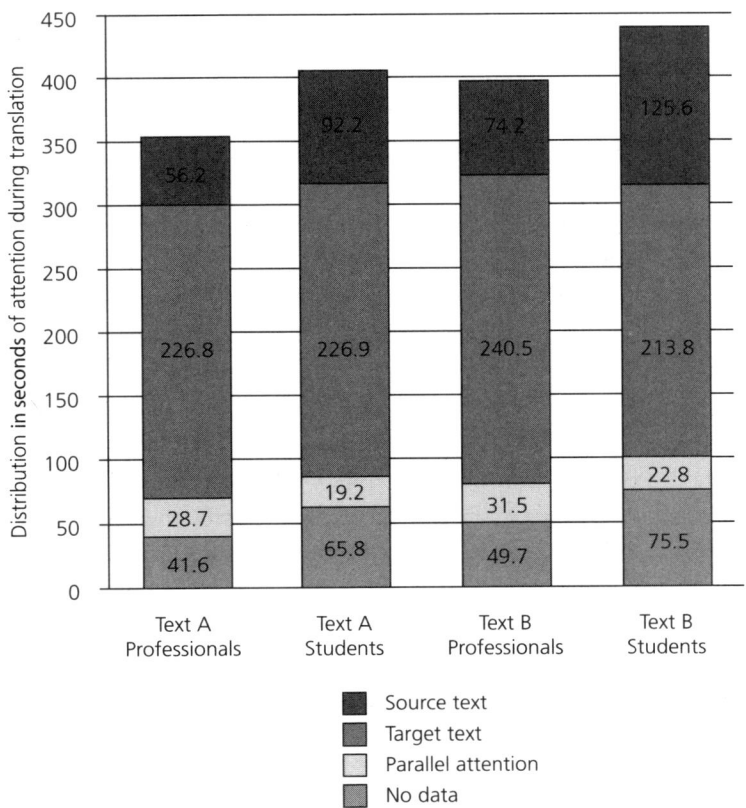

Figure 1 Distribution of attention during translation in seconds

than professional translators carrying out the task: 395.9 seconds and 437.7 seconds for Text A and Text B respectively. Figure 1 illustrates the distribution of attention in absolute mean values.

For both students and professionals, most attention is directed to the TT during the translation of both texts; the means ranged from 213.8 seconds to 240.5 seconds. Proportionately less attention is directed to the ST; the means ranged from 56.2 seconds to 125.6 seconds. Parallel attention is found for both groups in both texts, mean values ranging from 19.2 seconds to 31.5 seconds, corresponding to between 5 per cent and 8 per cent of the total task time. Finally, 'no data' is registered during parts of the translations, mean values ranging from 41.6 seconds to 75.5 seconds.

Mean values are reported in the following comparisons. For both groups, text complexity seems to affect the distribution of attention. For professionals, Text A involves less ST attention than Text B, i.e. 56.2 seconds vs. 74.2 seconds respectively. This seems to be the case also for students, where ST attention amounts to 92.2 and 125.6 seconds for Text A and Text B respectively. With respect to TT attention, Text A involves less attention than Text B for professionals (226.8 seconds and 240.5 seconds, respectively) while, surprisingly, for students, Text A requires more attention than Text B, i.e. 226.9 seconds vs. 213.8 seconds, respectively. There seems to be very little difference between the amount of parallel attention registered during the translation of Texts A and B for both professionals and students (28.7 seconds ~ 31.5 seconds, for professionals; 19.2 seconds ~ 22.8 seconds, for students). Parallel attention during translation will be examined more closely below.

The level of expertise also affects the distribution of attention. For both texts, professional translators allocate less attention to the ST than students. There is no difference, however, between professionals' and students' TT attention during the translation of Text A (226.8 seconds and 226.9 seconds), while professionals direct considerably more attention to the Text B TT than do students, i.e. 240.5 seconds and 213.8 seconds, respectively. For both texts, more parallel attention is observed for professionals than for students (28.7 seconds ~ 31.5 seconds and 19.2 seconds ~ 22.8 seconds, respectively).

Attentional shifts and number of segments

Assuming that the transition from one type of attentional segment to another represents a shift in attentional focus, we are able to calculate the number of times a participant shifts his or her attention during a translation task.

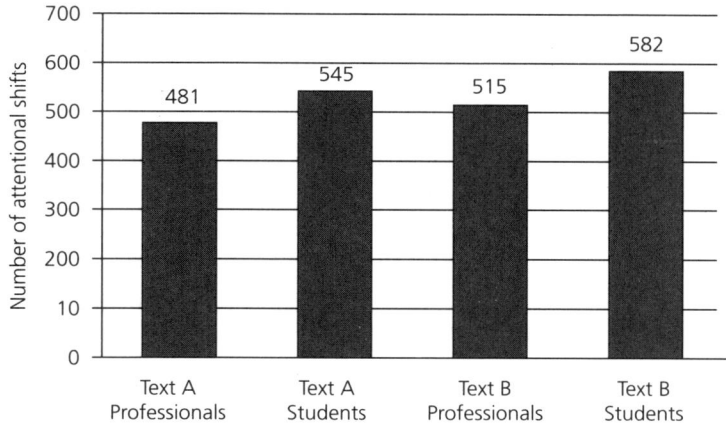

Figure 2 Mean number of attentional shifts

In Figure 2, the mean numbers of transitions between ST segments, TT segments, PA segments and 'no data' blocks have been calculated across groups and texts.

For both texts, students make a higher number of attentional shifts than professional translators (Text A: 13.3 per cent more shifts; Text B: 13.0 per

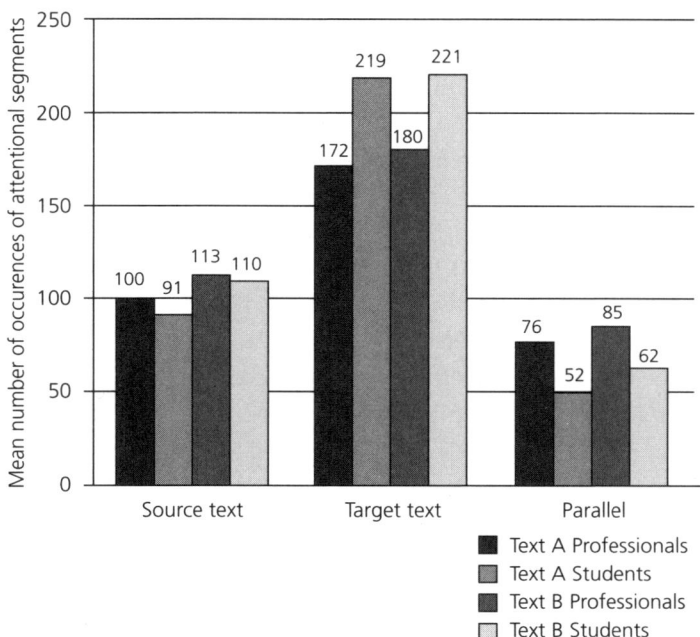

Figure 3 Mean number of occurrences of each type of attentional segment[5]

cent more shifts). Text complexity also seems to affect the number of attentional shifts (professionals: 7.1 per cent more shifts in Text B than in Text A; students: 6.8 per cent more shifts in Text B than in Text A). The amount of attentional shifting is closely connected to the numbers of each type of attentional segments. Statistical analyses of the numbers of occurrences of each type of segment are carried out below.

Each attentional shift represents a transition from one attentional segment (or in some cases from a 'no data' block) to another. In Figure 3, the mean numbers of occurrences for each type of attentional segment are presented for professionals and students.

For both groups and both texts, the number of TT attentional segments is higher than the number of ST segments. For professionals, there are 72 per cent more TT segments than ST segments in Text A. In Text B, the difference is lower, with 59 per cent more TT than ST segments. For students, the same pattern emerges, although the difference is greater: in Text A there are 141 per cent more TT segments than ST segments, and in Text B the difference is 101 per cent more TT than ST segments. In addition to ST and TT segments, we can also observe segments during which simultaneous (or parallel) ST and TT attention occurs. PA segments occur less frequently than ST and TT attention (professional translators, Text A: 76 segments, Text B: 85 segments; students: Text A: 52 segments, Text B: 62 segments). In a three-way ANOVA, the difference between the number of occurrences of ST, TT and PA segments was highly significant (F = 60.32, p< 0.0001). Tukey's post hoc tests showed that all the pairwise differences between ST, TT and PA segments were significant.

Additionally, there was a significant interaction between SegmentType and Group (F = 4.15, p = 0.02). However, in a Tukey post-hoc test, the group differences did not occur between segments of the same type; in other words, there were no differences between students and professionals for any of the three segment types. Rather, the interaction seems driven by relatively trivial differences across both group and segment type, e.g. between student TT and professional PA.

Despite the significantly lower number of PA segments, the data indicate that parallel processing does occur to some extent in the sense that comprehension and production efforts seem to be activated simultaneously. Thus in contrast to the vertical translation view, the data would support the suggestion that translation is not exclusively a serial task. This will be addressed more closely in the section on Attentional segment duration below.

It is not possible to make a quantitative estimate of the amount of effort involved in each segment on the basis of a segment count only. Segment counts are insensitive to the duration of the individual segments, and therefore mean segment duration values need to be included in the analysis.

Attentional segment duration

In Figure 4, the mean duration values for each type of segment are presented across groups and texts.

A three-way analysis of variance (ANOVA) was carried out to test to what extent attentional segment duration was affected by Group, TextType, and SegmentType. The ANOVA showed a significant main effect of segment type

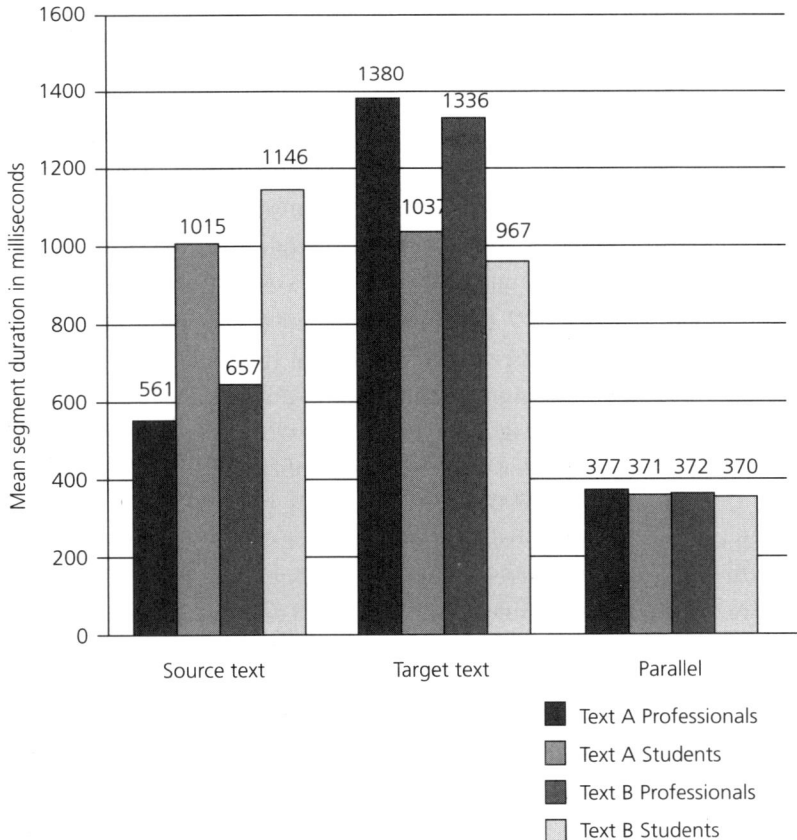

Figure 4 Mean segment duration for each type of segment[6]

(F = 473.78, p< 0.0001). A Tukey HSD (Honestly Significant Differences) post-hoc test showed that all pairwise differences between SegmentType were highly significant (p's< 0.0001). The ANOVA also showed a significant main effect of Group, in that the professionals' segment durations are shorter than the students' (F = 4.59, p = 0.03). There was no significant main effect of TextType.

The ANOVA also showed two significant interactions. Firstly there was an interaction between SegmentType and Group (F = 163.87, p =<0.0001). All post-hoc pairwise comparisons were significant with two exceptions: There was no difference for parallel segments between students and professionals (p > 0.9), as is also clear from Figure 4. There was also no difference between ST and TT segments for the students (p = 0.07). The professional translators' TT segments are significantly longer than their ST segments: Text A: 146 per cent longer; Text B: 103.3 per cent longer (p< 0.0001). The students' Text A TT segments are slightly longer than their ST segments (2.2 per cent longer). However, the students' Text B TT segments are somewhat *shorter* than their ST segments (18.5 per cent shorter). Differences in the students' ST and TT segment durations do not reach significance (p < 0.0709).

The other significant interaction in the duration ANOVA was between SegmentType and TextType (F = 5.44, p = 0.004). Here, post-hoc tests showed that Texts A and B differed in the duration of ST segments (p = 0.015), while the two texts did not differ for parallel attention segments (p > 0.9) or TT segments (p > 0.8). Within each text, the pairwise differences between all segment types were highly significant (p< 0.0001).

One explanation for the significantly shorter duration of the professional translators' ST segments might be that they are able to distribute their attention between the ST and the TT more efficiently. It is, for instance, possible that they only read those ST words or phrases that relate to the rendering of a particular translation unit and are thus able to allocate more time to the TT segments, thereby perhaps enabling them to produce higher-quality translations. This assumption would of course have to be tested by having their translation products evaluated. Students, on the other hand, would appear to translate less efficiently. They allocate considerably more time to each ST segment, presumably either reading more words than necessary to translate the ST segment, or reading the same word multiple times. These findings correspond well with those of Sharmin *et al.*, who found that students struggle more with L2 ST comprehension than professionals (2008: 48).

The professional translators' and students' PA segments, for both Texts A and B, are of similar duration ($+/-7$ ms). Tukey's HSD test for post-hoc comparison was performed to analyse differences in segment duration across groups and text types. No significant differences were found for either group ($p > 0.9$) or text type ($p > 0.9$).

One explanation for these strikingly similar PA segment duration values could be that there is a limitation on cognitive processing. The uniform mean duration values could indicate that there is a universal parallel processing constant that manifests itself over time. Thus the participants may only have a limited amount of parallel processing capacity.

Whether parallel attention takes place during *other* parts of the translation process is difficult to measure with the present data, since explicit manifestation of parallel attention in this paper requires evidence of typing. It certainly cannot be ruled out that comprehension and production may be activated simultaneously during reading of the ST, in which the translator considers various translation options. Similarly, we may see false examples of parallel processing. Short typing activity segments (i.e. < 180 ms) may be observed as occurring simultaneously with ST reading. Since typing is expected to occur with a delay of at least 180 ms,[7] we risk registering parts of the translation process as parallel when in fact they are not, and we risk not capturing parallel processing when there in fact is some.

PA segments are significantly shorter than the ST and TT segments (p, 0.0001). This does not come as a surprise since parallel processing cannot take place without considerable cost (Gazzaniga *et al.* 2002: 247–252), and the translator will presumably not have sufficient cognitive resources to engage a great deal in this type of processing.

Attentional shifts at word level

Above, we have examined the distribution of attention, how frequently attention shifts, and how many ST, TT, and PA segments occur in particular translation tasks. We have also examined the duration of the segments based on segment type, text type, and level of translator expertise. Thus, the analyses and discussion have so far focused mainly on overall trends and patterns. In this section, we will examine more closely what takes place during translation at word level. The analyses are limited to translations by two random participants (one student and one professional) of the compound expression *Police officer*, which is found in Text A. Table 1 shows attentional shifts for the student.

The student chooses to translate 'Police officer' as 'Politikommisær', which would back translate into 'Police superintendent'. The translation is somewhat more explicit than the context allows. It takes around 8 seconds, during which time the student makes a total of 15 shifts between ST and TT, or manifests parallel attention. In addition, four 'no data' blocks are observed.

During Segment 1 (S1), which is the longest attentional segment in the extract, it is likely that the participant reads the ST word and starts constructing a meaning hypothesis which she tests for plausibility (Gile 1995: 103). In S2, no eye or key activity is registered, but various translation options are probably being evaluated. In S3, we assume that a meaning hypothesis has been partially constructed, which is realized when she types the first part of

Table 1 Extract showing attentional shifts during the student translation of the expression 'Police officer'. (Colour codes: Grey: ST segment; dark grey: TT segment, white: PA segment, light grey: 'no data' block.)

KEY	TYPE	DURATION	END	START	SEGMENT
	ST	1774 ms	1774 ms	0 ms	1
	No data	618 ms	2392 ms	1774 ms	2
Politi	TT	1077 ms	3469 ms	2392 ms	3
	ST	279 ms	3748 ms	3469 ms	4
	TT	399 ms	4147 ms	3748 ms	5
	ST	738 ms	4885 ms	4147 ms	6
	TT	618 ms	5503 ms	4885 ms	7
	No data	259 ms	5762 ms	5503 ms	8
kommi	TT	877 ms	6639 ms	5762 ms	9
	No data	60 ms	6699	6639 ms	10
s	TT	199 ms	6898 ms	6699 ms	11
	No data	200 ms	7098 ms	6898 ms	12
æ	TT	239 ms	7337 ms	7098 ms	13
r	Parallel	178 ms	7515 ms	7337 ms	14
	ST	460 ms	7975 ms	7515 ms	15
	TT	219 ms	8194 ms	7975 ms	16
	No data	115 ms	8309 ms	8194 ms	17
(...)	ST	(...)	(...)	8309 ms	18

the compound, i.e. 'Politi' (English: 'Police'). Interestingly, between S4 and S7, which last 1.2 seconds, attention shifts between ST and TT three times. No typing takes place during this interval, presumably because the participant is considering how to translate the second part of the compound, 'officer'. In S8, no eye or key activity is registered, but since TT activity involving typing takes place in S9, the participant is most likely looking at the keyboard to locate the 'k'-key. From S9 to S13, spanning 1.6 seconds, she nearly completes typing the translation of the second part of the compound. Although attention shifts between TT and 'no data' blocks four times, it is reasonable to assume that TT processing is taking place in all five segments. The two 'no data' blocks (S10, S12) are on the face of it triggered by the participant's poor touch-typing skills as she is locating the 's' and 'æ'-keys, respectively. In S14, she is engaged in parallel processing in the sense that she is both typing and looking at the ST simultaneously. In S15, she rereads the ST word 'Police officer', and in S16 she proofreads her translation. In S17, no data are registered, and in S18, ST processing of the next word (Chris) begins.

Table 2 Extract showing attentional shifts during the professional translator's translation of the expression 'Police officer'.

SEGMENT	1	2	3	(4)
Start	0 ms	916 ms	1295 ms	4439 ms
End	916 ms	1295 ms	4439 ms	(…)
Duration	916 ms	379 ms	3144 ms	(…)
Type	ST	Parallel	TT	ST
Key		P	olitibetjent	

Table 2 is an extract from a professional translator's rendering of the same expression. He chooses to translate it as 'Politibetjent', which is more neutral than the solution chosen by the student. The translation is completed in approximately 4.5 seconds. During this time, the professional translator makes two attentional shifts from ST to parallel to TT. There are no 'no data' blocks. In S1, which lasts 0.9 seconds, he reads the ST word. In S2, parallel processing takes place in that ST reading and TT output occur simultaneously. In S3, the translation is completed. In S4, ST attention to the next ST word to be translated (Chris) begins.

Comparing the two extracts, we can see that the student spends considerably more time completing her translation and performs far more attentional shifts than the professional translator. The most obvious explanation for these findings is probably related to insecurity. The student starts translating the second part of the compound after nearly 6 seconds, while the professional translator promptly translates the compound in one single segment in less than 4.5 seconds.

The two examples above may help us understand differences between students' and professional translators' translation processes. The applicability of this methodology is obviously not restricted to examining expertise, but could for instance be useful in investigating the processes behind the translation of complex and simple sentences and the translation of low-frequency and high-frequency words.

Conclusion

The aim of this paper has been to investigate how attention is distributed during translation. An additional objective was to study the frequency of shifts in attention and the duration of attentional segments. Finally, we wanted to investigate if translation involves serial processing, parallel processing, or a combination of both.

Eye-tracking and key-logging data from 12 professional translators and 12 students of translation were subjected to analysis. We assumed that ST visual attention indicates ST processing, TT visual attention indicates TT processing, and keyboard attention indicates TT processing. Simultaneous ST and TT attention was seen to be indicative of parallel processing of both ST and TT.

The data showed that in translation by far the most attention was devoted to the TT. This applied to both professional translators and students. Conversely, the ST received proportionally less attention. An equally interesting finding was that manifestations of simultaneous ST and TT attention (i.e. parallel attention) was seen to take place to some degree in both groups. The amount of parallel attention, as reflected in the proportion of explicit PA segments, was 8 per cent for professional translators and 5 per cent for students of the total task time. Thus a mix of parallel and serial processing appears to take place during translation.

Mean segment duration was examined across segment type, group and text type. Professional translators' ST segments were found to be of significantly shorter duration than their TT segments, while students' ST segments and TT segments were found to be approximately equal in length. It was speculated that the difference between professionals and students in this respect might relate to professional translators' efficient and appropriate distribution of attentional resources, in the sense that only words relevant to a particular translation unit receive ST attention. It was further speculated that students, on the other hand, read and reread ST that is not always relevant to the translation of a particular translation unit. In line with other findings, it was hypothesized that students struggle more with ST comprehension than do professionals.

The mean duration of segments in which attention to both ST and TT took place simultaneously (PA segments) were found to be surprisingly uniform. There were no significant differences across groups or text types. We have suggested that the uniform mean durations could be indicative of a cognitive parallel processing constant.

Extracts from two subjects (one professional and one student) translating the same word were compared. The professional translator spent approximately half as much time translating the word 'Police officer' than did the student, and the professional translator performed far fewer attentional shifts than the student. It was suggested that the relative increase in time consumption and the higher number of attentional shifts reflect insecurity on the part of the student. Based on the amount of attentional shifting and the overall task time, the student appears to be far more cautious than the professional, and experiences more difficulty in carrying out the translation. This method for investigating attention and processing during translation could be useful for examining other linguistic features.

The next logical step in order to improve the methodology is to develop a method to map ST and TT content to attentional segments automatically. At present we only know which segments occur when and where. What we do not know is what words are processed during attentional segments. Combining key logging and eye tracking has nevertheless proved to be a very fruitful procedure in terms of registering with high precision when the ST and TT receive attention. By automatically mapping attentional segments to ST/TT content as a next step, we will be able to say more about the sub-processes of translation: e.g. morphological, semantic, syntactic and pragmatic processing.

Notes

1 I thank my colleague Dr. L.W. Balling for carrying out the statistical analyses. I am also very grateful to Dr. I.M. Mees and two anonymous reviewers for many valuable suggestions.

2 Saccades are rapid eye movements that help to reposition the fovea to a new location (Duchowski 2007: 42).

3 U.S. grade level indices: Automated Readability Index (ARI), the Flesch-Kincaid index, the Coleman-Liau index, the Gunning Fog index, and the SMOG index. Non-U.S. grade level indices: Flesch Reading Ease Score index and LIX (Swedish abbreviation for *läsbarhetsindex* (i.e. *readability index*)).

4 Low-frequency words are defined as words that are among the 1,001–10,000 most frequent words (Cobb 2008; Heatley and Nation 1994). High-frequency words are defined as words that are among the 1–1,000 most frequent words.

5 During some parts of the translation process, no eye-tracking or key-logging data were registered ('no data' segments). Presumably, processing in connection with the translation task takes place, but lack of data makes it difficult to identify reliably what type of processing is taking place. The occurrences of 'no data' blocks are as follows: professionals, Text A: 134; professionals Text B: 184; students Text A: 138; students Text B: 192. For the purpose of this paper, no further analyses will be made of the 'no data' blocks.

6 The 'no data' block mean duration values are as follows: professionals, Text A: 311 ms; professionals Text B: 359 ms; students Text A: 357 ms; students Text B: 394.

7 Information based on a paper by G. Pfurtscheller, C. Brunner and R. Grabner presented at the EYE-to-IT workshop 18 September 2006.

References

Anderson, J. (2000), *Cognitive Psychology and its Implications* (5th edn). New York: Worth.

Cobb, T. (2008), Web Vocabprofile [accessed 19 August 2009 from http://www.lextutor.ca/vp/], an adaptation of Heatley & Nation's (1994) *Range*.

De Groot, A.M.B. (1997), 'The cognitive study of translation and interpretation: three approaches'. In H.J. Danks, G.M. Shreve, S.B. Fountain, and M.K. McBeath (eds), *Cognitive Processing in Translation and Interpreting*. Thousand Oaks, CA: Sage. pp. 25–56.

Dragsted, B. (2004), *Segmentation in Translation and Translation Memory Systems: An Empirical Investigation of Cognitive Segmentation and Effects of Integrating a TM-System into the Translation Process*. PhD thesis, Copenhagen Business School. Copenhagen: Samfundslitteratur.

Dragsted, B. and I.G. Hansen (2008), 'Comprehension and production in translation: a pilot study on segmentation and the coordination of reading and writing processes'. In S. Göpferich, A.L. Jakobsen and I.M. Mees (eds), *Looking at Eyes: Eye-Tracking Studies of Reading and Translation Processing*. Copenhagen Studies in Language 36. Copenhagen: Samfundslitteratur. pp. 9–30.

Duchowski, A.T. (2007), *Eye Tracking Methodology: Theory and Practice*. London: Springer.

Gazzaniga, M., R. Ivry, and G. Mangun (2002), *Cognitive Neuroscience: The Biology of the Mind* (2nd edn). New York: W.W. Norton.

Gile, D. (1995), *Basic Concepts and Models for Interpreter and Translator Training*. Amsterdam/Philadelphia: John Benjamins.

Grainger, J. (1993), 'Visual word recognition in bilinguals'. In R. Schreuder and B. Weltens (eds), *The Bilingual Lexicon*. Amsterdam/Philadelphia, John Benjamins. pp. 11–25.

Hansen, G. (1999) (ed.), *Probing the Process in Translation: Methods and Results*. Copenhagen Studies in Language 24. Copenhagen: Samfundslitteratur.

Heatley, A. and P. Nation (1994), *Range*. Victoria University of Wellington, NZ. [Computer program, available at http://www.vuw.ac.nz/lals/].

Jakobsen, A.L. (1998), 'Logging time delay in translation'. In G. Hansen (ed.), *LSP Texts and the Process of Translation*. Copenhagen Working Papers 1. pp. 71–101.

Jakobsen, A.L. and L. Schou (1999), 'Translog Documentation Version 1.0.' In G. Hansen (ed.), *Probing the Process in Translation: Methods and Results*. Copenhagen Studies in Language 24. Copenhagen: Samfundslitteratur. pp. 9–20.

Jakobsen, A.L. (2005), 'Investigating expert translators' processing knowledge'. In H.V. Dam, J. Engberg, H. Gerzymisch-Arbogast (eds), *Knowledge Systems and Translation*. Text, Translation, Computational Processing 7. pp. 173–189.

Jakobsen, A.L. and K.T.H. Jensen (2008), 'Eye movement behaviour across four different types of reading task'. In S. Göpferich, A. L. Jakobsen and I. M. Mees (eds), *Looking at Eyes: Eye-Tracking Studies of Reading and Translation Processing*. Copenhagen Studies in Language 36. Copenhagen: Samfundslitteratur. pp. 103–124.

Jensen, K.T.H. (2009), 'Indicators of text complexity'. In S. Göpferich, A.L. Jakobsen and I.M. Mees. (eds), *Behind the Mind: Methods, Models and Results in Translation Process Research*. Copenhagen Studies in Language 36. Copenhagen: Samfundslitteratur. pp. 61–80.

Just, M.A. and P.A. Carpenter (1980), 'A theory of reading: from eye fixations to comprehension'. *Psychological Review* 87, 329–354.

O'Brien, S. (2006), 'Pauses as indicators of cognitive effort in post-editing machine translation output'. *Across Languages and Cultures* 7, 1, 1–21.

O'Brien, S. (2009), 'Eye tracking in translation-process research: methodological challenges and solutions'. In I.M. Mees, F. Alves and S. Göpferich (eds), *Methodology, Technology and Innovation in Translation Process Research*. Copenhagen Studies in Language 38. Copenhagen: Samfundslitteratur. pp. 251–266.

Pavlović, N. and K.T.H. Jensen (2009), 'Eye tracking translation directionality'. In A. Pym and A. Perekrestenko (eds), *Translation Research Projects* 2. Tarragona: Universitat Rovira i Virgili. pp. 93–109.

Posner, M.I. (1980), 'Orienting of attention', *Quarterly Journal of Experimental Psychology*, 32, 3–25.

Rayner, K. (1998), 'Eye movements in reading and information processing: 20 years of research.' *Psychological Bulletin*, 124, 372–422.

Rayner, K. and S.C. Sereno (1994), 'Eye movements in reading'. In M.A. Gernsbacher (ed.). *Handbook of Psycholinguistics*. San Diego: Academic Press, pp. 57–81.

Ruiz, C., N. Paredes, P. Macizo, and M.T. Bajo, (2007), 'Activation of lexical and syntactic target language properties in translation'. *Acta Psychologica*, 490–500.

Seleskovitch, D. (1976), 'Interpretation: a psychological approach to translation', In R.W. Brislin (ed.). *Translation: Applications and Research*. New York: Gardner, pp. 92–116.

Sharmin, S., O. Špakov, K. Räihä, and A.L. Jakobsen (2008), 'Where on the screen do translation students look, and for how long?'. In S. Göpferich, A.L. Jakobsen and I.M. Mees (eds), *Looking at Eyes: Eye-Tracking Studies of Reading and Translation Processing*. Copenhagen Studies in Language 36, pp. 30–51.

Appendix

(Text A) Killer nurse receives four life sentences
From *The Independent* (4 March 2008)

1   Hospital nurse Colin Norris was imprisoned for life today for the
2   killing of four of his patients. 32 year old Norris from Glasgow killed
3   the four women in 2002 by giving them large amounts of sleeping
4   medicine. Yesterday, he was found guilty of four counts of murder
5   following a long trial. He was given four life sentences, one for each
6   of the killings. He will have to serve at least 30 years. Police officer
7   Chris Gregg said that Norris had been acting strangely around the
8   hospital. Only the awareness of other hospital staff put a stop to him
9   and to the killings. The police have learned that the motive for the
10 killings was that Norris disliked working with old people. All of his
    victims were old weak women with heart problems. All of them could
    be considered a burden to hospital staff.

Number of characters with spaces: 837
Length of headline in characters with spaces: 41

(Text B) Spielberg shows Beijing red card over Darfur
From the *The Times* (13 February 2008)

1   In a gesture sure to rattle the Chinese Government, Steven Spielberg
2   pulled out of the Beijing Olympics to protest against China's backing
3   for Sudan's policy in Darfur. His withdrawal comes in the wake of
4   fighting flaring up again in Darfur and is set to embarrass China,
5   which has sought to halt the negative fallout from having close ties
6   to the Sudanese government. China, which has extensive invest-
7   ments in the Sudanese oil industry, maintains close links with the
8   Government, which includes one minister charged with crimes
9   against humanity by the International Criminal Court in The Hague.
10 Although emphasizing that Khartoum bears the bulk of the respon-
11 sibility for these ongoing atrocities, Spielberg maintains that the
    international community, and particularly China, should do more to
    end the suffering.

Number of characters with spaces: 856
Length of headline in characters with spaces: 44

Glossary of Terms

Area of interest
A term used in eye tracking to denote a specific area on a stimulus (text, web site, translation tool etc.). Usually abbreviated to AOI. Multiple AOIs can be defined by the researcher by highlighting the specific area(s) using eye-tracking analysis software. Fixation and gaze time data can then be calculated for each AOI to ascertain how much attention was given to each AOI during a task.

Automatization
Refers to when a procedure becomes so routinized in the brain that it is performed in a relatively automated way, with the result that there is no trace of that procedure in short-term memory, and consequently there is no evidence of it in a concurrent think-aloud protocol.

Camtasia Studio
A software product developed by the company TechSmith. It is used to record the desktop activity of a computer user. See www.techsmith.com/camtasia.asp for further information.

Cognitive Translation Unit
The bundling of problem recognition – solution proposal stages in the translation process.

Electroencephalography (EEG)
Refers to the use of electrodes to measure activity in the brain, in a millisecond timeframe, in response to different stimuli or emotions.

Eye blink frequency
The rate of blinking measured by an eye tracker and seen to be an indicator of cognitive load.

Eye-mind assumption
Attributed to Just and Carpenter (1980). The assumption is that there is no appreciable delay between the fixation of the eyes and what is being processed in the brain during a specific task. The eye-mind assumption is one of the foundations for the use of eye tracking in information processing research.

Eye tracker
Equipment used to record a user's eye movements when reading, translating, viewing content or using software on a computer or on other interfaces. Infrared light is bounced off parts of the eye so that it is possible to record the position of the eye on the interface. Other data, such as number of fixations, length of fixations and pupil dilation can also be recorded.

Eye tracking
The process of using an eye tracker to record information on a user's eye movements during various task types.

Fixation
The term used when eyes pause on a particular part of a screen or text for a number of milliseconds. The number of fixations (Fixation Count) and their duration (Fixation Duration or Fixation Length) are taken to be indicative of cognitive effort, i.e. the more there are and the longer they are the more effort is deemed to be involved in processing the information. There is currently no agreement on how long a meaningful fixation is, but a mean fixation of between 200 and 250 milliseconds is reported in reading research (see Jensen, this volume).

Functional Magnetic Resonance Imaging (fMRI)
Measures blood flow and oxygenation in the brain. fMRI is used to diagnose medical conditions relating to the brain. It is also used in cognitive research to record which parts of the brain are activated under specific conditions.

Galvanic skin response
A skin-response test which measures the flow of electricity through the skin. The flow increases when the rate of perspiration increases in response to specific emotions. It is used in human-computer interaction research to measure emotional response to specific conditions (e.g. frustration, stress etc.)

Gaze path

Refers to a type of data output from an eye tracker which shows a static representation of the eye movement data of a participant or group of participants in a task. Each fixation is usually represented by a circle and a sweep of the eyes from one fixation to another is represented by a line. The fixation circles are numbered, so the sequence of fixations and the exact scan path of a user's eyes are easy to determine. Also known as gaze plots.

Gaze time

The amount of time spent looking at a specific stimulus (e.g. text, website) as measured by an eye tracker. Gaze time usually only includes time spent in fixations. However, it is also argued that cognitive processing continues during saccade time and that gaze time should also take saccade time into account.

Heatmap

Refers to a type of data output from an eye tracker which shows the areas on the user interface where most fixations occur for a participant or group of participants. The highest concentration is usually assigned a specific colour (e.g. red), with medium and lower concentrations being assigned different colours (e.g. yellow and green). Areas on the user interface with relatively few fixations have no colours burned onto them. Also known as hot spots.

Keyboard logging

Involves the use of specially designed software to record all keys used on a keyboard as well as mouse actions and inaction (pauses). Keyboard-logging tools typically allow the text production process to be replayed in the form of an AVI (or similar) file. Statistics and log files showing which keys were used and how often are also generated. Translog is an example of a keyboard-logging tool that was developed in the Copenhagen Business School specifically for translation process research. Inputlog is an example of one that was developed for researching writing processes. Also known as keystroke logging or key logging.

Metacognition

Defined broadly as the conscious, volitional, strategic control over complex cognitive tasks. (Shreve 2009)

Problem Nexus
A term used by Angelone (this volume) to denote the confluence of a given textual property and level (lexis, term, collocation, phrase, syntax, sentence, macro-level feature) and a deficit in cognitive resources.

Prompting
The automated suggestion of words and phrases to a translator, writer or editor, based on what s/he was already typing in an editing interface.

PROXY Pro
Screen recording software. Can also be used for remotely accessing another user's computer. Developed by the company Proxy Networks. See http://www.proxynetworks.com/products/screen-recording-edition.html for further information.

Pupillometry
The measurement of pupil size (dilation and constriction) recorded by an eye tracker. Changes in pupil size are known to be indicative of changes in cognitive load and emotional state.

Saccade
A rapid movement of the eyes from one point on a screen or text to another. Saccades can be forward or backward in direction and occur between fixations. Forward and backward saccadic movement is typical of normal reading behaviour.

TAP – Think-aloud protocol
An oral explanation (also called a verbalization) of what is (or was) going on in a person's mind while they are (or were) performing a specific task. In translation process research, it refers to the oral explanation (and the transcription of that explanation) given by a translator while s/he is engaged in a particular task (a concurrent protocol) or after completing a task (a retrospective protocol).

Translation asymmetry
Imbalances in cognitive loading observed when translating between different language directions, i.e. L1 to L2 compared with L2 to L1.

TPP – Translation process protocol

A term used by the TransComp research group to refer to transcribed protocols containing not only what was said during the translation process but also actions such as consultation of a dictionary or adjustment of the head-set.

User-activity data

A combination of keystroke-logging and eye-tracking data, used to give a more detailed account of user activity. In this context, the user is the translator.

Index